Ethics and Policy in Scientific Publication

Other books published by the Council of Biology Editors, Inc.

Financial Management of Scientific Journals. 1989
Illustrating Science: Standards for Publication. 1988
Editorial Forms: A Guide to Journal Management. 1987
CBE Style Manual, 5th edition. 1983
Scientific Writing for Graduate Students. 1968, reprinted 1976, 1981, 1983,
    1986, 1989

Ethics and Policy in Scientific Publication

Editorial Policy Committee, Council of Biology Editors
John C. Bailar III, Chair
Marcia Angell
Sharon Boots
Evelyn S. Myers
Nancy Palmer
Melanie Shipley
Patricia Woolf

PUBLISHED BY
COUNCIL OF BIOLOGY EDITORS, INC.
BETHESDA, MARYLAND
1990

Library of Congress Cataloging-in-Publication Data

Ethics and policy in scientific publication / CBE Editorial Policy
  Committee.
     p.   cm.
    Part two of this book constitutes the proceedings of a conference
held at the National Academy of Sciences in Oct. 1988.
    ISBN 0-914340-09-3
    1. Technical publishing—Standards. 2. Technical publishing—Standards—Congresses. 3.
    Science—Moral and ethical aspects. 4. Science—Moral and ethical aspects—Congresses.
    I. CBE Editorial Policy Committee.
    [DNLM: 1. Authorship. 2. Authorship—congresses. 3. Ethics, Professional. 4. Ethics,
    Professional—congresses. 5. Publishing—standards. 6. Publishing—standards—
    congresses. 7. Scientific Misconduct. 8. Scientific Misconduct—congresses. Z 286.S4 E84
    1988]
T11.E84   1990
174′.95—dc20
DNLM/DLC
for Library of Congress   90-2681
                                                       CIP

CONTENTS

PART I
THE CBE SURVEYS

PART II
CONFERENCE PROCEEDINGS

PREFACE

The processes of scientific research and publishing are receiving more public attention today than at any other time in history. The attention is partly a result of the general appreciation of the long-term benefits of scientific and technical research, but many other factors are involved. Whether it is manifest in new medical therapies, new agricultural methods, safer and more effective consumer products, new sources of raw materials, or modifications of environmental policies, technical and scientific information affects the public in both obvious and subtle ways. The complications of scientific inquiry now influence the public more rapidly and more profoundly than ever before. However, although the justifications for funding scientific research often look to the ultimate utility of projects, observers of science have noted that, in the short term, science is conducted primarily to satisfy the needs of other scientists whose own progress depends on the results.

Although many kinds of research will not affect practical affairs for years, the results of other kinds are thought to be of such immediate significance that they are publicly announced as soon as, or even before, they are published. Sometimes there is pressure to release scientific findings even before they are reviewed by other scientists and approved for publication by editors. That is not surprising—it is both a cause and a consequence of the public's post-World War II investment in research. In the United States, the great preponderance of all research conducted in academic institutions is paid for with funds appropriated by the federal government. Furthermore, the public has become more interested in and better informed about science. That is partly because of the efforts of a new cadre of professional science writers; partly because of public information programs of organizations like the American Association for the Advancement of Science, the Federation of American Societies for Experimental Biology, nonprofit and public-interest groups with a focus on specific diseases or other problems, and the Scientists' Institute for Public Information; partly because of the work of a few talented scientists who are also gifted writers; and partly because critics of science, legislators, and even members of the general public have stirred interest in issues related to the appropriate conduct of research.

In this social context, attention is increasingly focused on the quality of individual research efforts still in progress, as opposed to the nicely packaged final reports of definitive studies. As scientific journal editors have become important arbiters of the quality and import of scientific research, their own activities have attracted public attention. Questions about function and effectiveness of peer review figure in discussions about the validity and value of published work. Attention to peer review has in turn raised many ethical and policy issues that bear on the quality of published research.

Although ethical principles are rarely articulated, they have been a part of science since its beginnings, and the norms of integrity, testability, and credibility have been guideposts for the scientist. Even though research is not yet a spectator sport, public attention to science is considerably more focused than it was a short time ago. The modern era has seen a transformation of many sciences, particularly the biomedical sciences, from an essentially amateurish venture to a highly professional, success-oriented, big-business enterprise. Beginning with the notable successes of science in World War II, burgeoning support from government, private philanthropy, and industry has produced armies of full-time researchers. Their livelihoods and their future research careers depend on their being granted some of the substantial but limited public funds allocated to research support. The growth in numbers of scientists has been accompanied by an increased variety of research specialties and journals. Given the intense competition for grant support, it is not surprising that the compelling desire to understand scientific problems has been exacerbated by the pressure for status. Because status is attained largely by publishing, and because one can publish more and faster if one cuts corners, some scientists have been tempted to breach the ethical norms of science. In fact, the rapid growth of science has reduced the sense of community and confidence in shared values, and it is no longer clear that traditional norms are even understood in the same way as in earlier eras. The evidence about violations is more anecdotal than comprehensive, but it indicates that some problems do exist. The issues have become a matter of concern to the public, as well as to the scientific community.

Questions of ethics almost invariably involve the publishing process, directly or indirectly. Although some editors have objected that the tasks of detecting and controlling unethical behavior are beyond their mandate, the editorial and peer-review process is widely accepted as the foremost and traditional mechanism for evaluating scientific papers. Recent publications dealing with the peer-review process and the responsibilities of authors have touched on the ethical issues; however, few publications have dealt with other problems that editors face daily.

This book discusses various practical ethical problems that have arisen in editors' work. It is intended first for those intimately involved with scientific publishing, but we hope it will serve the interests of others who study either ethics or publishing in general, including the increasing numbers of practicing research investigators who have an interest in the ethical issues of their profession.

The Council of Biology Editors (CBE), an organization that fosters education and improved communication in the life sciences and related fields, recognized that editors often face dilemmas of general interest to scientists. Therefore, the CBE Editorial Policy Committee conducted a survey of CBE members, cast in the form of questions about 19 scenarios, to identify and define some of the ethical issues in publishing research results, with the hope of eliciting a wide range of responses. The last nine scenarios (designated K through S) were also submitted to some editors of journals in the physical and social sciences. The survey stimulated much formal and informal discussion and careful thought about issues that editors have faced as individuals and for which they are now considered to be publicly accountable.

As our analysis of the scenarios progressed, and as we considered the range of reasonable but often incompatible responses to the surveys, we found that wider discussion of some issues could be helpful to us and to readers of our report. The committee therefore organized a conference, supported by the National Science Foundation, which was held in the auditorium of the U.S. National Academy of Sciences from October 14 to 16, 1988. About 175 distinguished invitees attended the conference and participated in spirited discussion of a broad range of ethical and policy issues. Two of us (John Bailar and Patricia Woolf) served as chair and cochair of the conference, another committee member (Nancy Palmer) played the leading role in preparing the proceedings for publication, Sharon Boots played a major role in arranging for the conference, and other committee members took responsibility for developing conference sessions. We also divided the responsibilities for initial analysis of the scenarios, but met frequently and worked so closely together that the final text is in every sense a joint and indivisible product.

On the whole, the reception of the survey results and the conference was so favorable that we were encouraged to present the material to an audience wider than the CBE membership. Furthermore, we recognize that different and incompatible views are often very strongly held and that the range of views could in itself be informative.

Ethical issues often involve legal and policy issues as well. Sometimes, two of the three types of issues, or even all three, seem to blend together, possibly becoming indistinguishable. That blending sometimes reflects genuine problems in sorting among them, but sometimes one version of a problem is invoked to avoid facing another. In particular, there appears to be a tendency to seek legal solutions to ethical issues—for instance, to disapprove a paper that might contain fraudulent data because of concern about possible legal consequences. Although it is often appropriate to determine the legal consequences of a particular action, doing so does not and should not determine the propriety of the action.

Similarly, policy issues can often be construed as ethical issues, and vice versa. For instance, some questions about duplicate or redundant publication of data raise issues of copyright, others involve both ethical and policy considerations of limited publication resources, and still other cases could be treated simply as matters of journal policy—for instance, when authors are forthright about wanting their manuscripts to be published twice. Often, editors admit that they avoid ethical problems and treat them as policy issues. For instance, an editor who suspects fraud, because the data in a manuscript seem "too good to be true," might reject it ostensibly because the subject is inappropriate for the journal. Interactions of ethical and policy issues are often confused and confusing, so we have attempted to sort out the types of issues when analyzing the problems raised in the scenarios.

The first part of this book presents the 19 scenarios and our comments on them. Each scenario discussion stands alone, in that each deals with a specific problem that a journal editor might expect to face. The experiences that are described are not cumulative, except that each lesson teaches that the editor's first impulse might not be the most appropriate one. But readers should feel free to skip around, reading only those of most interest. The second part of the book presents the papers and two invited discussions from the conference, with selections from the open discussions that contain additional points of broad interest.

Four of the seven committee members involved in the preparation of this book have a primary scientific base in biology or medicine; two committee members are chemists; and one member is a sociologist. A few other CBE members (and survey respondents) are from other disciplines, and we conducted limited surveys of editors in physics, chemistry, and the social sciences, using the same sets of scenarios sent to CBE members. It appeared to us that neither issues nor solutions are peculiar to biology and medicine, but apply across the whole range of science. That is reflected both in some broadening of the text of this book and in a title that includes the whole of scientific publishing.

Throughout both the scenarios and the conference, we have tried to focus on issues. Fabrication of data, in itself, is not an issue, in that everyone (including its few practitioners) agrees that fabrication of data is wrong. But what should we do about unconfirmed allegations of fabrication? Similarly, there is universal agreement that plagiarism—the unauthorized appropriation of another's words and ideas—is wrong; but what about covert self-plagiarism in the form of repetitive and undisclosed publication of the same material? These and other matters have no ready and agreed-on solutions. They raise truly ethical questions, in which deeply held values come in conflict—such values as the integrity of science versus fairness and due process, and rights in intellectual property versus over-burdening the channels of scientific communication.

This book, then, is for everyone who is concerned about current ethical dilemmas in science. Whatever else you, the reader, get from it, we hope that it creates an awareness that allows you to evaluate more critically the many possible responses to ethical problems in scientific publishing. If we nudge you into more thoughtful ideas and more thoughtful decisions, we will have succeeded. No ethicist was involved in the production of this book; therefore, important abstract considerations have not been dealt with, but we discuss some direct practical approaches to recurring problems and the experience of the editors who have used them. The committee hopes that you learn as much from reading this book as we did from writing and preparing it.

Council of Biology Editors
Editorial Policy Committee

John C. Bailar III, Chair
Marcia Angell
Sharon Boots
Evelyn S. Myers
Nancy Palmer
Melanie Shipley
Patricia Woolf

ACKNOWLEDGMENTS

We gratefully acknowledge our very large debt to many persons and groups that made substantial contributions to our work. The Council of Biology Editors supported the development and initial analysis of the first 10 scenarios with its own funds and has continued to provide critical administrative and support services. The National Science Foundation, through its grant to CBE, made possible our study of the remaining nine scenarios, the conference, and the development of this book itself. We are especially thankful to CBE Executive Director Philip L. Altman, Ms. Joy Williams of the CBE staff, and Dr. Rachelle Hollander of the National Science Foundation for their generous and patient labors in support of our work.

We also acknowledge with gratitude the contributions of two former committee members, Drs. Karl Heumann and Sidney Weinstein, who did much to get us off to a strong start, but were not able to continue their work as committee members.

Four commercial publishers—Byrd Press, Mack Printing Co., Waverly Press, and Elsevier Science Publishing Co.—provided generous financial support for social functions related to the conference. Such functions are not frivolous; they can be critical in easing interactions among strangers from different disciplines and in ensuring that sharp disagreements are dealt with productively.

Ms. Lali Yurukoglu provided the full range of technical support for the conference. Ms. Meredith Hecht typed and retyped successive drafts in the late stages of manuscript development. Members of the CBE Publications Committee offered helpful suggestions throughout the development of the book and made all technical arrangements for its production, including design, choice of printer and binder, and oversight of the production process.

We thank Kathleen Case for her many helpful comments, Corinne Buterbaugh for coordinating production of the book, and Karen Cannon for proofreading it.

We are especially grateful to the 175 conference attendees, including not only the invited speakers and discussants, who are acknowledged individually in this book, but the many others whose acute responses to the presentations made the open discussions an independent source of insight into some critical issues.

Mr. Norman Grossblatt and Mrs. Kate Kelly edited the manuscript.

The Committee

Part I
The CBE Surveys

Introduction to the Surveys

The Editorial Policy Committee is one of 11 standing committees of the Council of Biology Editors (CBE), an organization that fosters education and improved communication in biology and related fields. The committee is composed largely of editors, each with a unique combination of responsibilities and duties, but all concerned, directly or indirectly, with the day-to-day problems of communicating scientific and technical knowledge. The committee was established to serve as a resource in matters of editorial and publishing policy in the biologic and biomedical sciences. Its charge is to study and analyze, as it deems appropriate, such matters as procedural, ethical, and economic policies related to the editing, review, and publishing of manuscripts. On request, it may review issues that editors or others bring to its attention, and it may render opinions.

It is clear that editors face increasing numbers of complex issues related to the ethics of scientific publishing. In the spirit of its charge, the committee canvassed CBE members to identify, clarify, and assess the prevalence and seriousness of a variety of ethical problems that editors face. The problems were presented in two surveys—the first included Scenarios A through J and some background information, and the second included Scenarios K through S. The surveys, like this book, were not intended to define "right" and "wrong" responses, although the committee has offered recommendations based on the actions and consequences that several editors reported and on the deliberations of its own members.

When the committee members had agreed on the content of the surveys, the committee as a whole developed the survey items. The first survey was tested on a random sample of 35 CBE members, revised slightly, and then sent to all CBE members except those in the test sample. Responses from both groups were combined before they were analyzed. The second survey was not pretested.

The surveys were designed to elicit a range of views, rather than to establish frequencies of specific opinions or to yield rigorous conclusions. Because these were surveys of CBE members, not of journals, some journals might be overrepresented and many CBE members who are not editors have had an input. We hoped that the surveys would give us an idea of the kinds of ethical problems CBE members have actually faced, how seriously they regard the problems, who should be responsible for their resolution, and how the problems and their solutions impinge on the policies and duties of scientific editors.

In the questionnaire, each scenario was followed by four questions, to which members were asked to respond:

1. Should anything be done at this point? If yes, whose responsibility is it? The editor? Someone else? (Specify.)
2. Does this situation pose a serious or important problem for publishing in science? Do you think that the general problem illustrated above is common?
3. Has anything like this happened to you or your journal? (If yes, please describe below.)
4. How do you think this sort of problem should be handled? (Please describe below.)

Respondents were told that replies to the surveys would be kept anonymous, but might be quoted or paraphrased in a publication. Individual questionnaire forms were not identified, and replies were sent directly to the CBE office to emphasize the protection of anonymity. The anonymous approach precluded following up on unreturned questionnaires. A total of 212 questionnaires was returned from the first survey (33% of those mailed), and 225 (26% of the larger CBE membership at that time) from the second. Several dozen late returns were scanned briefly for possible contributions, especially from the anecdotal material they contained.

The next 19 chapters contain discussions of the 19 scenarios—short illustrations of problems that journal editors might face. Each chapter begins with the scenario presented to the respondents. We divided the discussion of each scenario into sections related to issues raised, responses, actions to consider, and conclusions and recommendations. The discussions make liberal use of quotations from the respondents (often lightly edited to improve clarity or consistency of style).

Although the scenarios were designed to elicit responses to single, rather well-defined problems, each also included or implied other questions of ethics or policy that would have substantial implications for both the impact and the resolution of the primary problem. For example, Scenario E focused on problems of financial conflicts of interest among authors, but also raised the question of whether anonymous accusations should be investigated. The committee does not regard such multiplicity as a special virtue or defect of its surveys, but rather as a general characteristic of ethical and policy issues in publishing and perhaps in other fields. In these issues, as with "Dry Bones," it sometimes seems that everything is ultimately connected to everything else. We have dealt with critical multiple issues in our discussions of the individual scenarios, but take up and develop some of the cross-cutting themes in a separate chapter.

Half the respondents considered their primary publication to be medically oriented. The remaining half were split evenly between biologic disciplines and all others. "All others" were still very much related to medicine and biology and in some cases could have been included in one of those categories, rather than "other."

More than one-third of the respondents had doctoral degrees. These included 56 with a PhD, 16 MD, one DDS, one DVM, and three PhD with another doctorate. Master's degrees were reported by an additional 22 respondents. Of the respondents who listed their publications as related to medicine, 40% had doctoral degrees; 53% of the respondents who listed their publications as related to biology and other fields had doctoral or master's degrees. Those are minimal figures; many respondents did not list their degrees.

Most respondents had multiple roles in publishing: 67% specified that they were scientific editors, 46% managing editors, 26% editorial-board members, 54% authors, 46% reviewers, and 16% other (nearly all author's editors). Half those who called themselves scientific editors were also heavily engaged in writing and reviewing; only 5% of those who considered themselves primarily managing editors were also authors and reviewers.

About half the respondents listed professional societies as the owners of their publications, 22% listed commercial publishers, 8% listed government sponsorship, and 7% and 14% listed nonprofit and "other," respectively. "Other," when specified, was usually a university.

Of the publications classified as medical, 57% were the products of professional societies; 25%, 6%, and 12% were products of commercial, government, and other publishers, respectively. Of the biologic publications, 50% were the products of professional societies, and 17%, 9%, and 18% were products of commercial, government, and other publishers, respectively. The remainder were categorized as 43% professional society, 12% commercial, 12% government, and 33% other.

Thus, the survey respondents were a highly diverse group of persons, although they shared a common interest in and usually a professional commitment to scientific and technical publishing. As is evident in the scenarios, their views about many ethical and policy issues are also strikingly diverse.

Scenario A

Allegations of Falsification of Data

Four authors submit a technical paper that is favorably reviewed, revised, approved, and published. Ten months later, the journal editor receives a conference telephone call from authors 1, 2, and 4: They have just discovered that author 3 "fabricated" the data in the only part of the paper that he wrote (two paragraphs and one table of molecular weights of some proteins—not a critical part of the paper). Author 3 has privately admitted to them that he "cooked" the data when he failed to get the results he expected. The editor replies that a retraction (perhaps with corrected data) must be published, and authors 1, 2, and 4 agree to prepare a short statement for publication. Then nothing happens. The first followup inquiries from the editor elicit vague excuses, and later inquiries are not answered at all. Meanwhile, the editor finds that other work by author 3 (with different coauthors) is retracted for similar reasons. The paper in question is becoming widely cited, although the citations do not seem to refer to or depend on the suspect data on molecular weights.

ISSUES

Falsification of data is perhaps the most serious transgression of the ethics of scientific research and is clearly and universally recognized as such, but scientific administrators and editors are often faced with complicated situations like the one in this scenario. The language used to describe specific events conveys uncertainty about the facts and embarrassment about how to proceed. In our example, "cooked" is used to mean selected or altered to present a predetermined result; the term does not necessarily imply out-and-out fabrication. "Trim" and "fudge" are also used to describe misleading selection or manipulation of original observations. Those slang terms were first used by Charles Babbage in the nineteenth century to describe research malpractice, and their casual ring continues to distract from the seriousness of the offenses. Note that authors 1, 2, and 4 say "fabricated," whereas author 3 admits only to having "cooked" data.

When fraud or the suspicion of research malpractice comes to light before an article has been published, an editor's duty is clear: The consequences of delaying or denying publication are considerably less serious than the consequences of publishing false scientific information. Editors who have had to publish retractions of fraudulent papers have found the experiences to be damaging to their scientific specialties, to their journals, and to their personal reputations for editorial acumen. The publication of fraudulent research is also damaging to coauthors, to authors' institutions, and—most of all—to the transgressors.

The present scenario, in which allegations are made about an article that has already been published, illuminates several of the problems that an editor might face. They include the difficulty of assessing contradictory signals from the authors, the editor's responsibility to the journal's readers (especially those who have cited the article), the role of the dubious data in the paper as a whole, the editor's relationships to other editors and to the institutions where the research was conducted, and the potential legal liabilities associated with inappropriate action.

The scenario also raises the issue of appropriate timing and due process: How much time should an editor allow the authors who first raised the issue to clarify their position? When, if ever, is an editor obliged to communicate with an author whose credibility has been challenged?

As the mass media have brought research transgressions to public attention, government agencies and funding sources have become concerned; fraud can no longer be handled as an internal matter in the professional research community. Scientific educators have asked themselves whether and how they might have failed to inculcate professional values as well as knowledge. Scientific societies and organizations have made explicit statements about standards of practice that were once taken for granted. Several funding agencies have issued guidelines for handling cases of suspected fraud.

Journal editors are regarded as principal arbiters of quality control in science, and they have actively examined their role in the detection and prevention of fraud and in reducing adverse consequences when questionable research is published. *Index Medicus* has established a method to associate formal statements of retraction with the work retracted. Editors will need to work closely with secondary services to ensure that retractions can readily be associated with the original articles.

RESPONSES

Most respondents to the CBE survey felt that some middle course of action was called for, at least while allegations of fraud are unconfirmed, but there was a broad spectrum of strongly worded opinions. The responses cited here were provided in the mid-1980s and do not reflect the rapid development of consensus, since that time, that authors' institutions, rather than journals, have the leading role in the investigation of research fraud.

Underlying some of the differences in opinion are different views of the functions of journals and of the relationships of editors to their readers. Some respondents see journals principally as a means of disseminating facts and authors' interpretations; others see them as forums where differences of opinion can be aired. Views probably vary from specialty to specialty and depend on such things as the number of investigators in a field and the nature of its opportunities for informal communication.

Although views of the functions of journals vary, there appears to be broad agreement that the integrity of a journal rests on the ethical behavior of both authors and editor. One respondent put it this way: "The integrity of a peer-reviewed journal for publication of primary results depends on the integrity of its authors and editors to disclose all facts of materials, methods, and results." Another said:

> All parties involved have an obligation to the truth; ideally, all parties will cooperate to that end. Noncooperation by any party constitutes a breach of ethics (whether by author or by editor). Any individual's subjective judgment of the "minor impact" or "insignificance" of known falsification is not a sufficient reason to rationalize away the obligation to see the issue through to a retraction.

A respondent whose views differed from that approach wrote:

> The science journal editor may monitor the materials as presented for publication, but should not play the role of investigator of the benchwork. The scientific community (at the benchwork level) excludes the journal editor, and it should handle the given problem (as the first coauthors have done when they did not respond to the editor's further queries). Here, the editor has no documentary proof.

One editor specifically indicated that as often as possible he chooses reviewers who know the authors, so that he can get as much extra information as possible; his statement illustrated the interaction of informal with formal communication networks.

The great majority of respondents favored some sort of retraction when there was a serious suspicion of fraud. A large number favored retracting the article after notifying the authors that a retraction notice would be published unless the authors themselves responded. An almost equal number did not explicitly mention communicating with the authors, but they might have assumed that such contact would occur. Several thought that the problem would have been less serious if action had been taken sooner. One respondent said that "the editor should have printed an explanation after the conference call, not waited (weeks? months?) to alert readers."

Should the editor communicate with the authors again? A minority of respondents explicitly mentioned getting in touch with either "all" the authors or author 3.

A large minority of respondents were concerned about legal liability. For instance:

> I realize that there is a risk of legal action.

> Contact legal counsel for advice!

Don't hesitate because of litigious overconcern.

Editor should print a notice of the failure of the writers to retract and should give a brief synopsis of the problem based on his correspondence. Then, await letters from lawyers threatening to bring suit. [The scenario referred only to a telephone call.]

Another large minority of respondents mentioned communicating with the administration of the authors' institutions, but they did not always specify how, or why, or what such contact should be meant to accomplish. Some reasons offered were to elicit more information, to force the authors to retract, and to punish the offending author.

Very few respondents explicitly expressed concern about protecting future scientists from reliance on fraudulent work, and the questionnaire did not specifically ask about this matter. A slightly larger number expressed concern about the reputation of the journal.

Responses ranged from a discreetly evasive omission of any response and a candid "I don't know" to the confidently emphatic "Publish as is" or "Reject!" (although the paper was already in print). Still others felt that the decision about a response should be deferred to other parties. Some suggested the editorial board; others felt that more reviewers, especially statisticians or biostatisticians, should have had a role in the initial review process.

Other respondents suggested that the editor put some teeth into his bite by calling or threatening to call lawyers, department chairs, deans, or heads of institutions. Others thought that the threat not to publish any further works by the authors would persuade them to retract. None mentioned the possibility that such coercive action might discourage future, more complete, reporting of possible problems.

Many agreed that the primary responsibility for the authenticity of submitted manuscripts rests with the authors under whose names articles are published. However, if an article is published and later found to be fraudulent, an editor has a responsibility (some say the ultimate responsibility) to tell readers that the published information is not what it was warranted to be.

DISCUSSION

There is now widespread agreement that responsibility for the investigation of allegations of fraud belongs with the institution of the person alleged to have behaved fraudulently. Journal editors cannot themselves conduct such investigations, because they are removed from the scene and do not have the needed resources, expertise, or investigative powers. They do have a responsibility, however, to refer substantial concerns about possible misconduct to the appropriate authorities at the researcher's institution and to insist that they themselves be informed of the outcome of any investigation, so that they will know whether and how to correct the record. The National Institutes of Health

(NIH) now requires all institutions that receive NIH funding to have in place procedures for investigating allegations of fraud.[2]

In the scenario, the editor has heard only one version of the problem, and his informants have pulled back even from that. The editor now has no convincing evidence that fraud has occurred, but does have reason to be concerned and to follow up on the telephone call. He should begin by trying to talk with all four authors, to ascertain the nature of the problem. He could probably be confident of their willingness to discuss the matter with him, if he would inform them that otherwise he will go to their department chair or dean. Depending on the outcome of that conversation, he might then go to the responsible authorities at the institution with any remaining concerns about misconduct and ask that they look into these concerns and inform him of their findings. In view of the NIH requirements and the increasing attention to this problem, it is unlikely that the institution would refuse to address the editor's concern about possible misconduct.

We are told in the scenario that other papers by author 3 have been retracted "for similar reasons." Almost certainly, the institution has already investigated allegations of misconduct by author 3 and reached a determination. If that is the case and author 3 has been found guilty of fraud in other work, the editor could ask the institution either for formal assurance about the work in question or for a retraction.

Although the editor cannot conduct an investigation of allegations of misconduct, he is obliged to publish a retraction of any work that is duly determined to be fraudulent after he has published it. The International Committee of Medical Journal Editors has published its recommendation on the form of such a retraction.[1]

CONCLUSIONS AND RECOMMENDATIONS

The committee believes that a suitable response has two important aspects: the first involves the editor's responsibility for prompt correction of the published record of science; the second concerns the editor's goal to maintain constructive relationships with the authors. Although correcting the record has higher priority, the two goals can interact heuristically.

The editor must ensure that he and the journal do not engage in illegal practices; it is also important to avoid unnecessary legal problems that might prove expensive, distracting, or otherwise damaging, even if any legal counteraction would be unsuccessful. However, editors must not let lawyers define their roles or functions.

Before taking action, the editor must make sure that the written record of events is as complete and accurate as possible, even when it reflects unfavorably on the editor or the journal. It should include a memorandum for the record as detailed as possible regarding the initial telephone call and each later contact. One hopes that the record will remain available only to the editor; but if things go wrong, it could provide crucial protection of both journal and editor.

Although the editor is obliged to follow up on the allegations of fraud, he is not in a position to determine whether fraud has occurred or, if it has, who is guilty. In most cases, the editor would not be the appropriate person to issue a retraction; if there is to be a retraction, it must come from the authors or from appropriate authorities at the institution where the research was done (which almost surely received the grant in the authors' names).

In the present scenario, the editor should attempt to get in touch with all the authors and tell them that, if they are evasive, he will refer the matter to the appropriate authorities at their institution. Unless he hears from all of them, he should do that. If, after communicating with all the authors, the editor has serious concerns about the integrity of the published work, he should refer the matter to the institution.

Once the institution has determined whether fraud occurred, the editor should be notified. If it has, he is then obliged to publish a retraction, signed either by the authors or by appropriate authorities at their institution. The committee concurs with the recommendation of the International Committee of Medical Journal Editors[1] as to the form of the retraction:

> The retraction, so labelled, should appear in a prominent section of the journal, be listed in the contents page, and include in its heading the title of the original article. It should not simply be a letter to the editor. Ideally, the first author should be the same in the retraction as in the article, although under certain circumstances the editor may accept retractions by other responsible persons. The text of the retraction should explain why the article is being retracted and include a bibliographic reference to it.

REFERENCES

1. International Committee of Medical Journal Editors. Retraction of research findings. Br Med J 1988;296:400.
2. Responsibilities of awardees and applicant institutions for dealing with and reporting possible misconduct in science. Federal Register 54, No. 151 (August 8, 1989). Rules and Regulations.

READINGS

1. Broad WJ. Harvard delays in reporting fraud. Science 1982;215:478–82.
2. Knox R. The Harvard fraud case: where does the problem lie? JAMA 1983;249:1797–9, 1802–7.

Scenario B

"Ownership" of Data and the Freedom of Information Act

A large research study was supported for many years by a series of government contracts. The study was completed, and the resulting data were submitted to the contracting agency 3 years ago. However, the principal investigator and her colleagues have not yet published any of the results. An investigator not affiliated with any of those who did the research requested and was sent (as required by the Freedom of Information Act) a copy of the data, research protocols, and other materials. He has written a paper based on the data and submitted it to a journal; a footnote accurately explains the circumstances. In response to the journal editor's request for comment, the principal investigator replies that she has had a paper almost finished for 2 years, that she will immediately get a colleague to finish it, and that she will sue the journal if her competitor's paper is published. The author of the paper in hand says that the data were generated with public money and are therefore public property, that he has used the Freedom of Information Act as Congress intended it to be used, and that 3 years is long enough to wait for publication of important results.

ISSUES

The U.S. Freedom of Information Act (FOIA) of 1966 outlined criteria by which the American public could obtain information regarding federally administered operations and federally funded projects. The intent of Congress in passing the FOIA was to acknowledge the accountability of the federal government to its citizens, who pay for federally funded projects.

The original version of the FOIA was somewhat restrictive, in that it allowed "only persons properly and directly concerned" to obtain "matters of official record." A 1974 amendment stated that "any person" is entitled to federal agency records, regardless of motivation.

Society's right to an open government can sometimes conflict with the need to protect other societal interests, such as confidentiality of individual medical records, matters of national security, law-enforcement investigation and litigation related to law enforcement, and regulation and supervision of financial institutions. The FOIA recognizes exclusions in those matters, but none of the nine categories of exceptions to disclosure of information refers specifically to scientific or medical research data. One allows for the protection and anonymity of persons who participate in scientific and medical studies, but various courts have ruled that maintaining confidentiality is not sufficient reason to override the disclosure requirements of the FOIA as long as individual identification is not possible.

Trade and commercial secrets are protected from disclosure under the FOIA, but scientific research is not, even though ideas are as important to the career and financial success of a scientist as trade secrets are to those of a business entrepreneur.

Scenario B raises several issues: Who has the right to publish? What is "intellectual property," and who owns it? What are the consequences of non-participating authors interpreting data? Conversely, what are the consequences of delaying or avoiding the publication of research, and when is delay justifiable? Should incomplete or unpublished data, complete data, and published data be regarded differently, with respect to the FOIA? What is the role of an editor when data acquired in ethically questionable ways are submitted for publication? How does an editor judge whether publication of such data would be inappropriate, harmful to the public, or unfair to the original investigators? How does an editor balance the responsibility to provide journal readers with the most accurate and timely information against the responsibility to respect nonlegal rights and proprietary interests of scientists? Does it matter whether the work was done under federal contracts (as in the scenario) or federal grants?

In 1973, files were requested under the terms of the FOIA on grant applications approved by the National Institute of Mental Health (NIMH) for research on the effects of drugs on children. When the Department of Health, Education, and Welfare refused to release the files, the Washington Research Project, Inc., filed suit. The NIMH investigators had not yet published the results or data. The U.S. District Court for the District of Columbia ruled that the plaintiff was entitled to the information for its use, *including publication*. The court ruled that exception 4 of the FOIA—covering privileged trade secrets and commercial financial information—did not apply to the NIMH research project.[1]

In 1980, the U.S. Supreme Court made an important distinction in *Forsham v. Harris* between data collected for use by the federal government or its agencies and data collected for investigator-initiated research funded by federal grants or by private organizations conducting research for the government.[3] The court found that the federal government typically is involved in research funded by a federal grant only to the extent of ensuring that the funded research is in compliance with the goals of the grant; it found that a private agency that receives a grant does not thereby become an agency of the federal government. In other words, because an investigator is neither carrying out a protocol designed by a federal funding agency nor providing data directly for use by the agency, work supported by a federal grant is not the possession of the funding agency.[5]

Editors should nonetheless be aware that several plaintiffs who had been denied access to information under the FOIA have recently succeeded in obtaining the same information through civil litigation—for example, where a study participant's privacy is not a primary concern.

RESPONSES

Most respondents felt that the journal editor was responsible for resolving the situation in Scenario B. More than half considered the issue to constitute a serious problem in scientific publishing. A large majority felt that the problem is fairly common, and some had encountered it themselves.

Many survey respondents commented that data reported by a nonparticipant are particularly susceptible to inaccurate interpretation. One respondent wrote that "data do not have a life of their own apart from the design of a study or the methods used to collect them." Another said:

> Scientific investigation includes not only numerical data, but also the subconscious and conscious awareness of circumstances surrounding acquisition of data that may influence their interpretation. Factors which may influence the ultimate interpretation of data by the original investigator may not necessarily be included in a compendium. Some examples of this might be experiments which may have been interrupted, experiments which may never have been completed, and experiments which may have been excluded from consideration for other reasons.

One respondent pointed out that the reasons for delay of publication of results by the principal investigators need to be considered, because they might be related to the scientific validity of the study:

> By controlling the disclosure of his data, an investigator can prevent release of unfounded hypotheses and possibly misleading or incomplete data. Secondary authors do not know the circumstances of data acquisition or the strengths and weaknesses of the work. They would not be capable of making a thorough and unbiased presentation of the data, nor would they be able to validate them without collaboration with the principal investigators.

Not-yet-validated clinical trials might be destroyed by premature disclosure, analysis, or release of data obtained under the FOIA. The fear that outside parties will gain access to preliminary data can seriously compromise the compliance of study subjects and research results.

Many respondents argued strongly that investigators' ideas and methods are their intellectual property and so deserve protection, as do trade secrets and commercial information. One wrote that "authors should retain control of their work until it is published and hold a valid interest in protecting ideas and methods uniquely their own and developed in the pursuit of their profession."

Publication of shoddy analyses that result from poor comprehension of theories or methods by secondary authors and possible duplication of published material were concerns of some respondents. Some believed that investigators, in an attempt to protect their ideas, might provide incomplete or unusable data in grant applications (the FOIA provides virtually unlimited access to successful grant applications submitted to federal agencies) or in response to requests made under the FOIA. Many scientists believe that acquisition of data under the FOIA disrupts scientific research, because, as one respondent said, "studies are then less controlled and blind and thus, less scientific in their conclusions. Federal scientists . . . must work in a 'fish' bowl under the FOIA statutes and are put at a professional disadvantage."

However, some respondents felt that the principal investigators in the scenario had been negligent in failing to disseminate their data in a timely manner and that the irresponsibility was especially serious in that the study had been supported by public funds. One wrote that "taxpayers do not support research for private gain. Investigators who receive these funds for their research should be aware of the status of tax-funded research and thus be willing to compromise their individual interest at some point to meet legitimate public interests." Another stated that, "if principal investigators do not show due diligence, it is the duty of the editors of scientific publications to make public scientific results available. Journals exist to disseminate information and are not vehicles for the establishment and/or protection of individual reputations."

Another argument that supports publication of an article by a nonparticipant is that the free exchange of scientific ideas enables scientists to build on the discoveries of others and thus helps to reduce the expense of duplicate research efforts.[5,6]

A few respondents pointed out that the monitoring of scientific data by the press, the public, or other investigators is a good review process through which errors made in the original evaluation can be checked. Others argued that, although peer review is already in place and is used by primary scientific and medical journals, it applies only to data chosen by the author for inclusion in a submitted manuscript.

Stallones[5] wrote:

> FOIA has been used to obtain grant applications, research data from projects in progress, and files from studies that have been published. Of these, release of work in progress is potentially the most damaging and should be exempted from FOIA by Congressional amendment. Next in order of serious consequences is the pirating of research ideas from grant applications. Thievery is thievery, whether recognized by the courts or not, and thieves are not likely to be inhibited by a call for voluntary restraint. Publication of the names of people who request this information should have salutary effect, but the best, most obvious solution is to add grant applications to the list of exemptions in the FOIA. Re-analysis and re-publication of research data already published may be the only means of rectifying errors. To employ FOIA to secure data for re-analysis is inherently adversarial in an arena where collegiality should be the modal basis for exchanges between

scientists. In most instances, we scientists should request our colleagues to release their data, and we should be willing to acquiesce to such requests. If a voluntary approach fails, and the public interest must be served, then the use of FOIA is justifiable and necessary.

DISCUSSION

Many survey respondents emphasized both the delicacy and the seriousness of the situation in Scenario B and felt that a predetermined journal policy is crucial to its resolution. A recent publication of the National Academy of Sciences deals more broadly with the sharing of research data and sheds much light on the issues raised by this scenario.[2]

In January 1978, a group of editors of some major biomedical journals published in English met in Vancouver, British Columbia, and decided on uniform technical requirements for manuscripts to be submitted to their journals. The group, referred to originally as the "Vancouver group," has evolved into the International Committee of Medical Journal Editors (ICMJE). The group published revised requirements in 1982 and again in 1988.[4] These have been adopted by hundreds of other journals and now come close to an international standard for preparation of English-language manuscripts to be submitted for journal publication. Some of the requirements deal with instructions for authors on such matters as the title page, abstract and key words, text, references, and tables and illustrations. Other sections discuss prior and duplicate publication, authorship, and acknowledgments. The ICMJE agreed on a statement of responsibilities that should be accepted by authors preparing and submitting papers for journal publication.[4] The following is an excerpt from the statement:

> Authorship credit should be based only on substantial contributions to (a) conception and design, or analysis and interpretation of data; (b) drafting the article or revising it critically for important intellectual content; and (c) final approval of the version to be published. Conditions (a), (b), and (c) must all be met. Participation solely in the acquisition of funding or the collection of data does not justify authorship. . . .
>
> A paper with corporate (collective) authorship must specify the key persons responsible for the article; others contributing to the work should be recognized separately (see Acknowledgments and Other Information).
>
> Editors may require authors to justify the assignment of authorship.

Scenario P cites the statement of the ICMJE at greater length. Other sections of the committee's statement define responsibilities in acknowledging technical assistance and financial support.

More than 400 scientific journals throughout the world require authors to subscribe to the ICMJE criteria. If a journal's policy required authors to meet both requirements of (a) of the guidelines—"conception and design" and "analysis and interpretation"—publication of data obtained under the FOIA by nonparticipating authors might be precluded. Editors would simply return such manuscripts to the authors and cite journal policy. However, use of that avenue of exclusion might also preclude publication of secondary analyses after a primary publication, even when the primary authors consent.

One survey respondent wrote:

> If the editorial policy of a journal precludes publication of any data other than original investigation performed by participating authors, but the information contained in a manuscript submitted by a nonparticipating author is deemed important and would normally carry a high priority, the journal editor must proceed cautiously in resolving the issue in order to guarantee fairness to all parties involved and at the same time fulfill the responsiblity to disseminate information through publication as accurately as possible.

For journals whose policies do not bar manuscripts written by secondary authors, publication of both manuscripts as confirmatory or complementary papers was highly recommended by some survey respondents. One respondent wrote that, "if another group can add to the interpretation of the data or clarify them, then science has been helped." That idea is distinctly different from the one involved when authors are unwilling to do their own "legwork," but instead simply obtain data and results to add publications to their lists.

A critical issue in the solution of this problem is the determination by the editor of an adequate interval during which investigators should prepare a paper for publication. Is 2 months after completion of the study a fair amount of time, or is 2 years? An editor must consider the circumstances surrounding each instance. What are the authors' reasons for delay in publication? Are their reasons valid? Has some recent development in the field negated the findings of the study in question?

If the original investigators' data are accurately referred to as having been obtained under the FOIA and if the secondary authors have included some of their own data, publication might present no conflict. One editor wrote that "use of unpublished data as a stepping stone furthering the original work of the secondary author in a manuscript concerning his original work would not represent a digression from currently acceptable publishing policy."

Editors might request personal communication from the principal investigators granting permission to a secondary author to use their data, but this could become a problem if they refuse (as in this scenario). Many respondents suggested that the editor attempt to negotiate coauthorship between the principal investigators and the secondary author or that coauthorship be made a requirement for publication.

Some respondents recommended that a manuscript from a nonparticipating author be processed in the usual way, regardless of how the data were obtained. If the work received a high priority for acceptance, the respondents felt, the editor should publish the work with full disclosure of all pertinent information.

Many respondents suggested that editors recommend to secondary authors a review or summary format for their work, inasmuch as publication of an idea or method usually confers credit on the author. Journals that publish review articles, analyses of work already published, or letters to the editor have a wider choice of format for the publication of material submitted by a nonparticipating author.

The following prospective solution was offered by the editor-in-chief of a medical publication: "Agencies contracting with investigators should include in initial agreements a requirement for publication of data within a specified amount of time after completion of the work."

CONCLUSIONS AND RECOMMENDATIONS

The committee believes that an editor who must decide whether to publish data reported by a nonparticipating author should first determine the position of the investigators who generated the data. Those investigators should tell the editor the expected dates of submission and publication of a manuscript or explain why publication has not occurred or will not occur.

The committee recommends that original investigators be encouraged to publish. However, we also recognize the limitations of this approach. It is not always possible for authors to submit their best manuscript within a specified period, an editor has no formal relationship with primary investigators before submission of a manuscript, and an editor might receive a poorly conceived and poorly presented report from the original investigators after declining to consider a better manuscript from nonparticipating authors.

The possibility that the primary investigators will never publish the data is most serious if their work cannot be repeated—for example, because too few patients are available, critical circumstances are rare, or the data set is prohibitively large or too expensive to compile. An editor then must determine whether investigators are "sitting" on and blocking the use of data that might be of substantial public value. The free flow of information is nearly always to be preferred to restriction of its availability. But the system of research credit works against openness, and the damage that can be done by faulty, uninformed reporting is more visible than the damage done by restricting the availability of information.

If the primary investigators have been advised of the situation and have failed to meet the deadline set by the editor for submission of a manuscript or if the manuscript they have submitted is unacceptable for publication, the committee recommends the following: coauthorship between the original investigators and the secondary author if they consent and agree on a manuscript, or peer review of the nonparticipating authors' manuscript with disclosure to the referees about the acquisition of data and then publication, including the editor's explanation, of the circumstances surrounding the data and publication.

REFERENCES

1. Brody EB. The freedom of medical information. JAMA 1975;233:145–6.
2. Fienberg SE, Martin ME, Straf ML, eds. Sharing Research Data. Washington, D.C.: National Academy Press; 1985.
3. *Forsham v. Harris.* 445 U.S. 169 (1980).
4. International Committee of Medical Journal Editors. Uniform requirements for manuscripts submitted to biomedical journals. Ann Intern Med 1988;108:258–65.
5. Stallones RA. The effects of the Freedom of Information Act on research. Am J Public Health 1982;72:335.
6. Yolles BJ, Connors JC, Grufferman S. Obtaining access to data from government-sponsored medical research. N Engl J Med 1986;315:1669–72.

Scenario C

Redundant Publication

A paper describing a small but useful scientific advance is published. The editor soon discovers that it had already been published in another journal in identical form, except that the authors have rewritten the abstract, introduced a few editorial changes elsewhere, changed the tables and figures to include results in subjects recruited since the first publication (about 3 times the initial number, but with little change in overall results), and added a sentence with an ambiguous reference to the earlier publication, which is now listed in the bibliography. In response to an inquiry from the editor, the authors say that the large number of new subjects justified publication even with nearly identical text and that the second paper gave adequate notice to the editor and reviewers (as well as readers) that it was updating an earlier one. The editor reviews the file and concludes that the correspondence and the ambiguous reference could in fact be interpreted as the authors claim, although the wording of the text seems to be deliberately deceptive.

ISSUES

The major theme in this scenario is redundant (sometimes called repetitive or duplicate) publication, that is, publication of essentially the same study more than once without clear notification to editors, reviewers, and readers. Most scientific journals have a policy of considering for publication only manuscripts that have not been submitted or published elsewhere. Thus, redundant publication is proscribed.

In this scenario, the second paper differed from the first in the large increase in the number of study subjects and in a few details of presentation. Its reference to the first publication was ambiguous, so it was not clear to the editor and reviewers that the second was an extension of the first. The scenario raises several issues: What constitutes repetitive publication? Why do most journals have policies proscribing it? Under what circumstances might it be justified?

What constitutes redundant publication is not always clear. Obviously, publishing a paper more than once in identical form is repetitive. But suppose that a study is reported in two journals with different readerships and that the presentation is made somewhat different to emphasize aspects of interest to each separate readership. Or suppose that the second paper is published later and, as here, deals with a larger number of study subjects or with a longer followup. Other special situations include repetitive publication in controlled-circulation reports, government reports, published abstracts or proceedings, publication in different languages, public or professional news reports of salient data, in-house reports, and commercial scientific newsletters. What obligation for disclosure should authors of repetitive or overlapping publication, editors, and others assume? How much should authors say about specific similarities to earlier reports? How, indeed, is "earlier" determined? Finally, how should an editor respond who first learns about overlapping publication when the later publication is already in print?

In one simplistic view, repetitive publication in any of its forms does not constitute a problem; after all, why not disseminate a report of a scientifically valid study to as many people as possible? But the matter is not so simple.

Certainly, a case can be made for repetitive publication in some circumstances. For example, regional publications and materials published in developing countries might be virtually lost unless they are republished.[7] Some consider the problem of hindrance of exchange of information because of language or regional barriers serious enough to justify deliberate republication on a large scale. A U.S.-U.S.S.R. agreement on the exchange of information on biomedical research resulted in the duplicate publication in English and Russian of three U.S.-U.S.S.R. monographs on cancer research and then in the appearance of jointly written articles in U.S. or international cancer-research journals. The *Journal of Soviet Oncology* and the *Journal of Soviet Cardiovascular Research,* both quarterlies, were introduced in the United States in 1980 to make selected U.S.S.R. research reports available in full to as many non-U.S.S.R. cancer, cardiovascular, and other researchers as possible.[5]

Another kind of repetitive publication generally considered legitimate by journal editors is publication of a full research report after publication of a meeting abstract or an in-house communication. Those forms of prior publication are widely permitted to encourage the free and rapid exchange of information among colleagues.

The type of repetitive publication of main interest here is the publication of duplicate or substantially overlapping reports in the primary scientific literature directed to the same audience. This form of repetitive publication is often fueled by authors' desire to build a long bibliography and by the desire of institutions and research groups to be seen as productive. The economic costs alone of this form of repetitive publication are very high and generally outweigh the perceived scientific benefits. The management of scientific information is expensive, as are writing, consulting, reviewing, revising, editing, typesetting, proofreading, printing, distributing, abstracting, cataloging, storing, retrieving, and reading one report. Repeating the whole process for exactly or essentially the same information entails a cost that society should not have to support. The argument that repetitive publication is necessary to reach all who might be interested has lost much of its strength as electronic means to search the literature have become increasingly available and effective.

The scientific costs of repetitive publication are also high. Because of the incentives for scientists to publish frequently, the scientific literature increasingly consists of "least publishable units," that is, reports containing the smallest amount of information that an editor will accept for publication.[4] The literature has become so large and fragmented that it is difficult to use. Adding the burden of repetitive publication increases the loss of information in the mass of published material. Already, readers must scan titles, rather than read papers, and most scientific reports are rarely read and never cited. Furthermore, when the same information is published more than once, it receives more emphasis than it warrants. Readers might even "double count" a single finding, not recognizing that they are reading the same report twice. Finally, repetitive publication wastes the time and expertise of reviewers, whose energies should be reserved for original reports.

RESPONSES

The respondents generally agreed that this scenario describes repetitive publication, apparently in part because the authors were less than candid about the earlier paper. The respondents saw repetitive publication as a frequent and important problem in science. Although they felt that it was first the authors' responsibility not to attempt repetitive publication, they felt that it was the editor's responsibility to ensure that it did not happen and, once it did (as in the scenario), to respond to it.

There were exceptions, however, to the consensus view that repetitive publication is an important problem and that the scenario describes it. Several respondents thought that the additional data in the second paper might have justified publication and that the referees' judgment as to whether publication was warranted should have been heeded. That presupposes that the referees knew about the earlier publication and did not mention it to the editor—perhaps an unlikely situation. One respondent wrote that "the relative importance of a new and larger study population could be assessed by statistical analysis of the power of both studies, on which basis a case might be made that the second, larger study did merit publication because it might establish new facts." Another wrote that "we will publish such a paper if the new series means a statistically significant change in results."

Some of the respondents cited examples of repetitive publication from their own experience. One reported:

> I had a case of simultaneous publication, except that in the other journal the manuscript wasn't edited as stringently as in mine. The data were the same. I wrote the author and the editor of the other journal, pointing out the duplication, and got a letter from the author's attorney! It took about 6 months of letters before the matter was finally dropped.

Another wrote:

> An author submitted a paper which was reviewed favorably and published by us in Canada. A reader from South Africa wrote to complain that the same materials had been published within the year in the U.S. and in England. I wrote the offending author twice, the second time by registered mail, saying that I was planning to print the letter from South Africa and offering him the chance of explanation or rebuttal. There was no answer so I published the letter, with a prominent heading.

Although the scenario deals with a fait accompli, many respondents emphasized the need to prevent repetitive publication. According to one, "prophylaxis will obviate the need for a cure." One specific recommendation for prophylaxis was the publication of a clear statement of policy concerning repetitive publication—in instructions for authors, on the copyright form, and in occasional editorials. Authors might also be instructed to submit with their manuscript a list of all previous publications dealing with the same subject and a covering letter affirming that there was no duplication. One respondent called for departmental review of all papers at the author's institution before submission to any journal.

Many respondents stressed the negligence of the reviewers and the editor in the scenario. They felt that the reviewers should have been aware of the duplication and should have called the editor's attention to it. The committee recognizes the near impossibility of maintaining a full range of knowledge in a rapidly developing field. Reviewers are generally selected for their knowledge of a field, but broad knowledge of recent developments in one field might not be accompanied by knowledge of experimental methods or awareness of implications for a related field. The costs of review are such that we cannot multiply reviewers to solve this problem.

Once the editor discovers the publication of an overlapping paper, what should be done and who should do it? Respondents' answers ranged from "once burned, twice warned" to a suggestion that the editor charge the authors with copyright violation. Most felt that the editor should reprimand the authors in some way. Some favored private reprimand, others public. Some respondents also suggested that the editor should inform the chair of the author's department or another authority in the institution. Many felt that some sort of blacklisting was in order, either implicit or explicit. Implicit blacklisting included telling the authors that for a stated period their work would not be considered for publication by the journal and informing other editors of the circumstances through a list of "chronic regurgitators" circulated among editors. One respondent suggested the publication of a notice in the journal— "This paper is very similar to Paper X in Journal Y"—to put pressure on both the author and the editor. Only one respondent suggested that the editor telephone the author to discuss the problem: "I think it would be worth while for the editor to phone the author and 'jawbone,' leaving the impression that the threshold for future publication by that author in that journal is very much higher."

In addition to making recommendations for dealing with the specific conditions of this scenario, many respondents spoke to the more general problem of repetitive publication. They suggested encouraging tenure committees to reduce the emphasis on numbers of publications in their guidelines for faculty promotion, creating a joint committee of journal editors to issue a statement on dual submissions and repetitive publication, and altering journal format to include "preliminary communications" and "addenda to previously published work." Some suggested that a letter to the editor is an appropriate vehicle for updating previous work.

DISCUSSION

Respondents to the survey pointed out that much of the problem of redundant publication has to do with incentives and practices within the research system as a whole, not just in connection with journals. At its most fundamental level, the responsibility for avoiding repetitive publication lies with authors. It should be a part of scientific education and practice to publish only what the scientific community needs to know. Occasionally, there is room for legitimate doubt as to when a study is ready for publication, for example, when the accumulation of more data justifies a followup report. It is essential in such situations that the editor be informed of the possibility of overlapping publication, so that the editor and the reviewers have the opportunity to make their own judgments.

The suggestion of more widespread policies for departmental review of all papers before submission to any journal is potentially important. Such an approach is already in force in many large research institutions, and perhaps others should consider it. Attempts to submit duplicate or overlapping manuscripts could be identified at the institutional level and perhaps dealt with there.

When a clearly duplicative or overlapping manuscript has been submitted without reference to the original report or disclosure, but is recognized as such, what should the editor do? Possible responses can be considered in three broad categories: private chastisement, reluctance to consider future submissions, and public exposure.

Private chastisement includes telephoning or writing the authors to educate them about the proprieties and policies of scientific publishing. If the duplicate publication was willful, the authors might not be dissuaded from future attempts at repetitive publication merely by an editor's displeasure.

The second category of response entails raising the threshold for acceptance of future articles from the authors or refusing to publish their work, indefinitely or for a given period. Such blacklisting might or might not be revealed to the authors. A major problem is that such a response remains private, leaving the authors free to send their duplicate publications to other, less wary journals. Even the disincentive of the threat of being barred from one journal is lost, of course, if the authors are not informed of the reasons, although the journal can increase its own protection from publishing duplicate articles. Abelson[1] has suggested that this type of response can be made stronger by eliciting explicit and concerted action from all the journals that had inadvertently published manuscripts from the offending authors.

The third category of response, public exposure, is probably the most effective. It entails publishing a notice about any duplicate publication that was not brought to the editor's attention until after publication. Examples are the announcement published in the correspondence columns of the April 12, 1985, *Journal of the American Medical Association*[3] and an editorial[2] and letters to the editor[6] in the May 4, 1989, issue of the *New England Journal of Medicine*.

CONCLUSIONS AND RECOMMENDATIONS

The committee favors the view that publication of the same study, regardless of details of presentation or differences in intended audience, constitutes repetitive publication and should in general be discouraged. The committee believes also that repetitive publication is a serious problem in scientific publication and that it raises several kinds of issues that should not be blurred or merged.

The definition of "redundant publication" might in some cases be primarily a scientific issue and in others primarily a policy issue. If new data are collected, it is a matter of judgment as to whether and where a new publication is warranted. Even if substantial new information is not added, repetitive publication in journals with different readerships might not violate the policies of the journals involved. Publication in a different language is a special case in which repetitive publication might often be justified. When the authors are forthright about what they are doing, the committee does not consider these sorts of judgments to involve ethical issues, but rather policy issues with substantial practical implications.

The committee believes that the scientific and policy issues become ethical issues when authors are not forthright about their earlier publications. Our system of rewarding scientists provides an incentive to publish as frequently as possible, so researchers might be tempted to engage in unjustified repetitive publication to add to their bibliographies. Such researchers might not disclose the existence of earlier publications emanating from the same studies, if they fear that the editor will recognize that later publication is unjustified. Most respondents seemed to feel that that was the situation in this scenario. The addition of study subjects or longer followup might or might not justify publication, but authors should be explicit about the existence of earlier publications, so that reviewers and editors can make their recommendations and decisions in the light of all the evidence. Failure to provide such information is a breach of publishing ethics. Later manuscripts should, of course, refer clearly to any earlier publications.

The committee makes the following recommendations:

1. Instructions for authors should clearly state journal policies about repetitive publication and should require that authors inform the editor at the time of submission of all possibly overlapping papers that have been published or submitted elsewhere, with supplementary notice to the editor if other possibilities of duplicate publication arise. Copies of the other papers— reprints if they are published, manuscripts if they are still pending—should be enclosed.
2. Reviewers should be informed of this policy. If a reviewer fails to call the attention of the editor to an instance of repetitive publication that is discovered later, the editor should inform the reviewer of the details.
3. Violations should be brought to the authors' attention. It is probably not justified to blacklist the authors—to refuse to publish their future work— because that might deprive the scientific community of important information. But it is reasonable to inform the authors that the threshold for the acceptance of future work might be higher.
4. Repeated submission of repetitive publications, egregious first offenses, and instances discovered only after publication should be brought to the attention of the authors' supervisor, who should be asked to deal with them and inform the editor of what has been done.
5. The editor should be prepared to publish a notice of the violation if duplicate publication occurs before discovery, as in this scenario. The decision should depend in part on action taken at the institutional level.

This measured, stepwise response combines the advantages of a private approach with the possibility of a later public response. When it is less than clear that the authors willfully engaged in repetitive publication, the issue can be clarified without damage to their reputations. When it is clear that the authors have deliberately behaved improperly, the issue can be dealt with at the institutional level, as well as (in some instances) publicly.

The scientific community must develop an acceptable and uniform approach to dealing with the all-too-common offense of unjustified repetitive publication.

REFERENCES

1. Abelson P. Excessive zeal to publish. Science 1982;218:953.
2. Angell M, Relman AS. Redundant publication. N Engl J Med 1989;320:1212-4.
3. Breaks and other bad breaks for breakers. JAMA 1985;253:2047.
4. Broad WJ. The publishing game: getting more for less. Science 1981;211:1137-9.
5. Pelikan J. Scholarship: a sacred vocation. Schol Pub 1984;16:1-37.
6. Saad MS, et al.; Benditt D. Publication of closely related reports. N Engl J Med 1989;320:1221-2.
7. Saunders JF. American-Soviet publications in the biomedical sciences. CBE Views 1982;5:4-7.

READINGS

1. Angell M. Editors and fraud. CBE Views 1983;6:30-8.
2. Council of Biology Editors Style Manual Committee. CBE Style Manual, 5th ed. Bethesda, Maryland: Council of Biology Editors; 1983.
3. Lock S. A Difficult Balance: Editorial Peer Review in Medicine. London: Nuffield Provincial Hospitals Trust; 1985.
4. Relman AS. Publish or perish—or both. N Engl J Med 1977;297:724-5.

Scenario D

Undisclosed Data-Dredging

A reviewer comments that a manuscript comparing the effect of two experimental treatments is incomplete; she knows from other sources that 10 treatments were studied. The reviewer has calculated that, with the larger number of treatments, one would expect that chance would produce at least one difference as large as that reported, even if the treatments are ineffective. The author replies that he did, in fact, choose to report only the largest and smallest effects, but that selective publi-

*cation of "positive" results has a long history, is not considered uneth-
ical, and indeed is encouraged by editors of leading journals. He also
says that the treatments reported were expected all along to be most
different, that the other eight treatments were included in the study to
provide a broad range of background material for other purposes, and
that it is inappropriate to add those eight to the analysis in the present
manuscript, because that would destroy the reported statistical significance and obscure the one important finding.*

ISSUES

This scenario describes a situation that might be one version of a practice
sometimes known as data-dredging—the sifting of a large body of data to find
"positive" results of research that was not specifically targeted to produce
those results. The technical problem raised by data-dredging is that any large
collection of data is likely to have some unexplained oddities just by chance
and that post hoc selection of such oddities as scientific observations distorts
the process of scientific inference. Data-dredging does have some clear and
important uses, and many major scientific advances have resulted from such
practices, although observations are likely to be confirmed by replication and
elaboration before publication. The situation here is less favorable: The positive finding was not replicated, and the investigator might well have misstated
(or perhaps misremembered) why only one comparison was presented.

The problem might be much deeper than exposition; it could involve the
deliberate manipulation of statistical analysis and data presentation to produce
a positive result, and hence a paper that is more likely to be published. The
editor has no way to verify the author's reasons for reporting only two of 10
studied treatments.

The main issue is whether and when an investigator is justified in data-
dredging, reporting only the positive result(s) and ignoring the rest. Related
issues concern the nature of scientific investigation and the relationship between an experiment and the manuscript that describes it and reports its
results. The situation also touches on aspects of the critical but informal and
collegial relationships among authors, reviewers, and editors.

This scenario poses several ethical and practical problems. First, should
all knowledge about the authors or their research techniques be part of the
editorial judgment process, or should a manuscript be judged for possible
publication strictly on its own merits and exactly as submitted (even, for some
journals, with authors anonymous to reviewers)?

Second, what is the role of reported statistical significance against the
background of limited statistical sophistication of most authors, reviewers, and
editors? Data-dredging is closely linked to the problem of multiple comparisons—the high probability that the calculation of a large number of statistical

tests will produce at least one "significant" value by chance alone. The problem is widely recognized, but rarely dealt with in specific analyses. Is it ethical to publish, as a scientific finding, a single result selected from a large set? How widespread among practicing scientists is ignorance (willful or otherwise) of this practical effect of the laws of probability? How widespread is the publication as significant of results that might be due to chance alone? How widespread is improper statistical analysis generally?

Third, is there a bias, as implied by the editor and recognized by the author, against publication of negative findings? It seems that authors widely (and probably correctly) believe that positive findings generally have a better chance of publication than negative findings. That perception has a profound impact on the whole scientific enterprise, from authors' selection of research topics and framing of hypotheses, through study design and implementation, to analysis, writing of reports, and choice of journal.

RESPONSES

Respondents offered a broad and often incompatible array of opinions on this scenario:

A simple letter to the editor would inform the general readership of the journal and would also allow the author to reply. This type of debate is good for research.

All publications involve some degree of selection. It is unreasonable to expect an author to discuss everything he has done.

This problem, a common one, shows that the author is a cookbook statistician.

One should never allow (if one knows) the conversion of meaningless data into meaningful results by statistical manipulation.

I specifically have a reviewer know the author (not double-blind review) so that I can get as much information as possible on the article.

The reviewer's own interpretations of the data are irrelevant—but the missing data are not irrelevant. If the author chooses to discuss the one really important finding, that is his/her prerogative. However, the reader should not have to find out from "other sources" that 10 treatments were studied.

The editor would have to depend on his well-qualified reviewers, not the author, to evaluate the statistical significance of the data.

I think some better training in statistical ethics (if one could call it that) is needed. . . . "Forcing" positive results is criminal and delays the results of good scientific inquiry.

Several editors reject papers like that in the scenario or said that they would do so. Almost half the respondents indicated that they had had some experience with this kind of problem, and several specific occurrences were cited in the responses. One respondent, sympathetic to the author, reported that he himself had been asked to present findings so as to make them appear more positive; but he agreed that all treatments should be mentioned, so that knowledgeable readers could understand the bases for selections and comparisons.

One editor first sent a paper to a reviewer who had seen it earlier and who knew that the reported number of subjects was smaller than the true number. Further information from the author differed from that of the reviewers, who then refused to comment on the revised manuscript. The editor felt that he was then obliged to accept the author's figures.

Another editor who had faced a problem similar to that in the scenario insisted on further explanation and improved statistical review; he eventually published a much improved paper, although he said that it still did not meet the standards urged by the reviewer.

In another case, it became clear that the authors had made the data fit the desired result. When the statistical reviewers challenged the significance of the results because the sample was too small, the authors withdrew the paper.

Some editors said that they would ask for further review or discuss the matter with their editorial boards. Many suspected that further technical statistical review would result in advice that the author "cough up the *whole* study," as one put it.

DISCUSSION

In their extreme, the views expressed in response to the scenario reflect and reinforce a serious misunderstanding of the role of statistical analysis. The core of the scientific method, and hence of science, is inference: learning about unobserved phenomena by studying and interpreting relevant data on observed phenomena. Because of its central role, inference must be protected, despite many contrary pressures, including pressures to publish. Authors submit selectively, editors approve selectively; we suspect even that readers read selectively. So inferences are wrongly drawn and interpreted.

The answer, though, is not an across-the-board interdiction of any look at results before a decision to submit, approve, or read a paper. Not every experiment worth doing is worth reporting in full, and not every possible outcome of a valid research study is of equal relevance to each reader. Some selectivity must be preserved in each of the three broad phases of scientific communication. We believe, rather, that a combination of smaller steps is appropriate. Authors should tailor the level of detail in a report to the needs of a majority of likely readers. Editors should insist on that, but in return should be more willing to publish brief "negative" reports. Readers should be alert to the pervasive and destructive effects of publication bias and interpret reported P values with caution, even when they are much more extreme than the usual 5% level. In addition, tenure committees and colleagues in general should put less weight on publication itself—whether of positive or negative results—and more on the research process as a whole (with, perhaps, some "extra credit" for restraint in publication when there is little to communicate).

The committee believes that, on balance, the author's refusal to disclose the data in full is bad science, although it is not outright fraud. No lie is told, but failure to tell the whole truth here distorts scientific inferences based on the data and hence is unethical. These matters have recently been discussed elsewhere.[1-7]

Statistics is the art and science of interpreting quantitative data. It includes framing questions that are answerable, designing the study, exercising quality control of the data to reduce both variance and bias, drawing inferences from data, and generalizing results to other situations. Those steps might or might not include computations of such values as means, variances, P values, and confidence limits.

Unfortunately, computation is widely misperceived as the whole of statistics. Furthermore, computation is commonly performed and interpreted by statistical amateurs, and the recent expansion of access to easy computation has seriously increased the problem by putting delicate, sophisticated, and powerful statistical tools in the hands of persons who do not know how to use them properly. Because of the frequent and serious problems of ensuring competent statistical analysis, some journals now make regular use of statistical consultants.

The positions of survey respondents, as noted, ranged from simple and prompt rejection of the paper to acceptance as is (and let the reader beware). Suggestions are listed below in order from the least to the most editorial involvement and commitment.

- Ignore the reviewer's comment and publish the paper as is.
- Publish the paper with a footnote or amplified discussion section.
- Request as a condition of further consideration that the author include a note to the effect that eight other treatments were assayed, with reasons for reporting only two treatments.
- Request as a condition of further consideration that the author submit the results of all 10 treatments.
- Ask the reviewer to write a letter to the editor, who then allows the author to reply in print.
- Publish the article as is, but write an editorial explaining the prepublication history of the manuscript.

- Ask the author to conduct additional experiments using only the two treatments and present an unbiased statistical analysis of the new data, with or without the old data.
- Disapprove on technical grounds.
- Disapprove on ethical grounds and notify other editors in the author's specialty about the problem and the author's refusal to correct it.
- Notify chairs, deans, and others at the author's research institution(s) that the author has submitted an incomplete and misleading manuscript.

CONCLUSIONS AND RECOMMENDATIONS

There is a growing awareness that many scientists are not adequately prepared to deal with more than the simplest statistical concepts and techniques and that their lack of sophistication has made many scientific conclusions less than valid. Reform movements and a growing literature are aimed at remedying those statistical deficits. The movement has also gained impetus from the recognition that experimentation involving human beings might be less than ethical when it does not have a reasonable chance of resulting in useful and beneficial knowledge.

The committee believes that, in a situation like that described in the scenario, the editor should require the author to describe in the methods section the whole of the experiment as it was conducted, including (if appropriate) differences in performance between the two treatments in question and the other eight treatments. In the results and discussion sections, the editor should allow the author substantial discretion in presentation of the two treatments that the author feels are most important, but should emphasize that the manuscript will be submitted for further review by a competent statistician and by someone in the field who also has a qualitative sense of the relative importance of the 10 treatments.

No further action is needed if the author withdraws the paper. If the editor notices that the manuscript is published elsewhere, the editor might alert the reviewer who first noted the problem; that reviewer, in the interest of improving statistical handling of data in scientific journals, could write a letter to the editor of the publishing journal.

REFERENCES

1. Bailar JC. Science, statistics, and deception. Ann Intern Med 1986;104:259-60.
2. Bailar JC. Louis TA, Lavori PW, Polansky M. A classification for biomedical research reports. N Engl J Med 1984;311:1482-7.
3. Bailar JC. Louis TA, Lavori PW, Polansky M. Studies without internal controls. N Engl J Med 1984;311:156-62.
4. Bailar JC, Mosteller F. Medical Uses of Statistics. Waltham, Massachusetts: New England Journal of Medicine Books; 1986.

5. Lock S. A Difficult Balance: Editorial Peer Review in Medicine. London: Nuffield Provincial Hospitals Trust; 1985.
6. Meier P. Current research in statistical methodology for clinical trials. Biometrics 1982;38(Suppl):141-53.
7. Snedecor GW, Cochran WG. Statistical Methods. 6th ed. Ames, Iowa: Iowa State University Press; 1968.

Scenario E

Conflicts of Interest

An author submits a paper on a new laboratory procedure that uses an expensive piece of equipment. The reviews are favorable, but the editor receives an anonymous note stating that the author of the paper has a large financial stake in publication and that his analysis is biased. There is no allegation of fraudulent data. The author admits on query from the editor that he has a substantial stock interest in the firm that makes the equipment, but denies that his judgment has been affected. (He says that he bought the stock because the product looked good.) He also denies that his private financial affairs are any business of the scientific community as long as his scientific work and its reporting are honest.

ISSUES

Relations among persons in academe, government, and business or industry have historically been viewed with suspicion accompanied by derogatory stereotyping and inferences of opportunistic financial alliance. Investigators have been required to maintain, and sometimes display, a balance of personal or professional financial transactions and independent scientific integrity. Editors are finding more and more that their roles have been expanded to include examination of the implications of the commercial affiliations of their authors.

In the field of recombinant DNA, many genetic-engineering firms, which patent laboratory-made genetic combinations and have vast potential profits, are owned in part by the same scientists whose work leads to the development of salable material. Many argue that it is unrealistic to expect scientists and physicians not to own stock in ventures or invest in capital growth in fields most familiar to them. As technology burgeons and academic collaboration with both industry and government increases, manuscripts submitted to journals more and more commonly list coauthors employed by the manufacturers of equipment or products used in the work. This scenario deals with an author's failure to disclose financial ties related to data submitted for publication.

Should manuscripts devoted to a single drug or piece of equipment be rejected? Should advocacy of any commercial technology or product be allowed? Should an editor's response to a manuscript depend on the authors' financial ties? Should editorial responses depend on whether results favor the commercial product at issue, and if so, why? To whom and to what extent should authors' involvement with a manufacturing company be disclosed? Does it matter whether the authors own a few shares of stock in a large corporation that holds an incidental interest in the equipment or product cited in their manuscript, versus 20% of the stock in a small company with no other product? What should be included in authors' disclosure statements to an editor—e.g., dollar amounts of financial transactions and dates of the authors' stock purchases? Is it necessary for editors to disclose such information to reviewers? Apart from those issues, should editors give credence to or take further action on the basis of information that reaches them anonymously?

RESPONSES

Most CBE members who responded to the survey said that they had dealt specifically with the subject of this scenario in their work. About half said that no deviations from the normal processing policies of their journals had occurred as part of their solutions to the issue. Although almost half the respondents did not consider the issue to constitute a serious problem in scientific publishing, most felt that it warrants serious consideration when detected, so that readers can be protected from author bias. According to the respondents, full disclosure of financial interests, support, and affiliations of authors is the most realistic tool available to alert editors, reviewers, and readers to the circumstances surrounding a manuscript with a potential conflict of interest.

The manuscript selection process, including peer review, was cited by more than half the respondents as a reliable tool for determining the appropriateness of publication, whether authors' financial ties to data are at issue or not. One respondent wrote:

> If referees judge the data to be fraudulent or unsupportable, interpretations and recommendations inappropriate, the procedures biased or invalid, or the study poorly executed or lacking in controls, the manuscript should be rejected. Data hold up or they don't; an author's arguments are sound or they are not.

Another stated:

> If equipment or products are thoroughly evaluated, particularly by comparison with established products or procedures, financial connections of the author

are issues moot to science. Financial interests or professional affiliations should not automatically imply dishonesty in the data or bias in the author's judgment.

DISCUSSION

It is the responsibility of the editor, editorial board, or publisher to determine what rules will apply to manuscripts that link authors to commercial products, equipment, or other financial interests and to set policy regarding criteria for disclosure. It is best for this determination to be made in advance, as a standing journal policy, rather than in response to a specific problem or possible problem. A policy should require that authors disclose their commercial or financial ties to products and the financial support of the work presented in manuscripts. However, the editors' responses to this information can depend on many things, including the nature of the work reported, the technical discipline, the type of financial tie, and other applicable journal policies.

An editor should not reject a manuscript or take other action solely because of information provided in an anonymous note. However, in circumstances similar to those in the present scenario, the editor should query authors to obtain whatever information is necessary to understand possible conflicts of interest and to apply any relevant policy fairly. The degree to which a manuscript is scrutinized by the editor or reviewers beyond normal journal procedures depends on the editor's perception of the potential conflict.

Journal policy might specify that an editor return manuscripts without considering them for publication when conflict of interest is likely. Such a policy might be designed for a small journal that does not have the resources—for example, staff or time—to accommodate deviations from normal processing. That also might be the policy for a journal that would not usually consider or publish works devoted to a single drug or piece of equipment.

To provide balance to the review process, an independent technical expert might be asked to review a manuscript to supplement and balance reviews by scientists.

In many disciplines, such as pharmacology and chemical engineering, it is common for a manuscript to be devoted to the evaluation of a single drug, piece of equipment, or technology. If a journal considers such manuscripts for publication, editors can invoke procedures or precautions that will help to ensure fair manuscript review and unbiased decisions regarding publication, and appropriate guidelines on journal policy can be made available to authors. Authors might be instructed that a manuscript devoted to a specific technology or drug will be considered only if balance is provided in the paper by adequate consideration of the use or results of other products or methods in the same category.

A policy of disclosure of possible conflicts of interest might be most effective when used preventively, instead of to resolve apparent conflicts as they are detected. The amount and type of information provided by the authors should be such that the editor can determine, before the manuscript is accepted for publication, that there is little likelihood that a conflict has affected the study results and interpretation or can pass the materials to the editorial board, reviewers, or readers to make their own determinations regarding conflict of interest.

New questions arise when the editor must decide whether to disclose the information to reviewers: Will it help them in their review of the data, including evaluation of how the data were collected, analyzed, interpreted, and reported? Can the referees remain unbiased, once cognizant of the authors' affiliations?

Editors must also exercise discretion in deciding whether to disclose such information to reviewers and readers. Special attention should be given to authors' rights to privacy in personal affairs. Editors must protect not only their readers and reviewers, but also their authors.

An editor who deems it necessary to disclose information regarding authors' personal financial affiliations should first determine what information is necessary to resolve the question of a conflict of interest and then seek the authors' permission to disclose it. Denial of permission would be sufficient grounds for the editor to withdraw the manuscript from consideration for publication. The editor might properly ask reviewers to give the matter special attention, whether supplementary information from the authors is included or not. The reviewers' heightened sensibilities and perceptions of a possible problem are likely to ensure that there is no oversight of possible conflicts of interest. Scientific standards, however, must remain constant. The validity and acceptability of data should be evaluated by reviewers in exactly the same way that other scientific reports are evaluated.

CONCLUSIONS AND RECOMMENDATIONS

The committee has become convinced that the best tool to be used to prevent questions of bias due to authors' financial affiliations is disclosure by authors to editors and, when appropriate, disclosure by editors to reviewers and readers. At the time of initial submission of a manuscript, authors should provide editors with adequate information regarding their commercial or financial ties to products and regarding financial support of the work presented.

Journals should include in their information for authors a requirement for statements from authors citing all sources of support for the research reported and possible conflicts of interest. Publishing such a statement moves responsibility from a journal to the authors. For example, the *New England Journal of Medicine* includes the following statement in its information for authors:[1]

> The Journal expects authors to disclose any commercial associations that might pose a conflict of interest in connection with the submitted article. All funding sources supporting the work should be routinely acknowledged on the

title page, as should all institutional or corporate affiliations of the authors. Other kinds of associations, such as consultancies, stock ownership or other equity interests, or patent-licensing arrangements, should be disclosed to the Editor in a covering letter at the time of submission. Such information will be held in confidence while the paper is under review and will not influence the editorial decision. If the manuscript is accepted, the Editor will discuss with the authors how best to disclose the relevant information. Questions about this policy should be directed to the Editor.

REFERENCE

1. Information for authors. N Engl J Med 1990;323 [published in first issue of each month].

READINGS

1. Prager DJ, Omenn GS. Research, innovation, and university-industry linkages. Science 1980;207:379-84.
2. Relman AS. Dealing with conflicts of interest (Editorial). N Engl J Med 1984;310:1182-3.
3. Relman AS. Dealing with conflicts of interest (Editorial). N Engl J Med 1985;313:749-51.

Scenario F

Withdrawal of an Accepted Paper

A report of a well-designed double-blind study of a new drug is submitted to a journal. It is reviewed, revised, and accepted. The acceptance letter points out that, because of the journal's backlog of accepted manuscripts, the paper will not be published for almost a year. The acceptance letter also requests a transfer of copyright; the senior author submits it with his own signature and those of the two coauthors. Six months later, the galley proofs are sent to the senior author, who replies that the paper is to be withdrawn. The editor telephones and asks why. The senior author replies that, without his knowledge, one of his coauthors submitted the paper to another journal, which accepted it. He himself prefers publication in the other journal, because it will reach more readers. He gives as another excuse the first journal's long publication lag.

ISSUES

When a manuscript has been accepted and the authors have signed a copyright transfer form, does a publisher have any recourse if the paper is withdrawn for a reason other than a finding that its data are invalid? What can be considered to justify the withdrawal of an accepted manuscript by authors? Is an unusually long lag between acceptance and publication of a paper a valid extenuating circumstance? Does the answer change when authors are well informed of the lag? Should publishers attempt to enforce the contract inherent in copyright transfer? The major subject of this scenario is withdrawal of an accepted paper, but several other subjects are of concern: copyright transfer, delays in publication, and multiple submission of a manuscript.

Copyright transfer. Before passage of the Copyright Act of 1976,[4] which became effective January 1, 1978, transfer of copyright to the publisher occurred automatically. Publishers now must ask authors to transfer copyright explicitly.

The timing of conveyance of copyright differs among scientific journals. Some journals require transfer before publication, but do not state explicitly when it will become effective; therefore, a considerable period remains undefined with respect to copyright ownership. One major medical publisher, the American Medical Association, asks for transfer on acceptance of the manuscript. The American Chemical Society originally stated on its conveyance form that copyright transfer became effective if and when a work was accepted for publication. It later changed its policy, so that copyright assignment, if appropriate, is effective when the form is signed by the author (or authorized agent, in the case of a work made for hire).

Fetzner[3] advised journals trying to decide whether to require copyright transfer at the time of manuscript submission to base their decision on their acceptance rate: "If it is less than 50%, wait until a manuscript is accepted. This reduces by more than half the number of transfer forms reaching the editor's desk."

The ethical implications of copyright transfer differ from the legal and management implications. The *CBE Style Manual*[2] notes:

> Some journals require transfer of copyright from the author to the journal, with such transfer required usually before final acceptance of the paper. From the ethical point of view, however, copyright does not belong to the journal until the paper is published. Until then, the paper must be regarded by the editor as belonging to the author.

Delays in publication. In this scenario, the delay between acceptance of the manuscript and its scheduled publication in the first journal was projected as almost a year and actually would have been more than 6 months. Most of the respondents to the survey believed that to be an extraordinarily long time.

However, it appears to be normal in some scientific disciplines and specialties, many of whose members publish journals that appear quarterly or less often.

A 1984 survey of 13 major U.S. and foreign psychiatric journals reported a range of 2.1-17.9 months between acceptance and publication; the overall mean was 7.6 months (personal communication, Evelyn S. Myers). The *Author's Guide to Journals in the Health Field*[1] gives similar data on several hundred journals, and wide variations are apparent; e.g., the lag time for the *New England Journal of Medicine* was 2 months, and that for the *Journal of Applied Psychology* was 1 year.

Many journals have mechanisms for rapid publication of material judged to be unusually important or warranting particularly timely publication (see Scenario I). Some journals require a manuscript to be in a special format to qualify for consideration in this category; others consider every manuscript as a possibility for the category, if its contents meet stringent criteria of originality and if it is judged to be of major and immediate importance. Of the 261 journals listed in the *Author's Guide to Journals in the Health Field*,[1] about 30% indicated that they had a procedure for rapid publication.

Multiple submission. As noted in the discussion of Scenario C (on repetitive publication), most scientific journals have a policy of considering for publication only manuscripts that have not been submitted or published elsewhere. The exclusive submission requirement assures reviewers and editors that they are not spending time in evaluating papers that colleagues are simultaneously evaluating for other journals, and it is intended to reduce the proliferation of printed material that results from duplicate publication. Journal-management considerations are substantial. Submission to more than one journal greatly increases the cost involved in the review process; if a manuscript is accepted and processed for publication by more than one journal, unnecessary expenses obviously are incurred by at least one of them. In this scenario, the withdrawn manuscript was already in the galley-proof stage.

RESPONSES

An overwhelming majority of the respondents noted that withdrawal of manuscripts by authors after acceptance was uncommon, but that the related problem—the long interval from acceptance to publication—was indeed common.

Most of the respondents believed that some action should be taken against the authors; nearly all of these believed that the responsibility rested with the editors of the journals involved. Others cited as having responsibility for resolving the matter were the editorial boards of the journals, the publishers, and the dean of the authors' academic institution. Although no respondents reported encountering the exact situation, one described a situation in which a coauthor, without the knowledge of the senior author, submitted a manuscript to a journal with a larger circulation than the journal that had originally accepted it. The coauthor claimed that his work would be more visible in the second journal and that visibility was important for his academic advancement. The editor of the original journal released the article, and it appeared in the second journal.

Respondents offered many suggestions for shortening the lag time; most were intended to decrease the backlog of accepted manuscripts. They included narrowing the journal's focus or dividing it among two or more journals, implementing stricter acceptance criteria, and increasing the number of published pages.

DISCUSSION

According to responses to the survey, a wide range of actions could be taken. They included the following possibilities:

- At one extreme is the "let sleeping dogs lie" approach—i.e., do nothing. One respondent stated:

  > The editor should consent to the senior author's request for withdrawal, even at this late and costly time. Reason: The senior authors, during the year of publication delay, might have other reasons than were stated, such as fault in the experiment or newer reports that either invalidated or outdated the report now in galley-proof form. If difficulties develop after the report is published, the journal editor is faced with a real dilemma and has no excuse.

- The editor of the first journal could confer with the editor of the second journal and agree on a course of action. One respondent wrote that "the editor [to whose journal the article was first submitted] should phone the editor of the other journal; it would be only decent for the other journal to refuse to publish under the circumstances."
- The authors could be charged for costs already incurred by the first journal. For example, the Institute of Electrical and Electronic Engineers (IEEE) has adopted the following as part of its Policy 6.16, "Charges for Withdrawal or Modification of Manuscripts": "If the author(s) of a manuscript request modification or withdrawal subsequent to acceptance for publication and distribution, and if compliance with such a request involves significant costs, the IEEE may levy appropriate charges . . ." (reprinted with permission of IEEE, Inc., New York, N.Y., from *IEEE Policy and Procedures Manual, January 1990*).
- Various kinds of sanctions could be imposed on the authors, including notification of their institution and their professional societies.

CONCLUSIONS AND RECOMMENDATIONS

The committee believes that the likelihood of legal recourse in instances of copyright violation is more apparent than real; even in cases of flagrant violation, damage is difficult to prove. In addition, a suit (whether successful or not) would divert substantial resources from more productive uses and could harm the reputation of both the journal and the editor.

The committee recommends the following actions to deal with the issues raised in the scenario.

- A statement of the requirement of exclusive submission and publication should be prominently displayed both in the instructions for authors and on the copyright-transfer form.
- Each journal should decide when its transfer of copyright will become effective and should state this explicitly in its instructions for authors and on the copyright-transfer form. Two possibilities with substantial merit are the date when the transfer form is signed by the authors and the date of acceptance of the manuscript for publication. We see much value in the development of a clear understanding between editors and authors that transfer is effective long before journal resources are invested in technical editing and typesetting. A statement like the following would also be appropriate: "If the paper is not accepted and published by [the publisher] or is withdrawn by the author(s) before publication, this agreement becomes null and void."
- When an author indicates an intention to violate a valid transfer of copyright to a journal, the editors should discuss the situation with the author and attempt to agree on a mutually satisfactory solution. However, regardless of the copyright situation, an author who wishes to withdraw a paper should be allowed to do so. An editor who insists on publishing a paper that an author wishes to withdraw runs a risk of serious long-term consequences for little immediate gain. Regardless of the reason given by the author for wishing to withdraw the manuscript, the editor should recognize the possibility of a serious but unstated problem, such as a late discovery of fraud, and should not publish the work.
- A journal should attempt to reduce inappropriate intervals between acceptance of a paper and publication. Authors should be made aware of the likely interval between acceptance and publication (even at the time of submission), if it is considered unduly long.
- Each journal should consider the merits of publishing the dates of submission and acceptance of each manuscript. (For further discussion of this issue, see Scenario I.)

REFERENCES

1. Ardell DB, James JY. Author's Guide to Journals in the Health Field. New York: Haworth Press; 1980: xxix.
2. Council of Biology Editors Style Manual Committee. CBE Style Manual. 5th ed. Bethesda, Maryland: Council of Biology Editors; 1983:4.

3. Fetzner, JM. Copyright transfer: developing policies and procedures. CBE Views 1979; 2:80-9.
4. 17 U.S.C. (1976) (Public Law 94-553, October 19, 1976).

Scenario G

Confidentiality of Reviews

An editor had informed the authors of a manuscript that their work might be acceptable if it were revised extensively to take account of the comments of Reviewer B. A revised manuscript is submitted, but deals only partially with the comments of Reviewer B. With it is a covering letter explaining that Reviewer B had identified herself to the authors at a meeting and that together they had negotiated the changes to be made in the manuscript. According to the authors, Reviewer B is now satisfied with the manuscript, and the authors assume that it will be accepted by the editor.

ISSUES

The main theme in this scenario is the role of reviewers in the editorial review process. The scenario raises several important issues. What is the proper role of a reviewer in the editorial process? Should reviewers serve in an advisory or in a decision-making capacity? If a reviewer makes editorial decisions, what is an editor's role? Should reviewers agree to remain anonymous, in part to maintain appropriate channels of communication among authors, editors, and reviewers? What are the policy and ethical considerations, and are they different if the journal specifically asks reviewers to remain anonymous?

Some journals require anonymity; others allow reviewers to disclose their identities. The committee believes that either approach is feasible, if it is clearly understood by authors and reviewers, but sees little merit in the occasional suggestions that reviewers should always be identified to authors, readers, or both.

RESPONSES

More than half the respondents described the situation in this scenario as common; approximately one-third had experienced a similar situation. Most felt that it presented no serious problem for editors. According to one, "the editor should not interfere with the channels of communication between reviewers and authors." In fact, many welcomed the reviewer's assistance in the editorial process. Two typical responses were the following: "I don't see any problem in the reviewer's having taken this approach; it may have been very helpful to the authors." "Negotiations between reviewers and authors are appropriate with or without anonymity." One respondent stated that "the editor should send the manuscript to another reviewer. Probably the interaction of the original reviewers and the authors has done nothing but good to the work; this reviewer ought to be named in the acknowledgments. I don't see this as an ethical problem."

A few respondents, however, felt quite strongly that the scenario presented two important problems. First, the reviewer might have violated an agreement of confidentiality with the journal by identifying herself to the authors. Second, the reviewer, by privately negotiating with the authors, overstepped the bounds of her role by assuming a responsibility that must remain with the editor. One stated that "the reviewer needs to be bluntly reminded that she is not authorized to negotiate for the journal, that decisions to accept or reject are the province of the editor." Another wrote:

> The editor should advise the author and reviewer that all decisions are made through the editorial office and not "in private"; Reviewer B needs a better education regarding the rights and responsibilities of reviewing. Either the editor did a slipshod job of explaining the journal's policies or this reviewer is clearly out of line.

Similarly, other respondents stated:

> The editorial decision about whether or not the manuscript can be accepted for publication resides with the editor, and the editor should so inform the author.

> The editor should (a) reprimand authors for dealing with the journal indirectly and (b) reprimand Reviewer B for revealing her identity.

> The editor should advise the reviewer that identifying herself is improper and that she is not in a position to negotiate changes with an author, because she is an adviser only to the editor.

DISCUSSION

Should something be done, once an editor has received a revised manuscript and is informed of outside negotiations between the authors and a reviewer? If so, who should do it? Most respondents felt that the editor should do something, but the recommended actions varied widely. The responses ranged from naming the reviewer in the acknowledgments of the manuscript to ceasing to use the reviewer altogether. Although some respondents did not approve of the negotiations, most felt that the editor should simply verify the author's account with Reviewer B and then accept the manuscript. Others suggested that the manuscript be sent to an additional reviewer, to balance the negotiations with Reviewer B.

CONCLUSIONS AND RECOMMENDATIONS

The committee is concerned that an eminent reviewer can exert improper pressure on a junior author—pressure that would not be possible if the confidentiality of review were maintained. Similarly, an eminent author can exert pressure on a junior, but highly competent, reviewer. In addition, an ethical issue is clearly raised if the journal described in the scenario had clearly informed Reviewer B of a policy of reviewer anonymity. Even when journal policy permits the identification of reviewers, the committee believes that contact between author and reviewer should take place only through the editorial office of the journal, with the editor's full knowledge and participation. That reduces the likelihood of improper pressure.

The committee is aware of a contrary opinion, rooted in concepts of "fairness," that reviewers' names should be disclosed to authors. But the requirement for fairness is satisfied when the editor makes clear, and the author accepts, the policy of the journal. In any event, the editor has the higher duty to protect the integrity of science. One powerful reason for anonymity is that it can protect reviewers from the temptation to avoid the displeasure of, or to curry favor with, authors by being inappropriately laudatory and uncritical. Another reason is that it protects more critical reviewers from having to engage in disputes with defensive authors. Excessively negative or personal comments should, of course, be deleted by an editor.

Sometimes authors would like to acknowledge particularly helpful reviewers in their papers or even include them as authors. The committee believes that constructive and critical reviewing is a part of investigators' commitment to the scientific enterprise and that public acknowledgment is neither necessary nor appropriate.

READINGS

1. Bailar JC. Patterson K. Journal peer review: the need for a research agenda. N Engl J Med. 1985;312:654-7.
2. Bishop CT. How to Edit a Scientific Journal. Philadelphia: ISI Press; 1984.
3. Council of Biology Editors Style Manual Committee. CBE Style Manual. 5th ed. Bethesda, Maryland: Council of Biology Editors; 1983.
4. Lock S. A Difficult Balance: Editorial Peer Review in Medicine. London: Nuffield Provincial Hospitals Trust: 1985.
5. Murray RGE. What is an editor for? CBE Views 1983;6:14-9.
6. O'Connor M. The Scientist as Editor: Guidelines for Editors of Books and Journals. New York: John Wiley & Sons; 1979:28-40.
7. Relman AS, Angell M. How good is peer review? N Engl J Med 1989;321:827-9.

8. Relman AS, Rennie D, Angell M. Greetings—with regrets (Editorial). N Engl J Med 1980;303:1527-8.
9. The Journal's peer review process (Comment). N Engl J Med 1989;321:837-9.

Scenario H

Noneditorial Use of Privileged Information

An author had submitted a paper that was rejected after two reviewers independently challenged the basic concepts of the reported work and criticized the research on the grounds of faulty methods and sloppy workmanship. The editor is now asked for his opinion on the promotion of the author to a tenured position. The request is accompanied by reprints of published articles by the author and positive evaluations by other colleagues. The editor feels that his reviewers' opinions were valid and that it is important to make an excellent appointment in the department in question, but he recognizes that some of his knowledge about the author is privileged.

ISSUES

The primary question raised in this scenario is whether editors may use for noneditorial purposes their knowledge of colleagues gleaned during the exercise of editorial functions generally held confidential. It is not apparent from the scenario whether the editor is familiar with the author's work other than through the editorial process, but the information gained through that process is not consistent with the general view of the author, and the manuscript was not published. Should information gained through the editorial process be off limits to everyone not involved in the publication of the journal, or is it sometimes justifiable to disclose such information? Does the answer depend on whether the editor has knowledge of the author through other connections, on whether the information gained through the editorial process is consistent with the general view of the author, or on whether the author's work is published or (as here) rejected for good cause?

RESPONSES

The following responses to this scenario reflect the spectrum of courses of action that the editor might consider:

Do nothing. Decline the invitation to give your opinion.

Reviewers' comments are indeed privileged. If the editor cannot write a recommendation that ignores reviewers' comments, he must somehow without prejudice avoid writing the letter.

The editor should abstain from such interference in academic promotions.

If the editor is not an expert in the field, he should disqualify himself.

The editor could explain tactfully to the tenure review board that some of the work this particular author had submitted had not been up to his standards in other work and that from his (the editor's) point of view it would be necessary to point this out, but also that it would be necessary to point out that the author should not be judged entirely by one paper.

I have been in this situation more than rarely. I have had no hesitation about giving my best judgment.

Report the situation to the tenure committee in its entirety with copies of supporting documents.

Too often sloppy researchers are rewarded because of an "old boy" system of friendly, forgiving colleagues. Any scientist, editor or not, should encourage excellence, not inferiority.

Tenure committees receive privileged information from many sources. I see no reason why an editor should not forward his experiences as well. He may, in fact, be a less biased source than many others.

As is apparent, this scenario evoked particularly varied responses, from an absolute proscription of recommendations that use editorial knowledge, through a suggestion of some sort of limited response, to the belief that the editor is obliged to divulge all the pertinent information he has.

Among those who recommended a limited response to the request for a recommendation, several suggested that the editor should become involved in the recommendation only if his field of expertise coincided with that of the author; the editor would have first-hand knowledge (as opposed to knowledge gained largely from reviewers) of the author's work and would not base an evaluation solely on the editorial experience. Those respondents felt that, if the editor's opinion of the author were based largely on the reviewers' comments, the editor would be basing a recommendation on a second-hand opinion; that would amount to hearsay, which would not be legitimate for the purpose of a recommendation. As a way to circumvent the reliance on second-hand information, some suggested that the editor decline to provide an assessment, but instead provide the names of the critical reviewers, who could evaluate the author's research abilities more accurately than could the editor.

In contrast, some felt that the editor could selectively disclose information about the profesional abilities of the authors, regardless of its source. And others held that, although the editor could legitimately base a recommendation on knowledge gained in the editorial process, he should not reveal details.

Thus, the editor should write a diplomatic letter disclosing in a general way that the situation was "not quite all right."

DISCUSSION

According to the responses to the survey, editors are asked fairly often to provide recommendations for colleagues, especially when the scientific interests of an editor are similar to those of a candidate. Each of the following possible actions received appreciable support from respondents.

- The editor declines to provide recommendations, on the grounds that it would violate the confidentiality of the editorial process.
- The editor provides a recommendation based only on extra-editorial activities and refuses to provide a recommendation if his only knowledge of the author is derived from his editorial activities.
- The editor provides a full opinion based on all information, including that obtained in evaluating the rejected manuscript. The editor's action might include sending copies of the rejected manuscript with copies of reviewers' comments.

The committee believes that this scenario involves a genuine ethical dilemma—the conflict between the editor's obligation to protect the confidentiality of the editorial process and his obligation to disclose information that accurately represents research quality. (The obligation of an editor to report fraud is not in dispute.) The wide range of responses indicates the respondents' various views on the relative importance of the competing obligations.

The scenario also raises other, somewhat different issues, and considering them might help in reaching a conclusion about the major conflict. The first is the distinction between recommendations based on personal knowledge of the candidate and those based on the quality of his work. A description of personal attributes is, by definition, subjective, and usually there is no necessity to offer evidence to support it. In contrast, an evaluation of a scientist's work is buttressed with evidence, primarily the body of the candidate's published writing. Thus, statements about the quality of a candidate's work offered in a recommendation can be questioned by members of the tenure committee, and they can, if they choose, form their own judgments by reviewing the writing. That is not the case in the scenario. If the editor makes a recommendation on the basis of a rejected manuscript, the tenure committee has no opportunity to evaluate the writing that supports the recommendation, and it will have to take the editor's word, itself based on the word of the reviewers, that the work was badly flawed. That outcome seems unscientific and perhaps unethical. The situation also confers too much power on the editor outside the journal office.

A response to the difficulty might be to send the tenure committee copies of the flawed manuscript with copies of the reviewers' comments, but this clearly would violate the confidentiality of the editorial process. Authors submit manuscripts to journals with the understanding that they will not be distributed without the authors' permission (including implicit permission for necessary peer review), and reviewers likewise offer their opinions in confidence. Editors do not have the right to distribute manuscripts that are not their property.

CONCLUSIONS AND RECOMMENDATIONS

Because the evidence from manuscript review might not be available to everyone and the editor may not distribute confidential materials, this committee strongly recommends against providing an evaluation of an author who is known to the editor only through journal submissions. There is also a practical reason for declining to offer recommendations based on editorial knowledge: doing so might result in the editor's very quickly becoming overwhelmed with requests for recommendations, precisely because he is in a position to have information not available to the scientific community at large.

A second additional issue concerns the distinction between knowledge gained as an editor and knowledge gained in another capacity, say, as a research colleague of the author. Might it be legitimate for the editor with both to offer a recommendation based only on the second? The committee does not believe that it is possible to compartmentalize impressions accurately according to where and how they originated; almost certainly, impressions formed outside the journal office will be contaminated by impressions formed during the editorial process. It might be possible for an editor whose field of expertise overlaps with the author's to offer a useful recommendation that is based heavily on published work and a view of the author's personal attributes. If the editor's evaluation is largely consistent with the general view of the candidate, that would offer few problems for the tenure committee.

There is a third additional issue: Does it matter whether the editor's evaluation is positive or negative? Probably it does. As just noted, an evaluation consistent with others' evaluations might not present problems. If, however, the editor's evaluation, based solely on noneditorial knowledge, is negative and the general view is positive, members of the tenure committee would almost certainly wonder whether that evaluation was based on unavailable knowledge gained in the editorial process. The evaluation itself might become difficult to evaluate and therefore not very helpful. The editor might decide to offer a recommendation only if it is based on published work and if it is largely consistent with the general view of the candidate. An editor who adopts that policy, however, should recognize that a refusal to offer a recommendation might be construed as implying the existence of knowledge from the editorial process that would be harmful to the candidate.

Taking all those issues together, the committee recommends one of two policies for editors who are asked for recommendations for colleagues.

1. An editor would be justified in adopting a consistent policy of not providing such recommendations, on the following grounds:
   - Knowledge of a candidate based on editorial work cannot be neatly separated from knowledge based on other activities. Evaluations would therefore be based at least in part on unavailable and confidential information.
   - An inconsistent policy—the occasional refusal to provide a recommendation—would suggest that unavailable and confidential information is involved.
   - Any other policy would lead to the editor's being overwhelmed with requests for recommendations because of the editor's special knowledge.
2. An editor would be justified in offering recommendations only when:
   - The editor has outside knowledge of the candidate.
   - The editor's evaluation is based only on published work and a view of personal attributes, and the editor makes this restriction clear in communicating with the recipient of the evaluation.

Scenario I

Sequence of Publication

A journal has a backlog of approved papers such that the average time from approval to publication is about a year. With the advice and consent of the journal's advisory board, the editor adopts a policy that some classes of papers will be published out of sequence: papers by authors who pay optional page charges; papers that seem to enhance the subject makeup of specific issues; papers by first-time authors; and papers that the editor, using the comments of reviewers, judges to be unusually important or urgent. Authors of favored papers like the policy, but other authors—their work now delayed even more—complain that the policy is unfair.

ISSUES

This scenario raises the following three sets of issues:

1. What sequence is appropriate? How should it balance competing interests? Should policy be explicit? Who should set the policy?
2. Journals and their editors have multiple responsibilities—to authors, readers, publisher-owners, the scientific field, the public at large, and perhaps

other persons and groups. This scenario can be read in part as an exploration of responsibilities to authors vis-à-vis other groups.

3. The journal with too large a backlog serves all its constituencies poorly; the journal with none leads a precarious existence and might from time to time have to publish material that does not attain reasonable scientific standards. How should an optimal intermediate point be defined, and how should editors try to attain it?

However a journal balances its responsibilities, it must attend in some way to the legitimate interests of a variety of stake-holders. If authors sense that they are being treated unfairly (whether in sequence of publication or in other matters), they will tend to send their work elsewhere. If readers find that their needs are not being met, they will curtail their reading—and their subscriptions. If publisher-owners perceive that a journal no longer serves their interests, they might reduce their active support; if it also loses money, they might sell it or even discontinue it. A journal that does not serve its scientific discipline might meet all those fates.

Editors tend to be in closest daily contact with authors, and perhaps for that reason they are most sharply aware of their dependence on and responsibilities to authors. Publisher-owners might be a close second, with readers, other subscribers (such as libraries), the field in general, and the public at large all much further behind.

This committee knows of no objective studies of optimal backlog size, although firm and incompatible opinions abound. The matter is in theory susceptible to statistical modeling. Given a more or less random rate of submission of potentially publishable papers, the approval rate must over the long term equal the publication rate; otherwise, the backlog will either vanish or grow without limit. Still, small adjustments in approval rate can be used to create a backlog that is just large enough to accommodate the expected degree of variation in submissions without making conditions for the journal so safe that the end of the backlog is never reached.

The problem is complicated, however, by variations. Some journals note a surge of submissions at about the time of annual meetings. Others note a substantial decrease during the summer, while investigators presumably are doing the work that will yield the next round of papers. Should backlogs be allowed to fluctuate in parallel with submission fluctuations, so that standards for acceptance remain constant? That would imply cycles in delays to publication. Conversely, if the delay is held constant, there might have to be undesirable fluctuations in acceptance rates and standards.

Less predictable are the rapid rise and fall of interest in the specific fields covered by journals and interruptions in the normal flow of publication by, for example, journal issues on particular topics. Should those be accommodated by adjusting backlogs? Problems are likely to differ between, for example, journals that publish weekly (for which a six-issue backlog might be tolerable) and journals that publish semiannually (for which it is not). How should policy reflect such differences? The committee has no general answers to the questions posed here, but believes that each journal should have a brief and clear statement of policy regarding size of backlog.

Each journal should also have a brief, clear statement about sequence of publication, and it should be made clear to both authors (in instructions for authors) and readers (when papers are published out of the journal's usual sequence).

RESPONSES

Survey respondents provided a remarkable diversity of opinions on the scenario, such as the following:

I think the editor's major responsibility is to the readers. Accordingly, the policy of first publishing unusually important or urgent papers seems reasonable.

This doesn't seem fair to authors who are asked to wait.

The authors . . . have the right to expect that approved manuscripts will be published in sequence.

Is a journal's primary responsibility to its authors or to its readers' need for the information?

The only one I would agree with would be payment of upfront page charges. This would allow printing of additional pages.

I suspect that giving priority to those who pay for publication risks converting the journal to a vanity publication.

The editor, not the date of submission, decides the order of publication.

The whole prejudicial preferential system should be discarded.

Priorities for publication are made on the basis of timeliness, content, and issue makeup, not . . . chronology of submission.

I favor publication on strict priority based on return of revisions. The deviation I will allow occurs when authors who are afraid of being scooped are willing to pay full page charges.

It is not ethical to require that authors pay for earlier publication. I think that this is in effect blackmail in a field in which *when* a paper is published is almost as important as *what* is published.

Editorial judgment is part of the responsibility of an editor. You can't make everyone happy!

Editorial policy is entirely up to the editor (and the editorial board). No ethical problem is involved.

There's no "right" or "wrong" here; each journal must assess this sort of policy on the basis of its own unique constraints and circumstances.

Except for page charges, I don't think it is ethical to move other papers ahead, and even payment of page charges is doubtful in a journal situation.

The fact that the editor-in-chief has allowed the situation to develop in the first place means that he is incompetent. A new editor-in-chief is needed—and *fast*.

I make no pretense of publishing lockstep. The dates of submission are published for each paper.

Many respondents said that one should publish only in acceptance-date order, and most suggested getting rid of the backlog by publishing larger issues or supplemental issues and at the same time raising the rejection rate. There was vigorous opposition to the payment of optional page charges to accelerate publication. The majority felt quite strongly that it was inherently wrong to "buy your way into a scientific publication"; only a few felt otherwise.

Most respondents were lukewarm about priority for first-time authors. Papers that seem to enhance the subject makeup of specific issues and those judged to be unusually important or urgent met with more acceptance; giving priority to important papers was considered the most acceptable of the choices. In fact, according to some respondents, many journals now appear to apply such a policy routinely.

Notification of journal policy was considered important. Many said that instructions for authors should describe the order of publication and that there would be no ethical problem if authors were aware of "out-of-sequence" policies before they submitted their manuscripts.

A problem can arise if a journal changes its policies without due notification to potential contributors. If a journal with an explicit policy of regularly publishing papers in acceptance-date order changes to another sequence when there is a large backlog, there might be a strong and damaging revolt.

Several respondents touched on the question, "To whom is the journal responsible?" Is a journal responsible to its whole potential readership—that is, to the scientific community—or to the much smaller pool of authors? Several respondents felt that the journal was responsible primarily to the readership and that the editor alone should always decide what appears in what issue, backlog or no backlog. The *New England Journal of Medicine* has published articles on the acquired immunodeficiency syndrome (AIDS) with a top priority, in an attempt to respond to intense concern over this epidemic. The editor decided that manuscripts dealing with AIDS that might be seen as having public-health implications should, at his discretion, be processed more rapidly than is routine. Readers (and, through them, the public) could then have information about AIDS as rapidly as possible. That sort of decision reflects the primacy of the interests of readers over those of authors.

Science suffered a problem with its large backlog and published a note stating that the journal had adopted a rejection rate of 90% and would maintain it until the backlog was gone.

DISCUSSION

Many respondents strongly believe that sequence of acceptance of manuscripts is the only, or nearly the only, legitimate criterion for sequence of publication. A smaller number prefer to use sequence of initial submission or of submission of the accepted version. But few discussed reasons; most respondents seemed to believe that reasons for their positions would be obvious. No respondent in the acceptance-date group made any allowance for variations in delays out of the authors' control, such as long delays in reviewing. Where exceptions were allowed, they were most often for papers judged to be unusually important or urgent. Some respondents stated, in various ways, that almost any policy would be acceptable if the policy were clearly articulated for potential authors and any new policy would not apply to papers already submitted (a "grandfather clause").

CONCLUSIONS AND RECOMMENDATIONS

The committee believes that editors should in general consider that their responsibilities to readers come first. Authors, publisher-owners, and others should also recognize that primacy; in the long run, a primary focus on readers will also benefit the other groups.

It seems nearly impossible to provide useful rules beyond that point. Sequence of publication is a matter more of journal policy than of ethics, although it has substantial ethical implications that might become dominant if authors are misled.

The committee also has some concern about the emphasis, sometimes approaching hysteria, on the moment of publication. It is a matter of much concern in some fields of science, but does not appear to have much importance to anyone except authors; even then it seems to be largely a product of group dynamics, with little rational foundation. One sometimes hears or reads that the emphasis on priority of publication is an important driving force behind the rapid progress of science, but we know of no data on that point, nor even of any careful dissection of the argument.

Committee members discussed the pros and cons of publishing dates of submission or acceptance. That also is a matter of journal policy, rather than ethics. There are arguments for and against any such policy. Having such a policy obviously lessens the pressure to publish rapidly, but it leads to excessive concern about priority. That might place additional pressure on editors to publish in rigid sequence, without regard for the relative importance of manuscripts or their fit in a given issue of a journal. Publishing submission dates also encourages the submission of rough drafts, rather than completed manuscripts.

Publishing out of sequence to enhance the quality and coherence of an issue of a journal is probably justified. It will arouse less anger in authors if the journal routinely publishes articles rapidly. An author's concerns will be greater if the journal is already slow (for example, if the journal is published bimonthly and has a 6-month delay). Publishing out of sequence on the basis of willingness to pay page charges serves only the financial health of the journal and is probably unjustified, as well as short-sighted. The committee recommends that, whatever policy is adopted, the editor ensure its full disclosure in such a manner that authors and other concerned persons will see and understand it.

Scenario J

Commitment to Publish

A manuscript is submitted, sent out for review, and returned with recommendations for extensive revisions. The editor asks the authors for the revisions, stating that acceptance is contingent on their being satisfactory. Shortly after sending the letter, the editor receives another manuscript on the same subject from a different group of investigators and finds that it is a report of a substantially better study.

ISSUES

This scenario illustrates an editor's conflict between the obligation to consider manuscripts in the order in which they are submitted and the obligation to publish the best data available, regardless of order of submission.

To whom is an editor responsible—to authors, with their perceived need to establish priority for their work through publication, or to the readers of the journal, with their expectations of receiving the best information available? Does an editor's responsibility include withdrawing a commitment to publish a manuscript, even if all conditions for its acceptance have been met? Should publication be denied to authors who have invested substantial effort in satisfying conditions of acceptance as outlined by the editor and referees, for reasons unrelated to these conditions? Would an editor's right to abrogate a commitment to publish a work at any time before final acceptance contribute to careless and hasty publication?

RESPONSES

Survey respondents almost unanimously placed responsibility for resolution of this conflict with the editor of the journal. About two-thirds said that the scenario represented a serious and common problem in scientific publication. Half the respondents indicated that they had experienced a similar situation at least once in their own work.

Most of the respondents recommended one of two actions: publication of both manuscripts or publication only of the better manuscript.

Respondents who recommended the first action felt that both manuscripts should be published if the first manuscript was satisfactorily revised, if the second manuscript also met journal standards for acceptance, if both added to the body of knowledge, and if journal space allowed; readers would ultimately judge for themselves which work was stronger. One respondent wrote that "the impact of the two studies with the same conclusion may be greater than that of one study; this may be helpful if the subject is particularly important. The journal is the marketplace where products (manuscripts) compete." Another commented that "a number of good papers on the same subject are needed to produce a reliable body of literature."

Respondents who recommended publication of the better manuscript, regardless of sequence of submission, believed that an editor's primary responsibility was not to authors, but to science. One respondent summed up that belief as follows: "Editors have an obligation to authors, but on the other hand a broader obligation to science and to the reader as the recipient of the best material available." Another said that "the better manuscript should be published. If the other study substantiates or negates that one, it can also be published." And a third simply stated: "Publish the best manuscript. Period." Respondents who recommended the second action felt that quality should be the deciding criterion for acceptance. One respondent wrote that "priority should go to the person or group who completes the study *properly* first." Another said, "Don't buy a pig in a poke by waiting for revisions from the first group. The revisions might never arrive, and too little too late gets very little in science." Yet another commented that, "if one is going to compete as an author, then one must learn that such a situation as described here goes with the territory."

A third, less common recommendation was to publish the first manuscript if the revisions were satisfactory and to return the second paper as a "priority reject," despite its superior quality. A few respondents said that the editor should make a final decision on the first paper on the basis of the revision *before* considering the second manuscript on the same topic. Some respondents used the word "contract" to describe the editor's commitment to the first group of authors to publish contingent on satisfactory revision. Thus, the editor should fulfill the contract to the first group, regardless of later developments. One respondent wrote: "What a quandary! Of course, the editor wants to publish the better manuscript, but he has made what might be considered a contract with the authors of the first manuscript." Another felt that no conflict existed, but "only an editor's disappointment," if journal policy precluded publication of two manuscripts on the same subject.

Several respondents discussed conditional acceptance of manuscripts. Most of them suggested that a conflict might ultimately be avoided if, instead of being conditionally accepted, papers were rejected with an invitation to resubmit only if changes were made. One respondent wrote that "a conditional acceptance is NOT an acceptance" and added that editors need to make that clear to authors.

A few respondents suggested coauthorship, mediated by the editor, as a possible solution. One wrote that "the best solution is for the editor to foster cooperation among the authors and propose a combined report, but realistically this is going too far and, at the very least, expecting too much." Another suggested that "the two groups might be persuaded to exchange manuscripts and cross-reference the two, pointing out similar or corroborative and differing or even conflicting results, interpretations, and conclusions."

DISCUSSION

Many editors must operate under serious economic constraints; publishing two manuscripts that report much the same results might be considered an inappropriate use of precious journal space. An editor who can accept only one manuscript on a particular subject should be candid with both groups of authors regarding the circumstances surrounding the consideration of two papers and explicitly outline the options available to both groups according to journal policy.

If an editor decides to stand behind a commitment to publish the first paper, its authors should be given a firm deadline for submission of their revision and an explanation of why a deadline is required. At the same time, the second manuscript should be returned to its authors as a "priority reject" with full disclosure of the reason for the decision. The editor should indicate to the second paper's authors that they may submit their manuscript elsewhere for publication or await the editor's decision regarding acceptance of the revision of the first manuscript; if the first manuscript is not revised satisfactorily, consideration of their manuscript according to regular journal processes can begin. One respondent said that

> editors should put the ball in the authors' court. In other words, if the first group of authors cannot revise their manuscript quickly, there is no reason not to proceed

with consideration of the second paper. Revisions can be stretched over an entire year's time and this would be unfair to the second group of authors, the journal's readership, and the scientific community in general.

A journal's policies about conditional acceptance should be clearly defined. Conditional acceptance by one journal might mean that an invitation to revise and resubmit implies an eventual commitment on the part of the editor to publish a work. One editor said that, when he sends a manuscript back to authors for revision, he writes:

> Your manuscript has been accepted for publication. If you do not wish to revise your work according to the criticisms outlined by the reviewers, please indicate your reasons for the editors. Revision according to all points raised in the enclosed critiques is not mandatory for publication.

CONCLUSIONS AND RECOMMENDATIONS

The situation described in this scenario seems to be sufficiently common for each journal to have a well-developed policy on the matter. The policy should be clearly communicated to possible authors, perhaps in the instructions for authors, and a letter of conditional acceptance should be clear about what commitment is made.

In the case presented here, the editor might wish to disclose the circumstances regarding both papers to the reviewers, to impress on them the need for expeditious review and to obtain as thorough and fair a review as possible. An editor might choose to send both papers to the same reviewers.

If an editor can publish only one manuscript on the same topic and, according to the journal's policy, conditional acceptance does not imply eventual acceptance, the editor should begin resolution of the conflict with disclosure to both sets of authors regarding the two submissions and the decision-making process to be used in deciding which manuscript will be published. It might then be appropriate for both manuscripts to undergo peer review according to normal journal standards, with publication of the first manuscript to be reviewed and revised to an acceptable form. That course of action seems to present some immediate problems, however, in that many factors that cannot be controlled by the editor or the authors can unfairly jeopardize the chances of one or the other paper. For example, if the editor sends each manuscript to different reviewers and one set of reviewers returns its critiques unusually fast, the corresponding group of authors will have an advantage in completing revision. An alternative to selection of one paper is for the editor to suggest collaboration or coauthorship to both groups of authors, but we are not persuaded that this would often work well.

An editor who has the luxury of being able to publish two manuscripts on the same subject also should begin processing each for consideration, with full disclosure to all authors regarding the circumstances. Here the major concern of authors will not necessarily be eventual publication, but the sequence of publication of the two manuscripts. Under these circumstances, an editor might or might not be bound to an original conditional acceptance. If a conditional acceptance stands, despite the later submission of a better manuscript, an editor can again issue a firm deadline to the authors of the first paper. The deadline might include a modest delay in publication, because readers could be well served by having the two papers back-to-back. The second manuscript can be considered and published in the same or a later issue only if it, too, meets the journal's standards for acceptance. If order of publication is decided in this way, dates of submission, revision, and acceptance of both manuscripts should be published. An editorial comment or explanation can sometimes be included that outlines the processing circumstances of the two manuscripts.

The committee strongly believes that a fair and orderly system of acceptance and publication enhances the scientific process, and hence serves the interests of readers, even if an editor must occasionally forfeit the publication of the better of two acceptable papers. It therefore recommends that the first manuscript described in this scenario be published, if it is revised in appropriate and timely fashion.

The committee also recommends that the following steps be used when publication of papers according to sequence conflicts with publication of papers according to quality.

- *Disclosure.* Regardless of the course of action chosen by an editor, the prompt disclosure of circumstances surrounding the submission of both manuscripts and of relevant journal policy should precede any other step. That should include full disclosure to both groups of authors and may, if appropriate or necessary, include disclosure to reviewers and readers.

    Editors should consider including a policy statement in their journals' instructions for authors regarding consideration of manuscripts on the same subject as it is related to order of submission; the alternative of informing authors only after the situation arises seems less satisfactory.

- *Priority of publication.* Editors should clearly outline and adhere to journal policy regarding priority of publication. When consideration of a second manuscript for publication is delayed, pending a decision regarding another paper on the same topic, the authors of the second manuscript should be so informed and given the option of submitting their manuscript elsewhere.

Scenario K

Bias Against Publication of Negative Results

*An author submits a paper concluding that a particular environmental
exposure has not harmed a specific forest area. Reviewers agree that
the work was well designed and well executed and that it eliminated
the possibility of a major harmful effect. However, the exposure in
question has not been a matter of serious concern, and the editor rejects
the paper on the grounds of low priority and low interest to readers.
The author protests, saying that the study was technically sound and
would have been viewed as a critical advance if the results had been
positive.*

ISSUES

Many investigators believe that there is a substantial bias against publication of negative results and that it can be a serious problem for them. The
perception itself presents a dilemma for journal publishers and editors. A
particular body of research is not complete until it has been made known to
the rest of the community. But not all research results are of enough interest
to warrant publication or, if published, to appear in the same kinds of peer-
reviewed journal articles. Resources are limited and must be used wisely at
each point from the posing of the research problem to the publication of
results. A further issue is "need to know"; negative results might be important
to other and fewer readers than positive results, and a different form, length,
and place of publication might be appropriate. In addition, it seems that many
negative studies are not properly completed and that negative reports are often
not written to the same standards as positive reports.

The issues raised in this scenario begin with whether the research hypothesis and protocol themselves had enough merit for the work to be supported.
If not, spending additional resources on publication is inappropriate. If so, at
least the opportunity for publication in some form should be available. The
editor decides whether that opportunity exists in his or her particular journal.
The editor, on initial screening, determines whether a paper meets the criteria
and falls within the scope of the journal; if so, the editor judges its importance
and the degree of interest in it in deciding whether to ask reviewers to invest
their efforts in evaluating it. Those are the editor's duties and prerogatives.
However, a widespread editorial bias against publishing negative results would
in effect censor some kinds of reports. It is not clear whether there are any
general principles about when the rejection of such papers is detrimental or
beneficial to science. Because space in any journal is expensive, rejection on

the basis of priority is common. If negative results are consistently rejected on the basis of priority, does the scientific community have a responsibility to provide an alternative mechanism for their dissemination?

Journal publishers are in some ways like newspaper publishers—they like to print "hot" news and very little unsensational news. And journal publishers must admit to doing that, at least to a small extent, for the same reasons—it sells! But the majority of studies probably have positive results, because researchers seldom start out in the dark and have some inkling of a positive effect. That is the impetus for a study. The operative words in this scenario seem to be "low priority" and "low interest." Most manuscripts that fit those words will report negative results, but there will still be manuscripts with negative results of research of high priority and high interest that should be published, as well as occasional reports of positive results of research of low priority and low interest that do not merit publication. Editors need to recognize their use of low priority as an excuse; negative results often get this label. "Editors should carefully weigh the importance of the new information."

The value of negative results is often as great as the value of positive results when they come from a bona fide study, not just the study of a straw man. In addition, a study's failure to show an effect can have many trivial reasons, particularly if the sample is small or the field of research is new and procedures are not yet well grounded. Environmental research (as in this scenario) often has so many variables that researchers do not always know what to look for. When negative results are related to the methods used and are indicative more of method sensitivity than of true effects, the publication of the results creates confusion and erroneous information in the literature. However, failure to attribute any importance to negative results can make it difficult to procure funding to support research, can create an incentive to submit fraudulent data, and can dilute the challenge to established, published hypotheses.

RESPONSES

A few respondents supported the editor's decision to reject the paper solely on the grounds of editorial prerogative—that it is the job of the editor to make the decisions to accept or reject and the editor's decisions are final. To those respondents, the merit of the paper, the basis of the rejection, and the author's protests are irrelevant. "What is this world coming to if an editor can be swayed by the first complaint of an author?" "The editor's job is to decide. He decided." "Editors decide what to publish, not a majority vote of reviewers."

Others supported the editor's right to decide on acceptance, but went on to say that the author has the option of submitting the paper elsewhere. Papers of great scientific merit are rejected by some journals and accepted by others.

Papers rejected by journals with particular standards of acceptance are accepted by journals with lower or different standards of acceptance.

Some respondents specifically suggested that the editor reconsider and seek additional advice from new reviewers, "other experts," or an editorial board or committee. "In the long run, the question of exposure will arise, and the editor is missing an opportunity to print an early definitive investigation in his journal." "The editor is not always qualified to judge the priority and interest for readers of a particular study." "The editor should carefully examine what his response would have been had the results been positive." However, no suggestions were given as to the criteria to be used by additional advisers.

Several respondents supported the editor's decision to reject on the basis of low interest and space-dictated priorities. They did not feel that the negative results were necessarily the basis of the low priority; the exposure was not of serious concern, and the results were therefore of low interest. It was noted that the problem with the research should have been identified earlier, so that it would not be the job of the editor alone to determine whether the question is trivial or important. That is, the initial error was misevaluation of the importance of the research. "Research administrators should see that inconsequential research [is] not . . . given the [indicated] time and attention." "The best scientists [engage] in important experiments where either outcome, positive or negative, is regarded as an advance and worthy of publication." Likewise, if reader interest is to be a deciding factor, it should be evaluated more critically when the paper is received in the editorial office, so as not to waste reviewers' time and to give the author an earlier decision.

Some respondents, while not faulting the editor's decision or right to make the decision, bemoaned the lack of an appropriate outlet for this type of report. A mechanism for archiving the information might be necessary. Are the results of competent science often lost because they are not considered important enough for publication?

About one-fourth of the respondents expressed support for publishing negative results; some felt that, under the conditions outlined in the scenario, the paper deserved publication. "Editors need to recognize that negative results are important in science." "Negative findings are as important as the opposite, but they receive little attention until a situation becomes critical." "If this study is the first to substantiate that the situation is in fact not of serious concern, such conclusions are valid and justify publication." "Negative studies that are based on credible experimental design and data deserve to be published to reduce repetition of useless studies, to inform about biologically harmless substances, and to allow other scientists to improve experimental designs in similar study areas." "Low priority and low interest should not determine whether a research report is published. A purpose of scientific publishing should be to conclude lines of research, as well as to stimulate others."

A review of the responses from editors not in the life sciences revealed the same conflict of responses. Some felt that negative results do impart information and that the paper should be published; some felt that priority and usefulness of the information should be the deciding factors. Editors in the social sciences noted that the dilemma of reporting negative results is widespread.

DISCUSSION

Despite widespread concern, the committee is not persuaded that bias against publication of negative results is either widespread (if "publication" is interpreted broadly to mean that persons who need the results know about them from meeting abstracts, comments in other papers, or even word of mouth) or important (given that negative findings might often arise from poor selection of a research problem, inadequate protocol design, or insufficient sample size and that many reports of negative studies are incomplete or otherwise flawed). These matters need careful research study; if the bias exists and has serious implications for science, editors might need to reverse the trend against publication of negative results.

CONCLUSIONS AND RECOMMENDATIONS

The editor can respond to the author by explaining more specifically why he decided to reject the paper. If it is the editor's bias to select only papers of high impact and reader interest, the author will use that information in directing future submissions. If the journal is more archival, the editor might be able to suggest how the paper could be recast to emphasize the importance of the study, or even how the study could have been done to make it of interest to this particular journal's readers; either can help the author in submitting the paper to other journals.

If the journal publishes letters to the editor, isolated summaries, or other types of brief technical communication, such publication might be a good way to present negative findings from well-done research. The author can, of course, offer in a short report to supply the full report on request.

The editor could reverse his decision and publish the paper in full. As a special case, if the journal has published positive results on the same subject (not an issue in this scenario), there might be special reason to publish the proposed paper.

High on the list of issues for an editor who is considering the value of a negative report is the question, "Who needs to know?" In some fields, many people might need to know about particular negative results—hence the necessity for wide dissemination through publication. In other fields, positive and negative results might be of interest and use to different sets of readers; this could be a cause of the low-interest low-priority reaction. Such information can be communicated in other ways, such as in research communications less rigorous than journal articles or through informal collegial networks. Those secondary routes of communication and dissemination might rob the author of publication credit, but that is not editors' chief concern.

The perceived bias against publication of negative reports is probably not serious and is offset by the availability of other information channels. Much negative information is in fact published, not necessarily as distinct, individual papers, but as parts of more comprehensive reports. Those who need to know—often other researchers studying the same problems—will acquire the information through the other channels.

Scenario L

Subsidized Journal Issues and Proceedings of Sponsored Meetings

A new editor is attempting to reduce a backlog of papers approved by her predecessor. A symposium steering committee asks her to publish the proceedings of a symposium about the use of a new and expensive research tool that is available from only one manufacturer. The manufacturer, on hearing about the journal backlog, proposes to subsidize an entire, expanded issue of the journal, so that the journal can publish the complete symposium papers early, as well as some of the backlog of other papers.

ISSUES

Publication of sponsored symposia is not new, but the current trend toward cooperative research and development ventures between industry and academe, industry and government, and government and academe might lend new importance to this matter. Reports of research findings are always suspect when the reporting is paid for directly by a party with an interest in the results, because the motives of self-promotion and profit can have so many subtle effects, not only on what is reported, but especially on how it is presented and interpreted. Government-sponsored symposia and special issues of journals can also be suspect, if the motives are considered to be political or agency-promoting.

The committee regards the sponsored publication of research results as a very serious issue of both science and ethics. Editors need to address whether and how financial support of publication of proceedings or special journal issues might pose specific ethical questions and what procedures are available to minimize detrimental consequences.

Some are concerned that papers from sponsored symposia are or are perceived to be of lower quality than other papers and question whether it is justifiable for journals to lower their standards for symposium papers. Will the quality of science presented in sponsored symposia lower the standards and reputation of the journal? Does the very fact that a journal publishes sponsored symposia lower its reputation? Will the pressure of financial gain lead to the publication of material that a journal would not normally accept? Will the necessity to publish a coherent whole require the inclusion of presentations of poor quality? If so, does that pose an ethical issue for the editor or publisher?

Sponsored symposia might be accompanied by a particular kind of bias that is broader than bias in single papers. If the sponsoring institution or company selects the participants, will properly varied points of view be presented? If not, does that pose an ethical issue for the editor or publisher?

A journal editor must have some freedom. The editors of scientific journals are widely accepted as the gatekeepers in the publication process. An editor has the major responsibility, with the advice of peer reviewers, for selecting new, important, and valid findings for publication; for detecting error and sometimes fraud; for protecting against misleading bias; for exposing poorly conceived or executed studies; and for preventing the publication of unsupportable data. Does the subsidy or sponsorship of a special issue, or of a meeting whose proceedings are made available through the journal, alter the editorial review process in an undesirable way by preventing the editor from carrying out those responsibilities?

Where does the editorial responsibility lie if a guest editor is chosen? What is the guest editor's relationship to the journal editor? Does the dilution of editorial responsibility pose ethical dilemmas?

One must assess the risks and benefits. Who pays? Who profits? The availability of extra funding might allow faster publication—certainly a boon and an incentive for participating authors. But what about other authors whose papers could be delayed to accommodate the special issue?

RESPONSES

As many as one-fourth of the respondents rejected the proposal summarily, for reasons related to the perception of compromising the journal's reputation or the editor's freedom of action. "We refuse to publish symposia that simply laud and promote the product of a single manufacturer; research papers about the use of that product constitute valid and important science and are welcome." Some respondents expressed a general concern about the overcommercialization of journals, but the alternative offered was to allow advertisers to support the publication.

Most of those rejecting the proposal felt that manufacturers should not be allowed to subsidize journals, because single-sponsor issues are inherently suspect. One respondent wrote that, "even if this doesn't affect editorial freedom, it will send the wrong message." Another noted that, "even if the editor does not allow the manufacturer to affect her editorial policy, no one else will know that."

A few respondents cautioned against any action that interrupts the orderly flow of papers and permits (here in the case of the symposium papers) the publication of some authors' work ahead of others' (see Scenario I). Symposium papers should be considered individually and in the normal order and be subject to the same scrutiny as any other submitted paper.

Respondents who saw no dilemma for the editor or who felt that any difficulties could be overcome were clearly in the majority. A few respondents recognized a potential conflict, but took a pragmatic approach. They acknowledged the financial windfall and noted that scientific publishers would be reluctant to turn away possible income ("the dilemma is whether it would appear the manufacturer is buying space and the journal is selling out; on the other hand, it is possible for the journal to remain pure all the way to bankruptcy court"), and they acknowledged the opportunity to relieve the backlog. Some saw little difference between this proposal and other types of subsidies, such as the priority given to authors willing to pay full page charges and the subsidy given to some society members for publication costs. One suggested simply letting the manufacturer buy more advertising pages as a way to support the cost of publishing the symposium papers. Several felt that the manufacturer's offer could ethically be accepted and that the only action required to maintain journal integrity would be publication of acknowledgment of the support.

Other respondents recommended acceptance of the offer only if no strings were attached. The editor must be in control and should not compromise standards, peer review must not be threatened, and regularly scheduled manuscripts must not be delayed. In that view, the decision of whether to accept the offer and publish the papers rests solely on results of assessment of the importance, validity, and scientific contribution of the information reported; any other concerns are irrelevant. The manufacturer should have no input into the selection of papers. Some saw no difference between this and any other grant, as long as editorial control would not be surrendered.

Some proposed that all difficulties could be addressed by requiring publication of a separate proceedings issue, completely distinct from regular issues of the journal and clearly labeled as a sponsored publication and therefore not compromising the journal.

A review of responses specifically from non-CBE editors who were not in the life sciences showed a sharp division of views on this scenario. Those who felt that the symposium proceedings could be published and funded by the manufacturer were clearly in the majority, but hung many precautions and restrictions on the process, requiring primarily that all papers pass peer review and that the editor have the final say on the merit of each paper. Those who rejected the manufacturer's offer did so vehemently, on the basis that such a conflict of editorial and financial considerations was unconscionable.

DISCUSSION

Few scholarly publishers operate with an excess of funds. Sponsorship can provide revenue needed to publish specialized information that is important to a limited readership. Faced with the circumstances of this scenario, publishers will have to determine whether a balance can be struck between financial sponsorship and independent scientific inquiry without a compromise of publishing ethics.

The right to publish should not be a commodity that can be bought and sold—either by authors or by sponsors. Otherwise, a company with the financial resources can bias the dissemination of scientific information and thus subvert science itself.

Bias can be introduced not only in the content, but also in the quality of the material to be published. One standard for acceptability might be set for symposium participants, and more stringent standards for authors who individually submit research reports. Stringent standards of content and quality of research are expected by the authors and readers of particular journals. That mantle of respectability should not be conferred automatically on, for example, symposium papers, because it would allow the manufacturer to capitalize on a journal's reputation without contributing to its mission.

However, different standards for a symposium as a whole might be acceptable. One has to consider how a symposium issue is used. A symposium issue can be useful to readers who need a review of a field; in such a case, care should be taken that it be representative. A symposium issue might be a good forum for reporting new ideas; reports of work in progress, by their very nature, would probably not meet standards that are applied to individual papers.

The arbiter of a journal's standard of quality and content is its editor. A guest editor might put collegial responsibilities over editorial responsibilities for guarding against fraud, bias, and poor science; i.e., a guest editor, who is in an essentially honorary position, might be passive and reluctant to make hard decisions that are unfavorable to some authors. Conversely, a guest editor can shield the journal editor.

A more subtle constraint on the editor in the case of a symposium issue is the necessity to make a block decision, rather than assessing each paper separately. One or more individual contributions might be top-notch; in the aggregate, do the papers form a balanced representation?

What about a more active influence? Bias could be introduced if the sponsor of a symposium expects to exercise some review of submitted manuscripts before they are accepted for inclusion. If the criteria of review are different from those usually exercised by the journal editor, the reputation of the journal and the expectations of its constituency have been breached.

What is the ethical impact? Should advocacy of a particular technology, product, or position be considered one of the rights that a sponsor receives in return for financial largesse?

CONCLUSIONS AND RECOMMENDATIONS

Although the scientific community might generally perceive and expect papers appearing in a symposium issue to be selected by standards different from those for individual peer-reviewed research accounts, papers presenting an overview of a particular topic are, in fact, welcomed and sought by editors, because many readers want them. However, the committee believes that journal publication of a sponsored symposium is not a good option for obtaining financial relief and should if possible be avoided, because of inherent conflicts of interest. If, however, the option is chosen, a journal's editorial policy should address the weak points.

It is critical that the journal and its editor set guidelines that will avoid the compromising of standards. Although standards of content and coverage (scope) might appropriately be altered for symposium papers, standards of scientific and technical quality should not be. Hence, peer review is required. A guest editor can initially select appropriate papers and even recruit additional papers, if they are needed for a more complete presentation, but should not function as the peer reviewer. The journal editor must maintain authority over review, revision, and acceptance or rejection. A journal editor might also choose to publish material from transcribed discussions at a symposium, if it adds appropriately to the information and content and helps to give readers a more balanced view of the subject matter.

A specific, standing journal policy concerning symposium publication can prevent having to "write policy" each time the editor is approached, prevent ambiguity in editorial authority, and prevent compromising of financial arrangements. One approach is to publish proceedings only when there is a satisfactory presymposium agreement between sponsors and journal, including the right of the journal to refuse the packaged proceedings of a completed symposium. The agreement could establish criteria—regarding subject matter, credentials of participants, quality of research, manuscript format, peer review, etc.—that a symposium's sponsor would accept in advance.

Scenario M

Results of a "Black Box" Procedure

An industrial scientist submits a paper that includes critical measurements made with a commercial biotechnical test kit that is said to be faster and more specific than current procedures. A reviewer returns the paper with the criticism that the protocol used to produce the critical biologic agent in the kit is proprietary and therefore not known to the reviewer or to readers who might want to undertake further research. The reviewer contends that science is not advanced by the use of a research tool that is the subject of a trade secret. The author replies that his company will not invest money in research without hope of economic advantage through exclusivity and that, as long as other scientists can obtain satisfactory results with the "black box," it is not necessary for them to know how it works.

ISSUES

Reviewers are routinely asked to evaluate the methods sections of papers according to the criterion of repeatability of the reported work. Thus, the secretiveness of scientific research and the purposeful withholding of information from reports submitted for publication have been matters of concern to scientists for some time. As both industrial research and academic research become more competitive and monetary stakes become higher, it is possible that less and less of the actual methodology involved will reach the scientific literature in a manner that is useful to scientists.

Are journal editors today finding that many submitted papers concern "black boxes" or have methods sections with important omissions?

This scenario raises the question of how much detail is needed in a methods section. Does the answer depend on the journal and the editorial niche that it has carved for itself? Does it depend on the importance of the subject and how timely the paper is? Does it depend on whether the important omission was intentional and has commercial overtones? Does it depend on whether the particular "black box" has been used for some time and has gained respectability because of its use and purported usefulness? It also raises a question about the relative value of the paper in reporting new, important findings made possible by the black box versus commercial promotion of the black box itself.

RESPONSES

Slightly more than half the respondents recommended rejection of the manuscript because the method was incompletely disclosed and the investigator failed to provide enough information for other scientists to repeat the work (except perhaps by purchase of the black box). More than half felt that this was a serious problem in scientific publishing; few felt that it was a common one. Almost half the respondents recommended that publication be considered if some criteria (described below) were met.

Those who recommended rejection raised one serious concern. Journal standards commonly dictate that methods or experimental sections contain enough detail to permit qualified scientists to repeat the work and attempt to duplicate the reported results. One cannot expect a reviewer to evaluate the scientific merit of a manuscript properly if the methods section is so incomplete as to prevent thorough and acceptable peer review. Several respondents pointed out that the purpose of scientific publication is to advance science and that progress in science requires full disclosure of information.

Others indicated that companies can distribute such information to the appropriate community efficiently in several ways. Manufacturers can send literature to many people via purchased mailing lists. Information can also be disseminated through advertising.

Several respondents felt that the company might have erred in not seeking patent protection first. One stated succinctly that "the editor should refuse to publish any paper that withholds critical information. The author's argument here is spurious, in that the company can protect its economic investment by applying for a patent before the paper is submitted."

Those who recommended acceptance raised questions about the particular paper and how it fit into the rest of the literature pertaining to this kit, or black box:

> If the paper only introduces the product and gives examples of what it can do, it belongs in the manufacturer's literature. However, if results are provided that compare this product with other methods and if it answers a specific research question that is worthy of study, it should be considered for scholarly publication on the same basis as any other article.

> There are many black boxes used every day in science, all with their special unknowns. Do we know the trade secrets of Kodak film or IBM PCs?

> I think the critical issue here is whether or not the black box can be proved to do what it purports to do without revealing its contents. I would accept the paper, provided that there is clear evidence from suitably controlled studies to ensure its effectiveness.

Others mentioned proper validation, e.g., "as long as the method has been tested for specificity, reproducibility, accuracy, and sensitivity, it's OK."

Some respondents thought that the mission of the journal might determine the editor's response. For example:

This depends on the orientation of the journal. A technical journal might be willing to evaluate and publish the paper, whereas a scientific journal whose readers expect fundamental explanations would not. In medicine, there would be an obligation to accredit a technique that could be shown to improve health or save lives, even if it were not fully understood. If the kit is unique (e.g., a quick, reliable test for AIDS), then publication is warranted, with a disclaimer as to the proprietary nature of the kit.

Others recommended that the editor publish the information (if the subject is of particular importance) in an abbreviated form, e.g., as a letter to the editor or "communication."

DISCUSSION

The editor must decide how each particular paper fits into the editorial mission of the journal. If an article appears to be more suited for an advertisement or manufacturer's literature, the decision appears easy. However, as with all articles, the editor must judge the importance and timeliness of the article, the necessity for experimental detail, and how readers would benefit from publication.

The editor should consider various questions when developing a policy or reaching a decision: Should it matter whether information was omitted intentionally by an industrial investigator who wished to protect a company's commercial interests or omitted unintentionally or by necessity by an investigator who lacked scientific information about the black box? If a clinical investigator in academe submitted an article that used a complex mixture of natural products to reduce blood cholesterol dramatically, would this black box be considered appropriate, because there seemed to be no commercial overtones? Is validation the important question here—not exactly how or why it works, but that it does so eliably for all investigators?

Most editors deal daily with two, often competing, concerns: the desire to disseminate important information quickly (albeit incompletely, for whatever reason) and the desire to publish complete accounts of a more fundamental nature. The latter ultimately are the only reports that satisfy scientists' "need to know."

Editors must decide daily about the suitability of manuscripts for publication. Editors who consider their primary role to be the dissemination of important and timely information as quickly as possible for immediate, practical application might not be seriously troubled by the use of black boxes, if the reported data are valid and important. Editors who consider their primary role to be the dissemination of basic or fundamental scientific information might attach much greater importance to reporting of the fundamental working of any black boxes.

CONCLUSIONS AND RECOMMENDATIONS

The committee recommends that journal editors proceed cautiously before relaxing the requirements for the complete description of the methods in scientific research. Editors who have been lax in insisting on complete methods sections are urged to re-examine their policies.

Withholding of information simply to maintain an economic advantage, as described in this scenario, is unacceptable. However, motives are not always clear, and editors might remain puzzled even after discussing apparent omissions from methods sections directly with authors.

Many scientific-journal editors probably attach less importance than they should to the repeatability of the methods described in papers. Acknowledgments often describe materials as "generous gifts obtained from J. Doe" or "thank R. Roe for the synthesis of compound X," with no references to the published scientific literature. In addition, many authors, both industrial and academic, avoid publishing complete methods via the "communication" route. Preliminary results should be followed promptly by definitive papers; often these never appear.

Each journal should establish guidelines as to how black boxes fit into its overall mission.

Scenario N

Prior Publication in a "Throwaway" Journal

A scientist reports in a controlled-circulation, or "throwaway," journal, produced and distributed free by his company, on an immunoassay for a class of compounds. He writes a similar account of the assay and results and submits it to a society journal. The report in the throwaway journal is already being cited in the peer-reviewed literature. The editor of the society journal rejects the paper on the grounds that the material has already been published, citing rules and arguments regarding duplicate publication. The author states that the earlier report did not constitute publication, because the throwaway journal was not peer-reviewed, not generally available through libraries, and not indexed and abstracted by secondary services.

ISSUES

The basic question raised by this scenario is: "What constitutes prior publication?" The time when the answer to this question would clearly rule out a throwaway (or controlled-circulation) journal has probably passed, although many would disagree. An underlying question concerns the need to supply journal readers with timely and accurate data while making the best use of expensive publication space. Another issue is the role and importance of peer review. Controlled-circulation journals used to forego peer review; the highly esteemed core journals availed themselves of it. However, at least one major core journal (*Lancet*) now subjects all its submissions to internal review, but not always to outside peer review; and some controlled-circulation journals now use peer review.

It is difficult to define "controlled-circulation journal" precisely. Such journals are usually supported by advertisers or corporate sponsors and are sent to recipients without charge. They are not generally available through subscription. Most (as the author claimed of the throwaway journal in question) are not peer-reviewed, are not available through libraries, and are not indexed or abstracted by the major indexing and secondary services; but that is changing, as will be noted later.

The International Committee of Medical Journal Editors (the Vancouver group) issued a strong statement against multiple publication that did not mention controlled-circulation journals specifically: "Multiple publication— that is, the publication more than once of the same study results—is rarely justified."[3] (That committee cited as a possible justification secondary publication in another language; see Scenario O.) A focus of much of the sentiment against multiple publication is the "Ingelfinger rule," described by Franz Ingelfinger in a landmark paper[2] published in the *New England Journal of Medicine* in 1977:

> The "rule" essentially states that anything already published in substance, especially if accompanied by illustrations and specific data, will not be published again by *The New England Journal of Medicine*, and it does not matter whether the first publication is in the form of a standard medical article in *JAMA*, a letter to *Lancet* or an article in *Medical Tribune*.

Ingelfinger also observed that, although initially the rule "provoked some vigorous repercussions," it survived, because it had the backing, with few exceptions, of the biomedical scientific fraternity. Arnold Relman, Ingelfinger's successor as editor, has continued to apply and defend the Ingelfinger rule.[4]

The Ingelfinger rule clearly includes controlled-circulation journals, but another point of view holds that material that has appeared in a controlled-circulation journal has not actually been "published" and that therefore the rule should not be applied. Day[1] cited as authority for that point of view the definition of "primary scientific publication" arrived at by the Council of Biology Editors in 1968:

> An acceptable primary scientific publication must be the first disclosure containing sufficient information to enable peers (1) to assess observations, (2) to

repeat experiments, and (3) to evaluate intellectual processes; moreover, it must be susceptible to sensory perception, essentially permanent, available to the scientific community without restriction, and available for regular screening by one or more of the major recognized secondary services (e.g., currently, Biological Abstracts, Chemical Abstracts, Index Medicus, Excerpta Medica, Bibliography of Agriculture, etc., in the United States and similar facilities in other countries).

Day commented: "Thus, publications such as newsletters and house organs . . . cannot serve as repositories for scientific knowledge."

House organs and other throwaways formerly were not usually indexed by the major secondary services; nor was the journal cited in the scenario. However, the secondary services' attitude toward controlled-circulation journals seems to be changing. In a seminar on controlled-circulation journals at the 1988 CBE annual meeting, a representative of the National Library of Medicine (NLM) commented that, although NLM has not been favorably disposed toward including controlled-circulation journals in *Index Medicus,* some of them are now included. In deciding which journals to include in *Index Medicus,* NLM focuses primarily on their content, but also considers their availability; it is aware that many controlled-circulation journals have limited accessibility. (In the scenario, the author noted that the throwaway journal was not generally available through libraries.) In the same CBE seminar, it was reported that some controlled-circulation medical journals, including *Postgraduate Medicine,* are peer-reviewed. Thus, two of the reasons for excluding controlled-circulation journals from the ranks of "acceptable" scientific publications—lack of peer review and lack of citation by the major secondary services—appear to have less validity than they did 15 or 20 years ago.

In a further complication of the situation, primary journals vary in whether they permit citation of controlled-circulation journals in reference lists in their own papers. Some permit it; some, including the *New England Journal of Medicine,* do not. Some permit such references in text, but not in reference lists.

The secondary services might establish a separate category for controlled-circulation journals. For example, in a session on "disposable" journals at the 1989 CBE annual meeting, Edward J. Huth, editor of *Annals of Internal Medicine,* expressed the opinion that controlled-circulation journals do not meet the criteria of scientific literature, in that they lack the connection with the past that "regular" journals have. He suggested that a separate category of "transient" or "ephemeral" publications be used by indexing and abstracting services.

RESPONSES

A substantial majority of CBE respondents believed that the editor was correct in rejecting the paper. A smaller majority of the non-CBE respondents agreed. Most CBE respondents thought the problem posed in the scenario was a serious one in scientific publishing; almost half the non-CBE respondents thought it serious.

Typical of the hard-line position that endorsed rejection were the following: "The paper should be declined absolutely. Manuscripts must be original to be published in the reviewed literature. The author can't have it both ways, and you can bet the throwaway is listed on his C.V." "The editor handled it just as we would—period. Prior publication is grounds for rejection. In this case, publication in a company throwaway simply doubles our grounds for rejection." Also favoring rejection, but with an interesting comment about the economics of publishing, was this:

> I would reject the report because it should be considered published, since it has been cited in peer-reviewed literature, even though it is not generally available to libraries nor indexed and abstracted by the secondary services. Although it has not been abstracted or indexed, it has most likely been widely distributed to scientists by the company. It would not be economically feasible for the manufacturer to keep quiet about a product whose development it financed. In the future, the scientist should have his articles peer-reviewed and published in primary journals. Those journals could then sell reprints to a manufacturer for distribution. Publishers need to make money, too!

On the opposite side were respondents who thought that the author was correct in saying that appearence in the controlled-circulation journal did not constitute true publication. Two respondents cited the CBE definition quoted earlier. One commented:

> Prior publication in a nonindexed journal or a journal of lower standards has been a frequent problem for us, and it is the essence of the Ingelfinger paradigm. The scientific journal's principal task is to accredit new work in the peer-reviewed literature, and this has priority over the journal's claim to absolute originality. I would give the author a stern lecture and then evaluate his paper.

The other had hard words not only for the editor in the scenario, but for those who cited the paper:

> The editor screwed up and so did anybody who cited the nonreviewed paper. The editor should know better regarding what constitutes publication. The editor's position is self-demeaning, as it implicitly places his or her journal on the same low-quality standard as a throwaway.

Some respondents took a somewhat equivocal position, believing that the editor has to make a decision based on the paper's merit. One wrote:

> The decision would depend entirely on what the study was. If it was trivial, the throwaway report may have been quite enough publication. If it was important, we would probably wind up publishing it, although the second paper would be expected to be quite different from (i.e., more complete than) the first.

Another said that the problem was essentially one of priorities: if the material was important, it should be in the indexed literature; an editor with more important papers whose contents had not already been published should try to help the author by suggesting other journals.

At least one respondent wanted to involve the journal's editorial board:

> I find the quandary of the editor quite baffling. Of course, the easy way out is to stick to his or her guns. Maybe that is too easy. Why not ask the editorial board what to do? Or the society's council? . . . Maybe the best (and first) step to take is to have the paper refereed—it may not stand and will have to be rejected on grounds other than prior publication.

One respondent who addressed the issue of whether publication in a throwaway was valid publication commented:

> These sheets/journals often appear very professional and are in fact designed to impress their readers that the articles have the cachet of publication. This leads to their being cited. I consider them in the same category as advertisement circulars, with as much reliability.

Also addressing the question of definition was the respondent who wrote:

> A difficulty in this matter might be whether everyone agrees on which journals are "throwaways"—journals that have peer review, but by reviewers who are not expert; journals that do not employ any form of review; journals that have been in existence only for several years; or journals that have rejected work by the person who applies the term.

As has been the case in other scenarios, some respondents opted for full disclosure. One wrote:

> Journals that have been wise enough to spell out this policy (e.g., no publication of work previously published) would have no difficulty in rejecting the paper. However, if the "throwaway" report was merely a brief outline of the work done, a "better" journal should consider publishing a complete research report for the use of readers and indexing services.

One respondent cited his own experience in suggesting the need for further discussion in the scientific community of what constitutes publication. The authors, he said,

> should get advice on what constitutes publication, or perhaps this matter should be more thoroughly discussed in the scientific community—maybe included in writing courses. I have run into this problem because I work both for a medical journal and for newspapers as a medical reporter. I have interviewed scientists about their work, and they have been so cooperative in giving both their work and results that if I had been a different kind of reporter—out for a "scoop"—I might have published their hard data; that on occasion has been construed as

publication, because a great deal of the work has appeared in a newspaper. I thank them for the complete information, caution them against handing out statistics and specific results, and couch their findings in words like "nearly one-third," "more than half," etc.

A few respondents commented that the problem of considering abstracts published for distribution at scientific and technical meetings as prior publication was similar to the problem posed by throwaways. One noted that his society had published proceedings of an international conference, specifying in the front matter that the publication was not a primary publication because the papers were abstracts. Nevertheless, a major journal later rejected several manuscripts from the conference, citing dual publication. The respondent believed that the scientific literature contains important gaps because of misunderstandings as to what constitutes valid publication.

DISCUSSION

The editor must decide not only what general rule is appropriate for the journal, but how to interpret and how strictly to enforce the rule against duplicate publication. Is the Ingelfinger rule applicable? A variant of it? Even if the Ingelfinger rule is applicable, the editor must consider whether there are exceptional circumstances (e.g., a finding of particular importance) that would warrant peer review and possible publication of a paper whose main content has already appeared in a controlled-circulation journal. In the latter case, should the editor seek advice of the editorial board?

A strong case can be made for attempting to keep the scientific literature "pure."[5] The committee is not convinced by arguments to the contrary.[6] That might include not only deciding that prior publication in a controlled-circulation journal should not be considered valid publication (not part of the scientific canon), but forbidding the use of papers in controlled-circulation journals in a reference list. However, we note the cautious moves by at least one of the major data bases (*Index Medicus*) to include some controlled-circulation journals. In addition, there is a lack of information, or at least a lack of clear definition, as to which journals are adequately peer-reviewed.

Duplicate publication should be discouraged. A journal that caters to researchers who use secondary services should not provide duplicate publications to them. A journal whose readers are practitioners whose continuing education consists of reading journals that land on their desks is responsible for providing readers with what they need, possibly including redundant material. The editor of a journal that caters to both groups must assess whether a specific piece of work already published elsewhere has enough interest, applicability, and importance to warrant a second publication, and regular standards for acceptance should not be relaxed.

CONCLUSIONS AND RECOMMENDATIONS

We recommend that publication in a controlled-circulation journal not automatically be considered nonvalid publication. However, second publication of material already published in a controlled-circulation journal should be governed by the general criteria governing duplicate publication. First, such publication should not occur without a strong and explicitly stated reason. Second, material already published as a new research contribution should not be published again with any implication that it is a new research contribution. It is particularly important that the second publication note any overlaps, lest the authors of later reviews, including meta-analyses, give double weight to duplicated material.

We recognize that there are substantial differences among journals and their purposes, and each journal should develop guidelines governing duplicate publication on the basis of its own readership and goals. When considering appropriate guidelines, the editor should take the needs of the readership into account. The editor should consider whether readers are mostly researchers who have access to the major secondary services and are likely to use them or are mostly practitioners, whose continuing education consists mainly of the journals that cross their desks. In a particular instance, an editor will need to determine and consider the accessibility of the original publication and whether it is indexed by the major secondary services.

In each journal's instructions for authors, the editor should clearly state the journal's policy regarding valid publication and duplicate publication. For example, meeting abstracts, other preliminary reports in scientific publications, letters to the editor, and reports in scientific and medical news media may be judged to constitute prior publication. The editor's statement should include the types of prior publication that absolutely preclude later publication; if publication in a controlled-circulation journal is included in the list of proscriptions, that should be specifically stated.

In a given instance, when—for a strong and explicit reason—duplicate publication is being considered, full disclosure should be the rule: by the author to the editor regarding prior publication, and by the editor to reviewers. If duplicate publication eventually occurs, a statement noting that and the reason for it should accompany publication.

REFERENCES

1. Day RA. How to Write and Publish a Scientific Paper. 3rd ed. Phoenix: Oryx Press; 1988:2.
2. Ingelfinger FJ. Shattuck lecture—the general medical journal: for readers or repositories? N Engl J Med 1977;296:1258-64.
3. International Committee of Medical Journal Editors. Uniform requirements for manuscripts submitted to biomedical journals. Ann Intern Med 1988;108:258-65.

4. Relman AS. The Ingelfinger rule. N Engl J Med 1987;305:824-6.
5. Rennie D, Bero LA. Throw it away, Sam: the controlled circulation journals. CBE Views 1990;13:31-5.
6. Siwek J. The great "throwaway" debate. CBE Views 1990; 13:65.

Scenario O

Non-English Publication

A scientist publishes a research report in a national scientific journal in a language known to few Western scientists and submits a slightly amplified version in English to an international scientific journal. Reviewers for the international journal support the validity and importance of the scientific findings, but the editor rejects the paper on the grounds of prior publication. The scientist argues that, although the first journal is covered by the scientific abstracting and indexing services, Western scientists will not know the content of the paper, because it was not published in English. The author also says that his government (the funding source) requires that he support his national journal.

ISSUES

This scenario pits a journal editor's responsibility to provide the most timely and accurate data to the journal's readers against the responsibility to make the best use of publication space. Accessibility of data is crucial to the advancement of science. If a published article is indexed or abstracted by the secondary services, its data are generally accessible. But obtaining, translating, and publishing material that is already available in a non-English-language journal raises all the issues of repetitive publication generally and might also vitiate the timeliness that is often critical to progress in scientific research. If an editor's primary function is to advance science through the dissemination of information, that very function might be hampered by strict enforcement of policy in the face of special extenuating circumstances. Is it time to distinguish between dual publication generally and two-language publication? Is it time for editors to look hard at the advantages of two-language publication, as well as its disadvantages? Should "linguistic imperialism," perceived by many to be practiced by primary English-language journals, be abolished or reinforced? The question is difficult to answer, because it involves important competing values. Accessibility of a work depends on the language in which it is written, the circulation of the publishing journal, and whether the work is indexed by the secondary services.

RESPONSES

Most of the respondents recommended publication of the paper in the English-language journal. And over half thought the issue not common, but serious and important.

Many respondents felt strongly that editors of primary English-language journals are obliged to ensure the widest possible dissemination of important scientific data. One respondent wrote that "there is a debt owed by developed countries to the underdeveloped, a debt that acknowledges both elements of the problem described in the scenario." Others felt that it was of the utmost importance to eliminate tones of "Western chauvinism" in scientific publication. That chauvinism is exemplified by these responses:

> Don't touch the paper with a 10-foot pole. If the paper were really important, the scientist would have had it published in ENGLISH. Don't play second fiddle to articles first published in a remote language. Intelligent scientists know the value of publishing in English first.

> The author and his sponsors should get real and publish in the lingua franca (OK, well, English) of science. The editor is right, and in the end, everyone *will* publish in English (which is, after all, the only language worth publishing in, surely).

Because of the advantages available in Western countries in science, many respondents insisted that a subtle form of domination had evolved. One respondent wrote that "the scientific community must tolerate political pressures from time to time. Prohibition against prior publication takes on 'sacred cow' status in this setting. Ultimately, research around the world should be encouraged, not discouraged."

Many respondents suggested that strict adherence to policy and rules leads to pedantry. But many felt that nonnegotiable policies regarding prior publication help to eliminate run-of-the-mill material that is normally the subject of this problem.

Many respondents who recommended rejection of the paper seemed to believe that, if a work is indexed and abstracted, it is previously published, regardless of the language in which the material originally appears and regardless of any differences in readership. Specifically, "duplicate publication is just that and is totally unacceptable in any language—scientific or otherwise." However, almost all these respondents were also sympathetic to the need for an appropriate forum for important data in papers previously published in non-English-language journals; many suggested publication of the abstracts in English, publication as special volumes of translated works, or publication of findings in letters to the editor. One respondent wrote that "authors can cite the first paper in their next English-language paper and provide as much detail as they wish." Another agreed: "There is no reason to publish a paper in more than one language. Unless the scientific community is willing to financially support multiplicity, no paper should be published, indexed, and abstracted more than once."

Many respondents agreed that the main purpose of scientific publication is to make substantial valid research accessible to scientists as soon as possible and in whatever format is most effective and that an editor's decision not to publish an important paper because of previous publication in a nonprimary journal seriously compromises the goal. They believe that editors should discriminate against previously published papers only on the basis of the likelihood that they will have been seen in both the national or nonprimary journal and the English version by the same reader. Many respondents stated that editors should ignore the rules regarding prior publication if duplicate publication of a work will benefit the majority of the research community. For example:

> It is wrong to withhold important results from the majority of the world's scientists, who are English-speaking. The American tendency is not to know a foreign language, as our European colleagues do. Americans are known to be linguistically chauvinistic.

> Publication in a national journal can be compared to presenting the material at a meeting—both reach a limited audience. Prior publication in a national language should not prevent proper publication in an international forum. If efficient dissemination of important data is the editor's goal, then strict adherence to prior-publication policy becomes an end, instead of a means to an end.

> I am collaborating with researchers in Italy, who must submit some of their research reports to national journals. Most probably, that work will not be read outside Italy.

> What if Aristotle were still available only in Greek? Prior publication is not covered in the Ten Commandments. Editors should look at each situation in context. Guidelines for duplicate publication and policies regarding previous publication should be applied in a way that is advantageous to readers.

Another respondent wrote:

> It would be nice to think that there still was such a thing as a polyglot, international community of scholars, but there is not. If the paper is not published in English, the abstracting and indexing service's English translation of the abstract is read, and the original abstract is never read. I am more tolerant than some academic journal editors of duplicate publication, whether in another language or for a different audience. We often publish material that has already appeared in a research journal in another form, because our readers will not see the other publication from one year to another.

Many researchers still request "English only" literature searches and cannot afford to translate foreign-language articles; they rely on abstracts (often incomplete) translated into English. In addition, budgetary restrictions levied on most libraries today allow subscriptions only to primary science journals; this often renders non-English-language materials, whether indexed and abstracted or not, in effect irretrievable. One respondent wrote that "we all have access to obscure journals and translators today if material is important enough. Multiple publication only clutters the flow of information. Secondary services should be used as the main resource for all languages, thus eliminating the need for dual-language publication."

Many respondents emphasized the importance of a journal's obtaining copyright permission from the original copyright holder and the importance of indicating in a bibliography dual entries that describe a single piece of research. Editors could avoid impeding scientific communication if they switched their focus from eliminating all duplicate publication to eliminating abuses that might result from justifiable duplicate publication, such as deceptively long bibliographies. Indeed, another respondent wrote that "padding bibliographies, particularly by non-English-speaking scientists, is common and probably encouraged by their national agencies, which purport that dual publication is a legitimate means of gaining international recognition. However, it only has an inflationary effect on all scientific literature." Another warned that "only when a previously published manuscript masquerades as an original is there a significant problem."

Another stressed the importance of identifying the issue of two-language publication as a minority-language problem, not an "Eastern" problem: "Journal editors must address this problem soon, because people who read English are not the only ones capable of rational thought. If two readerships are exclusive of one another, then a publication available to one would be denied to the other."

Many respondents felt that English-language scientists need to become more international-minded. As developing countries build their own scientific communities—for example, through an exchange of information in national journals—the number and quality of reports sent to Western journals from these countries will increase. Restricting a non-English-language scientist to submitting only papers never published elsewhere in any form leads to a vicious circle. It stunts the growth and development of the research process in the author's country. Authors who do not publish in their national journals might not receive funding for future projects.

Many respondents felt that, until non-English-language journals are more widely indexed and accessible, the mandate for editors to disseminate the best scientific data warrants duplicate publication in some instances: "Every rule has its exception. Editors who feel that a work is truly important to their readers should make some accommodation for publication." Others held fast to the principle that the absence of substantial new data remains one of the chief reasons for rejection of a paper.

DISCUSSION

For journals published entirely or largely in English, previous publication in other languages widely used in science, such as German, French, Spanish, *or* English could be considered prior publication. One respondent suggested that "valid publication" be defined (in part) as "publication in English."

The International Committee of Medical Journal Editors (the Vancouver group) recommends that there be at least a 2-week interval between publication of an international (English) version and a following second publication in a non-English-language journal.[1]

Important material already published in a non-English-language journal could be published as a translation in a primary English-language journal. However, it can be difficult to identify a good translation service, translation is expensive and entails substantial delays, and the possibility of introducing errors into the work during translation is considerable. An editor's note like the following could accompany the translation: "This article is being published in English (German/French/Spanish) for the first time, and this version is a translation of a paper originally published in (other language) in the *Journal of* . . . 1987;122:233-41." Inclusion of the name of the translator is important, because mistakes made in translation are those of the translator, and not of the authors. An editor's note could also explain why the circumstances justify a deviation from normal policy.

New or expanded data could be published in a letter to the editor. Such correspondence is indexed by the secondary services, and authors could include references to their original publications.

CONCLUSIONS AND RECOMMENDATIONS

As noted in the discussion of Scenario N and elsewhere, duplicate publication should be rare.

An editor should first establish whether new data are included in an English version of a paper previously published. Previously published material should not be published again as a new research contribution. In general, additional or more extensive data, better controls, more complete descriptions of methods, more elaborate discussions, additional followup of subjects, and better documentation are not substantial enough to qualify as "new" material, if the findings are essentially the same as those already published.

Individual consideration is required for classification of material that has appeared as proceedings of meetings and conferences. Conference organizers often assure authors that their findings are eligible for publication elsewhere without penalty; but, of course, no such assurance is appropriate. Other persons and organizations cannot dictate the policies of journals with regard to prior publication.

If information published in a non-English-language journal will not reach the wider Western journal readership unless published again and if reviewers and editors judge the work important, an editor might well want to help an author to find an appropriate format for disseminating the information. An editor might require authors to justify a second publication of their work by specifying modification of their manuscript to suit the second readership.

Whatever the circumstances, duplicate publication should not occur without a strong and explicit reason, which might include some of the following:

1. *Content.* For important and urgent research papers, editors need to determine and consider:
   - Accessibility of the original publication, including indexing by at least one major secondary service. A policy that precludes duplicate publication of important papers if they are accessible puts appropriate pressure on readers to use secondary services.
   - Substantial differences between the two publications of overlapping material.
   - Order of publication and requirements for a minimal interval between publications of the same or very similar material.

2. *Language.* For literature originally published in a language other than English, editors need to determine and consider:
   - Accessibility of the original publication, including indexing by major secondary services. Language is the key determinant of accessibility here: How widespread among potential users is knowledge of the language of the original publication?
   - Access to and cost of translation to or from English.

Journals have different purposes, so no general rule about prior non-English publication would be appropriate. Editors should clearly state the policies of their journals regarding duplicate publication, including the types of previous publication that preclude republication, in their instructions for authors.

When duplicate publication occurs, full disclosure on the part of authors to editors and of editors to reviewers, libraries, book editors, and secondary services is essential. A statement explaining the reasons for duplicate publication should accompany publication. Authors have a concomitant responsibility to disclose to editors all instances of prior publication.

All copyright requirements and restrictions need to be satisfied by the second publisher of previously published material.

REFERENCE

1. International Committee of Medical Journal Editors. Uniform requirements for manuscripts submitted to biomedical journals. Ann Intern Med 1988;108:258-65.

Scenario P

Disputes Over Authorship

A paper is submitted, reviewed, revised slightly, and approved for publication. The editor then receives a telephone call from a person who was acknowledged for "helpful discussion." The caller, who heard about the submission from one of the reviewers, says that he did most of the work, published an abstract (listed in the paper's bibliography) under his own name, essentially completed a full-length manuscript for publication, and then left the research organization. On inquiry, the editor learns that the director of research had moved the original author's name to the acknowledgments and named as author a person at the laboratory who, although knowledgeable about the work, had done no more than offer advice.

ISSUES

The primary question raised in this scenario is who should be treated as an author of a scientific publication. Are there appropriate guidelines for authorship? Have suitable guidelines been widely publicized, and have they received the endorsement of the scientific community? If so, what are they? Is the first step in the appropriate assignment of authorship the open and honest disclosure by each scientist as to his or her contribution to the intended published work? Should journal editors be involved in "enforcing" statements on authorship, or should the sponsoring institutions or corporations ensure that explicit guidelines are followed?

The International Committee of Medical Journal Editors has commented as follows on authorship and acknowledgments:[7]

> All persons designated as authors should qualify for authorship. Each author should have participated sufficiently in the work to take public responsibility for the content.
>
> Authorship credit should be based only on substantial contributions to (a) conception and design, or analysis and interpretation of data; (b) drafting the article or revising it critically for important intellectual content; and on (c) final approval of the version to be published. Conditions (a), (b), and (c) must all be met. Participation solely in the acquisition of funding or the collection of data does not justify authorship. General supervision of the research group is also not sufficient for authorship. Any part of an article critical to its main conclusions must be the responsibility of at least one author.
>
> A paper with corporate (collective) authorship must specify the key persons responsible for the article; others contributing to the work should be recognized separately.

Editors may require authors to justify the assignment of authorship.

At an appropriate place in the article . . . one or more statements should specify: (a) contributions that need acknowledging but do not justify authorship, such as general support by a departmental chairman; (b) acknowledgments of technical help; (c) acknowledgments of financial and material support, specifying the nature of the support; (d) financial relationships that may pose a conflict of interest.

Persons who have contributed intellectually to the paper but whose contributions do not justify authorship may be named and their functions or contribution described, for example, "scientific adviser," "critical review of study proposal," "data collection," "participation in clinical trial." Such persons must have given their permission to be named. Authors are responsible for obtaining written permission from persons acknowledged by name because readers may infer their endorsement of the data and conclusions.

Technical help should be acknowledged in a paragraph separate from those acknowledging other contributions.

This scenario raises two other issues: intellectual property rights and ownership of data (also discussed in Scenario B). The scenario implies that the management of the research organization shows little inclination to follow acceptable criteria regarding authorship or to acknowledge the intellectual property rights of the scientist who had been most involved in the work. Several questions arise: Should the individual property rights of the scientists carrying out the work be of primary importance in determining who should be considered authors, or does a company "own" all professional credit for the data produced by its staff, regardless of who they are and where they are when a manuscript is submitted or published? Should it matter whether the scientist had signed an employment contract, relinquishing all rights to data produced during the employee's tenure at the company? Of course, a company might also have legitimate reasons for concern as to who will be considered an author of a paper. Two of the more obvious concerns are related to the proprietary nature of the findings of company-sponsored research and possible damage to the company's reputation by the publication of work that is not of high quality.

The paper might describe data obtained in a long-term project. Designating someone at the company as the corresponding author allows the company to be "the official spokesperson" for the research. Acknowledgments tend to be overlooked by many readers, and the acknowledgments section is not a satisfactory place to alert readers to important information, such as where to send queries directed to the company.

In academic institutions, it is common practice for individual scientists to consider their work their own, and regard for intellectual property rights is entrenched. Institutions have thus far not acted to usurp power and assume ownership of researchers' data, although this could change in some ways as academic institutions are required to take more responsibility for work done by their employees.

Much of the current discussion of authorship revolves around two issues: how to define categorically and explicitly how much of a contribution an individual scientist needs to make to a paper intended for publication to be an author, and how much accountability an individual scientist needs to have for the whole of the paper. Science has become more complex, and interdisciplinary research is more common. Scientists now commonly collaborate with colleagues in different fields. If authors are to take public responsibility for the entire content of a paper, should they be held accountable for aspects of the work provided by other authors in fields remote from their own?

RESPONSES

Almost all respondents felt that the paper described in the scenario should not be published until authorship is settled to the satisfaction of all involved in the work. Some felt that the editor should attempt to settle the dispute and should be directly involved by writing the letters and making the telephone calls. Others felt that the editor should return the manuscript to the corresponding author and request that he straighten out the situation. The editor should request that any future correspondence with regard to the manuscript include statements from all involved in the work that concerns regarding authorship had been resolved to their satisfaction. Once that had been done, most seem to agree, the paper should be published.

A few recommended stronger action: "This is plagiarism pure and simple. The paper should be rejected outright and no revision of the manuscript allowed." "Reject the paper. Refuse to publish anything further from that organization." "The allegation needs to be investigated. If true, it is a serious breach of ethics and the perpetrator should be disciplined. If the perpetrator is 'the chief,' the journal should not accept papers from this organization for some period."

Some recommended that the supervisor of the director of research be informed; others suggested that the "slighted author" be invited to submit his own version of the paper. The following response suggests both courses of action: "The paper should be rejected and the research organization's CEO informed about the inappropriate alterations to the paper. The original author should be invited to submit a paper based on his own work, and its processing should be expedited."

Only a few respondents alluded to ownership of data: "Does the company have the proprietary right to the former employee's research?" "In a sense, it's the organization's paper, not the scientist's. Perhaps the editor should ask the director of research to exclude all names and use only the name of the organization." Another commented on this as both an ethical and a moral issue:

> The problem is one of ethics as much as one of copyright. If it was work for hire or, under non-U.S. legislation, work done in the normal course of employ-

ment, the employer organization would own the rights and would be able to submit the article to the journal under its own name. Moral rights provisions, whether under common law or Bern convention rule [on copyright], would give the original author the possibility of claiming paternity. Common decency (ethics) prescribes, in my view, that the editor tell the director of research or the "other" person that the article cannot be published unless the original author's name is mentioned as such.

DISCUSSION

Responsible authorship and ownership of data are both important aspects of publishing. Should journal editors develop, publish, and aggressively attempt to enforce standard criteria for authorship by requiring a written statement from all authors as to their contributions to a particular paper? Or should journal editors assume a more passive role and act only when there appears to be a flagrant abuse of authorship? For instance, in this scenario, should the journal editor return the paper once the abuse is uncovered and let all concerned know that the paper will not be considered until a written statement is obtained that indicates agreement among the group? That could lead to a plea-bargain situation in which the slighted author's name is added, but the person who had little involvement is still listed as an author to satisfy the company's management that someone currently in the company assumes responsibility for the accuracy of the data and for the conclusions. Should the editor allow such a compromise or should there be a system of "other credits," as suggested by Conrad (pp. 184-187, this volume)?

Should the editor, after the fact, educate those involved with regard to acceptable criteria for authorship? Is it important for the editor to determine the ownership of data? Do the data in the paper belong to the organization (work for hire) or to the person who did the work (intellectual property)? Should journal editors work with industrial concerns to develop guidelines regarding appropriate wording in "work-for-hire" contracts to protect both the individual scientist and the company with respect to criteria for authorship and ownership of data?

At least four professional societies (the American Chemical Society, the American Psychological Association, the American College Personnel Association, and the Endocrine Society) and two associations of editors (the Council of Biology Editors and the International Committee of Medical Journal Editors) have published explicit standards for authorship.[1-5,7] Research investigators should know about those standards. Huth[6] has recommended a collaborative effort of the Association of American Medical Colleges, the Council of Biology Editors, and the International Committee of Medical Journal Editors to develop a national standard for authorship in the medical sciences and clinical medicine that might be widely distributed by professional societies.

Perhaps an expanded group that includes, for instance, the American Chemical Society and the American Institute of Physics could develop even broader standards that would be applicable to the physical and biologic sciences, as well as to medical science and clinical medicine. (As science becomes more interdisciplinary, boundaries between the physical, biologic, medical, and clinical sciences will become less distinct.)

CONCLUSIONS AND RECOMMENDATIONS

Journal editors would be responsible for publishing the standards regularly, notifying institutions and corporations of their existence, and perhaps requiring all authors and coauthors to sign statements about their contributions to the paper and indicating that they each take responsibility for the entire content or specified parts of the content of the paper. It would be critical that such a signed statement be obtained for the final, accepted version of a paper.

Perhaps, in the interim, the standards of the International Committee of Medical Journal Editors[7] should be endorsed and publicized by journal editors. We recommend that journal editors also consider implementing the use of a signed statement in which all listed authors certify that they have actually participated in the work reported and meet the criteria for authorship in accordance with the standards.

According to Huth,[6]

> science is a method of collecting verifiable, replicable evidence from which we develop concepts useful for theory and application. The evidence is gathered in tests of hypotheses, explicit or implicit, or efforts to answer questions. The hypotheses are generated from previously generated and presumably supported concepts. Science proceeds fruitfully only if these concepts and the evidence supporting them can be relied on. Therefore scientists committed to supporting science as a reliable method of generating evidence and concepts that can be assumed as a basis for future work must be committed to gathering reliable evidence and reporting it accurately.

REFERENCES

1. American Chemical Society. Ethical guidelines to publication of chemical research. In: Dodd JS. The ACS Style Guide. Washington, DC: American Chemical Society; 1986:217-22.
2. American College Personnel Association. Statement of ethical and professional standards. J Coll Student Pers Assoc 1984;22:184-9.
3. American Psychological Association. Authorship. In: Publication Manual of the American Psychological Association. 3rd ed. Washington, DC: American Psychological Association; 1983:20-1.
4. Council of Biology Editors Style Manual Committee. CBE Style Manual. 5th ed. Bethesda, Maryland: Council of Biology Editors; 1983:1-3.

5. Endocrine Society Publications Committee. Ethical guidelines for publication of research. J Clin Endocrinol Metab 1988;66:1-2.
6. Huth EJ. Scientific Authorship and Publication: Process, Standards, Problems, Suggestions. Background paper prepared for the Institute of Medicine, 1988.
7. International Committee of Medical Journal Editors. Uniform requirements for manuscripts submitted to biomedical journals. Ann Intern Med 1988;108:258-65.

Scenario Q

Group Review

A journal's form letter to reviewers states that a selected reviewer who is unable to provide a timely review may ask a colleague to prepare the review instead. The editor receives a telephone call from the author of a paper that has been accepted but not yet published, complaining that the manuscript has been widely circulated among research competitors at another university. The editor asks the reviewer about possible leaks and learns that the reviewer routinely asks a closed group of people who attend his research seminar to review manuscripts as a group, because of the educational value of such review. The group includes faculty, fellows, and a few advanced doctoral candidates. The reviewer made copies of the manuscript and had five members of his group prepare independent critiques, which were then discussed by the entire group. The reviewer consolidated the comments, signed the form, and took full responsibility for the content of the group report. Further inquiry strongly suggests that the manuscript did not stray outside the reviewing group. The review itself is thorough and constructive.

ISSUES

This scenario focuses on the conflict between scientific openness and confidentiality. Secondary issues are the need for wisdom and clarity in the editor's instructions for reviewers.

At its best, scientific research is an open, collegial activity, in which ideas are freely exchanged and researchers benefit directly from the efforts (including the mistakes) of others. Thus, a reviewer's practice of asking the participants of his research seminar to evaluate manuscripts that he receives for review has educational merit. Such a review might well be more thorough and thoughtful than a review from one person. In addition, those in the seminar could learn much about the subject dealt with in the paper and, perhaps more important, have the opportunity to sharpen their critical abilities.

However, such easy dissemination of a researcher's work before publication makes it difficult to ensure that the researcher's ideas will not be used inappropriately by others. Plagiarism of the conception, design, and results of a study might occur. That is always a possibility in peer review, whether a manuscript is reviewed by one person or by a group, but the use of only one or two reviewers whose identities are known to the editor affords some accountability. In the situation described in this scenario, it might be nearly impossible to trace plagiarism to the guilty person or even to be certain that it had occurred.

Assuming that confidentiality is important and that the editor wishes to ensure it, are the instructions for reviewers in this scenario appropriate and clear? Permitting the reviewer to "ask a colleague" to review a manuscript if the selected reviewer cannot do it removes the responsibility for the selection of reviewers from the editor. Did the instructions mean literally that only one colleague could be chosen as an alternative reviewer, or that an alternative *or* alternatives could be chosen? Although the chosen reviewer might be considered to have specialized knowledge in the field that would result in a good choice of an alternative reviewer, the original reviewer might be less aware than the editor of possible risks or problems. For example, although it is important that reviewers be expert in the subject of the paper, they might find it difficult to be impartial if they are engaged in much the same kind of work or if they have had some collaboration with the author in the past.

Finally, one can wonder whether the circumstances in this scenario are teaching junior colleagues the wrong lessons about professional conduct.

RESPONSES

Most of the respondents felt that the reviewer's practice was wrong, but many were vague in their reasons. One respondent said: "I would 'fire' the reviewer! Using someone else's work as a teaching exercise before it has been published is a violation of confidentiality." Another said: "I would drop the reviewer. Manuscripts are confidential; this is *completely* unacceptable!"

A minority of respondents, however, did not object to the reviewer's practice, and many of these thought that it would enhance the review process. One said: "Sounds all right to me. I wish all reviews were that comprehensive." Another said: "I agree with the reviewer. Such a procedure can have educational value. The reviewer should take responsibility for the comments, if he or she has compiled and edited them. The author should be grateful for the additional feedback." Others pointed out that the nature of peer review exposes one's work to competitors. As one respondent said, "it is unavoidable that 'research competitors' be asked to review papers in their field of study."

Many respondents focused specifically on the intent and wording of the instructions for reviewers. One said: "Change [the] form letter to state that 'colleagues' may be consulted by reviewers, in 'confidence.' " But several respondents said that it was important for the editor to maintain control over the choice of reviewers. One said that "the journal's form letter should immediately be changed. If the recipient cannot provide a timely review, the manuscript should be returned to the editor."

DISCUSSION

An editor must first decide what he or she wants to achieve. If the highest priority is a thorough review, the editor might permit more than one colleague to assist a reviewer in the review process, and this should be stated in the instructions for reviewers. However, authors should be made aware that that is the policy of the journal; in this scenario, the editor was remiss in the obligation to make this policy clear to the authors and further remiss in not requiring that the chosen reviewer name any colleagues who helped in the review.

If preserving confidentiality is an editor's highest priority, the instructions for reviewers should stipulate that a reviewer is required to check with the editor before asking even one colleague to assist in the review. The instructions for reviewers for the *New England Journal of Medicine,* for example, include the following statement: "This manuscript is a privileged communication and is sent to you for your personal review. You are free to solicit advice from others, but please do not refer the manuscript to anyone else to review without prior approval by the editors. It is the property of the author and should not be photocopied."[1]

The instructions of the editor in this scenario were unclear and incomplete and did not accomplish the important goal of maintaining confidentiality.

CONCLUSIONS AND RECOMMENDATIONS

The instructions of the editor in this scenario were unclear and incomplete. The reviewer form for this particular journal stated that a colleague could be asked to prepare the review instead. The instructions did not mention obtaining prior approval of the editor. If the reviewer wished to ask a group to prepare the review, the editor should have been consulted beforehand and should have given his approval, because, in this case, the instructions specify "colleague," and not "colleagues."

What if the instructions to reviewers had stated that a collective review of a few people was all right, as long as the confidentiality of the review process was maintained?

Scientists do not work in a vacuum. They talk informally every day with other scientists about their work in progress. In addition, they present talks at scientific meetings, often doing nothing more than updating the field in which they are working and giving the latest unpublished results. If their colleagues or competitors wish to "steal" their ideas, they have ample opportunity to do so outside the confidential review process used by journal editors.

Much can be said in favor of a "group" review, provided that the reviewers and authors know the guidelines and the confidentiality of the review process is preserved. Both the National Science Foundation and the National Institutes of Health use "group review" to review research proposals, and much can be said for this type of discussion. The journal might wish to establish the number of colleagues who can assist in a review. Would five be appropriate, but 25 unwieldy and inappropriate, from an editor's standpoint? When does the size of the group suddenly make the discussion a "public discussion"? Should all participants be asked to sign the reviewer form? Should we or should we not attempt, on occasion, to use the review process to educate less-experienced scientists?

Review of unpublished work provides scientists with an opportunity to look for the weak points in an argument, gaps in data, and so forth. But critiquing published work that has already been subject to the rigors of thorough review will sometimes leave little for a young, untested scientist to evaluate.

The committee recommends that each journal establish a policy with regard to review of papers and that this policy be adequately publicized so that authors and reviewers alike understand it.

In this scenario, the editor has no choice but to remind the reviewer of the terms of the review for the journal and to apologize to the author.

REFERENCE

1. Information for authors. N Engl J Med 1990; 323 [published in the first issue of each month].

Scenario R

Possibly Unethical Research

A university requires each coauthor of a paper to approve the final draft of the manuscript before submission. An author consults the university's "author's editor" regarding a manuscript. The author's editor finds that university guidelines for animal experimentation have apparently been violated. Before the author's editor asks the senior author and coauthor to sign the standard approval form, he asks them

about the apparent violation. The coauthor supposes that the descrip-
tion of the experimental protocol is in error and is willing to alter it
and sign the standard form. The senior author signs the form and tells
the author's editor by telephone that the university regulation is too
strict, but that the author's editor could add a statement to the manu-
script that the animals were cared for "in compliance with generally
accepted standards."

ISSUES

This scenario illustrates how a single ethical issue can develop many ramifications. Irregularities appeared in a manuscript that was given to an author's
editor (that is, an editor who works in the author's behalf, rather than for a
journal or publisher, to prepare a manuscript for submission and publication).
A coauthor has an unsettling willingness to rewrite a report of his research to
make it comply with established university guidelines regarding research protocols while a senior author seemingly generalizes the issue into nothingness.

Does the nature or the extent of the violation make a difference regarding
the degree of seriousness of the situation or its solution, or does any violation
or manipulation of data inherently constitute misconduct? Whose responsibility is it to determine whether a violation of university protocol has taken place
and, if so, what actions should be taken to correct both the manuscript and
the actions of the authors? Does the responsibility rest with the author's editor,
the authors, the university, or the editor of a journal to which the manuscript
has been or is to be submitted for publication? Does the allegiance of an
author's editor belong to the authors, the authors' department, the institution,
the scientific community, or the public? What should a journal editor do when
such a manuscript, appropriate or not, arrives at the journal office?

RESPONSES

Only one-fourth of the survey respondents felt that the circumstances of
the scenario currently pose a serious threat to scientific publishing. But over
half felt that, when the situation does occur, some action must be taken to
resolve the discrepancies, preferably before the paper is submitted and defi-
nitely before it is published. One respondent wrote that "the problem this
scenario presents is not the mistreatment of animals, but the authors' cavalier
manner of [making misstatements to readers]. If an author is able to glibly
dismiss an [author's] editor's criticism, how can the [journal] editor or readers
be certain that the scholarly work is not just as glib?"

Only a few of the respondents to this scenario had participated in the
resolution of a similar situation. One author's editor wrote:

> My own involvement in dubious cases such as the one outlined here usually
> involves unethical behavior in very gray areas. Unfortunately, the problem becomes

one of publishing, rather than of research ethics, because an author's editor immediately becomes involved in a serious conflict of interest by questioning the integrity of authors employed by his or her own employer. In most instances, the only recourse is to notify the journal editor of possible problems and let the journal editor, who is in no danger of losing his or her job, question the author and institution.

Many felt strongly that resolution did not rest with the journal editor, because the discrepancies should be resolved before submission of the manuscript, and that a journal editor was unlikely to find suspicious the statement that the animal experimentation met "generally accepted standards" or to be familiar with various university policies. One respondent wrote that "the problem should be addressed at the source—ethical review by the institution—and not become part of the publishing process."

However, one-fourth of the respondents found the journal editor responsible for resolving the dilemma. One suggested that a journal editor's responsibility in this situation, if he knows about it, is to ensure that the university's regulations are not violated, no matter how inappropriate the regulations might be. Many suggested that a journal editor return the manuscript with a notice to the author's supervisor, explaining the reasons for the action of no review.

A few respondents said that a solution should depend on how extensive the violation of the protocol was and how central to the manuscript's conclusion—despite today's climate in which research funding sources require acceptance of and adherence to their standards. One wrote:

> Is the violation truly worth fussing over? The key point is not in the letter of the law, but in the actual suffering, neglect, or whatever to which the animals were subjected. If the food-bowl size was 2 cm too small, that's nonsense. If the animals were hung by their tails to simulate weightlessness, that should be reported.

Several respondents gave the journal editor authority to decide the fate of the manuscript:

> Scientists often are subjected to numerous administrative restrictions, complex permit requirements, red tape, etc., that inhibit legitimate work. Editors should look into the situation. If the university's regulations are excessive, the editor could follow the senior author's desires about adding the indicated statement. If the authors are trying to circumvent valid rules, then the paper as presented should be rejected. The editor must use judgment to distinguish between valid regulations and the plethora of "red tape" regulation.

> If a paper is good and valid, publish it. Guidelines vary from institution to institution. The purpose of peer review is to judge methods and results, not animal welfare. Journal editors are not obliged to follow any university's procedures.

One respondent reported that his editorial board would evaluate whether the rules of the university were too strict, compared with the currently accepted standards of the scientific community. And another said: "Let the article speak for itself. Publish it."

A few respondents suggested that both author's editors and journal editors can ignore questionable practices reported in papers when it appears that the work has made it through institutional administrative formalities. But one stated simply that "it is the primary responsibility of an author to abide by the rules and regulations of his university in research procedures; there can be no excuse for such behavior from authors. How can a compromise on morality be reached?"

A smaller group of respondents placed responsibility on the author's editor. Many felt that the author's editor should meet with all the authors for clarification of the procedures and of the authors' compliance with federal statutes.

> An author's editor should refuse to complete work on the manuscript until the university sanctions the experimental protocol used and the proposed wording in the manuscript. The author's editor should notify in writing his or her immediate supervisor and the dean of the institution of the status of work on the manuscript and the reasons behind the halt in processing it. All work on the manuscript should be stopped until the alleged violation of protocol is cleared or confirmed.

One respondent wrote:

> The scenario gives no indication of who is in charge of the authors or the author's editor. If the author's editor has final approval on a manuscript, no manuscript with an alleged violation of any kind should pass approval. If an institution does not allow an author's editor to stop or question such an issue, then an author's editor can either choose to notify [a journal] editor or let the paper pass.

Another suggested that, if an author's editor is not allowed to prohibit submission of a paper for publication, the author's editor should "anonymously leak the story to the student newspaper."

A few felt strongly that author's editors should not act as police officers and should not force any authors to respond to their concerns:

> Under no circumstances should the author's editor put himself between the authors and the publisher. An author's editor's function is to perform a service. He can check that policy is followed and alert the person responsible for the manuscript, but he is not at the level to enforce anything.

Other respondents variously named the authors' department chair, the authors themselves, and appropriate university committees as responsible for resolving such dilemmas. Many respondents felt that the requirement that scientists conform to research guidelines is nonnegotiable. A few felt that the author's editor should go around the author and take the matter directly to the university's dean or ethics committee. Others felt that the person or committee at the university responsible for approving the release of research results held the responsibility to stop publication of the work or send it forward.

In 1982, the Association of American Medical Colleges published guidelines for the maintenance of high ethical standards in research.[2] The guidelines state:

> The principles that govern scientific research have long been established and have been applied by faculties and administrators of academic centers and teaching facilities for the discovery of the new knowledge that is needed to promote the health and welfare of mankind. The maintenance of high ethical standards in research based on these principles is a central and critical responsibility of faculties and administrators of academic centers. . . . The primary responsibility of taking steps to prevent research fraud rests with the scientific community. In academic institutions, it can best be executed by the faculties.

A workshop sponsored by the joint American Association for the Advancement of Science-American Bar Association National Conference of Lawyers and Scientists found[1] in 1988 that

> the scientific community is characterized by its decentralized organization. The major institutions that represent this community include universities, government agencies, commercial firms, and private foundations . . . , and professional societies and journals that promote professional competence and the exchange of research results. The diverse and overlapping responsibilities among these institutions complicate the assignment of key roles in handling claims of research misconduct. . . . [Furthermore,] the universities are believed by many—including the government research agencies—to be the appropriate institutions to handle allegations of misconduct by their faculty, research staff, or students.

Most of the workshop participants agreed that universities should be the "front line" for resolving issues regarding misconduct, but many also felt that the universities are not the only "proper" institutions to take responsibility for allegations of misconduct by their employees.

DISCUSSION

Most respondents agreed that the resolution of this situation rests with the authors and their universities. Although authors are responsible for the quality, nature, and accuracy of work that they produce and report in compliance with guidelines established by their institutions, the authors' institutions should have some mechanism to control work that is produced in affiliation with the institution and its employees. When questionable work gets beyond the appropriate checkpoints, alleged misconduct on the part of authors or misrepresentations of research protocol included in manuscripts might become the problem of an author's editor and later of a journal editor. Journal editors and author's editors who have reason to suspect violations of protocol or misconduct might consider several types of actions.

Author's editors can attempt to resolve questions concerning protocols and discrepancies in manuscripts by meeting with all authors to clarify the relevant institutional guidelines and requirements and to determine the protocols used, so as to highlight any differences from required protocols. If no satisfactory resolution results from such a meeting, an author's editor can take documentation of the situation to appropriate department chairs, deans of universities or other institutions, or institutional review boards or ethics committees, for final decision that the work in question is ready to be submitted for publication.

If an author's university is funded in part by U.S. Public Health Service (USPHS) grants or contracts, author's editors can consult the USPHS *Policy and Procedures for Dealing with Possible Misconduct in Extramural Research.*

Journal editors can require signed statements by authors that all guidelines of their sponsoring institutions or funding bodies have been met, or they can include a statement regarding acceptable research procedures in their journals' instructions for authors. One primary cardiology journal includes the following statement:[4]

> *Ethics.* Published studies should be in compliance with human studies committees and animal welfare regulations of the authors' institutions and FDA [Food and Drug Administration] guidelines. Authors should indicate that human subjects have given informed consent and that the institutional committee on human research has approved the study protocol. Similarly, they should indicate that studies involving experimental animals conform to the guiding principles of the American Physiological Society.

If manuscripts with alleged violations reach journal editorial offices, editors can place the burden of resolving disputes on the authors and return the manuscripts unreviewed, indicating that the work will not be considered for publication until violations are confirmed or dismissed by the authors' sponsoring institutions. In other words, authors should consult with their appropriate university review boards, committees, or offices that are responsible for the protocols governing their research. The decisions should be submitted in writing to journal editors.

Some journals include some version of this question on the forms they send to reviewers: "Do you have any concerns regarding the ethical aspects of the experimental procedures?"

CONCLUSIONS AND RECOMMENDATIONS

The committee concludes that, regardless of the justification for institutional guidelines for research, authors must comply with the existing guidelines of their institutions. Authors' defiance of their institutions' research requirements is a serious act of misconduct, and it might constitute a legal offense.

The committee recommends that the resolution of situations similar to those discussed in this scenario not become the responsibility of journal editors. Such situations reflect institutional problems, and they should remain at the institutions until resolved. In addition, editors are likely to be poorly informed about critical aspects of the situation, and they have neither the authority nor the resources to investigate. Journal editors should not become enforcers of the regulations of other institutions.

A journal editor who has reason to suspect that a submitted manuscript is based on work that has violated institutional protocol or other standards of conduct by an author or contains misrepresentation as to protocol should return the manuscript unreviewed with an explanation for the action of no review. Such a manuscript should not be considered for publication until the journal editor is satisfied that the author's institution has approved the protocol on which the paper was based and is itself satisfied about the author's scientific conduct.

REFERENCES

1. American Association for the Advancement of Science-American Bar Association. National Conference of Lawyers and Scientists project on scientific fraud and misconduct: report on workshop number one. Washington, DC: American Association for the Advancement of Science; 1988.
2. Association of American Medical Colleges. The maintenance of high ethical standards in the conduct of research. Washington, DC: Association of American Medical Colleges; 1982.
3. Gilbert JR, Wright CN, Amberson JI, Thompson AL. Profile of the author's editor: findings from a national survey. CBE Views 1980;7:4-10.
4. Information for authors. Circulation 1987;75:6.

Scenario S

Lack of Informed Consent and Institutional Review Board Approval

An editor receives a scientifically sound manuscript from a developing country in which the use of postoperative analgesia after minor procedures is rare. The paper reports on a placebo-controlled randomized clinical trial of a new analgesic for postoperative pain. The journal's instructions for authors require that a manuscript specify whether patients have given informed consent and whether an institutional review board approved the study. The author's letter of submission says that

*informed consent is not a recognized concept in the author's country
and that there are no institutional review boards.*

ISSUES

This scenario raises several important issues. The most obvious is the
conflict between the claims of science (assuming that the trial yielded important
results) and ethical considerations. It is generally acknowledged in the United
States that clinical trials are ethical only if informed consent from patients is
obtained and that the need for informed consent outweighs any need for the
scientific results of a trial.

A second issue is the difference among countries in ethical standards.
Does the fact that this trial took place in a country with no apparent tradition
of or requirement for informed consent change the ethics of the trial? That is,
are some studies proper in one country, but not in another? Who sets ethical
standards in a community? Is there something absolute about them, or are
they a matter of custom?[1]

Finally, there is the issue of informed consent itself. Should informed
consent always be necessary? Is it always sufficient? For example, if a patient
gives informed consent to be maimed, does that relieve a researcher of responsibility? Can institutional review board (IRB) approval substitute for informed consent? What happens when neither is available?

RESPONSES

Most respondents thought that it was appropriate to publish the report.
They gave several reasons. Many thought that, if the ethics were in accord with
those of the country in which the research was done, people from outside that
country should not object. One did "not believe an editor should 'meddle' in
the affairs of a foreign state." Another said that it is "far beyond the responsibility of a journal to 'require' that all countries meet U.S. medical standards."
A third, evidently seeing the requirement for informed consent as journal
policy, rather than an ethical standard, said that "medical research ethics and
procedures of the country where the author resides must have priority over a
journal policy that may be completely irrelevant in [another] country or culture."

Many in the group that would publish the paper seemed to think that the
only or major criterion was the scientific merit of the study. "The value of the
paper is in its scientific merit." "This situation is all too common in the Third
World, and it won't change in the near future. Something must be done so
that this won't hamper the publication of high-quality investigation from those
countries. Perhaps a disclaimer? A footnote?" Others felt that scientific merit
might mitigate genuine ethical concerns. "There is certainly a sound of Hitler-
like indifference to painful procedures. However, the data may well be useful

and add knowledge not easily acquired in any other way or from any other source." Many who felt that publication was warranted if the manuscript had scientific merit suggested that the editor publish some sort of "disclaimer" or explanation of the circumstances in the researcher's country.

A somewhat smaller, but less equivocal, group of respondents thought that the paper should be rejected. One respondent wrote that "human rights transcend the 'advancement' of science in all cases." Some pointed out that permitting such violations, even if the immediate consequences might not be great, puts us on a "slippery slope" ethically. Others disputed the view that questions of ethics are merely national and pointed to international agreements. One said:

> The Helsinki Declaration is quite clear on this point. The manuscript should be rejected, since it violates the principles governing [the use of] human subjects in research. I am not bothered by the use of a placebo nearly as much as I am by the lack of review and the lack of informed consent.

Others who objected to publishing the paper looked at the issue much more narrowly, as involving only the standards or policies of the journal. One said that "the author should comply with the instructions for authors or resubmit to another journal that doesn't have the informed-consent requirement." Others felt that the ethical standards should be those of the country of publication, not the country of the research. A few insisted that ethics are not relative. One drew a distinction between the lack of informed consent and the lack of IRB approval:

> Informed consent is a recognized concept in clinical research everywhere today, even if it is not enforced in some places. IRBs are not. The lack of an IRB is irrelevant if the research was ethical, and IRB approval of unethical research does not convert it to ethical research.

A third group of respondents expressed deep uncertainty about what the editor should do.

DISCUSSION

The editor could publish the manuscript on the basis of its scientific merits, reject it, or publish it with an explanation, disclaimer, or editorial comment.

This scenario evoked remarkably divergent opinions that centered on two views of ethics. The first view sees ethics as relative, that is, properly different in different cultures or contexts. According to that view, journal editors should defer to the ethical practices and customs of the locality in which the research was done. Anything else would arbitrarily impose foreign standards and therefore be inappropriate. The second view holds ethical standards, like scientific standards, to be fundamentally absolute. Adherence to them might vary from place to place and time to time, but there is an irreducible set of ethical standards to protect human subjects that we all should make efforts to apply universally. According to that view, editors can help to uphold the standards by refusing to publish work that violates them, wherever that work originates.

In the United States, the rights of human subjects of clinical research are protected by federal regulations that make it clear that the value of research to society does not justify violating the rights of individual subjects.[3] Accordingly, human subjects have the rights to have their welfare held paramount by researchers, to refuse participation without penalty, and to participate only after giving informed consent. Those basic rights are not peculiar to this country. Similar requirements were spelled out in the Nuremberg Code of 1947 and the World Medical Association Declaration of Helsinki, revised in 1975.[2] The Declaration of Helsinki states that "concern for the interests of the subject must always prevail over the interests of science and society."

CONCLUSIONS AND RECOMMENDATIONS

The committee supports the view that human subjects must be protected from unethical research, which includes research in which the interests of the individual subjects are subordinated to those of the research. IRB approval, although helpful in ensuring ethical review of the design of research, is not a substitute for informed consent. Nor is informed consent sufficient to justify inherently unethical research, that is, research that would or might entail unjustifiable harm to subjects. Editors can and should play their part in upholding ethical standards by refusing to publish reports of work that violates human rights, even if the work seems scientifically valid and important.

REFERENCES

1. Angell M. Ethical imperialism? Ethics in international collaborative clinical research. N Engl J Med. 1988; 319:1081-3.
2. Beauchamp TL, Childress JF, eds. Principles of Biomedical Ethics. 2nd ed. Oxford: Oxford University Press; 1983:338-43.
3. Protection of human subjects in behavioral and social research. OPRR Reports. 45 CFR 46. Washington, DC: DHHS; 1983. (GPO publication 0-406-756.)

Cross-Cutting Issues

As the committee studied the comments of CBE members and thought more deeply about each scenario, we recognized that the scenarios are much more interrelated than we had expected. This chapter deals with several issues that cut across the lines of scenarios and with some basic approaches to resolving these and perhaps other issues of ethics and policy. The committee has become convinced that the individual issues raised in the scenarios reflect deeper issues and questions that face journals and their editors. Examples are in Table 1. If the study of ethics is largely the study of standards of conduct called into use when values are in conflict, what principles of conduct govern the work of an editor? Should all editors be encouraged to act in a specified manner, or should each editor base decisions on his or her own standards of conduct? Do authors, reviewers, and readers expect a particular type of behavior in editors? Should they?

An editor is responsible to authors, reviewers, readers, and others. What should be done when an editor's varied responsibilities collide? Editors place high value on the open exchange of scientific data, but also value the proprietary interest of the scientist who produces the data (Scenario B). Fabrication of data is perhaps the most serious breach of conduct in science today, and our sense of values impels us to condemn such fraud with utmost vigor, but we also recognize a need to protect possibly innocent persons and their reputations while allegations of fraud are being resolved. What should editors do if resolution never comes (see Scenario A)?

Our discussion here of those and other cross-cutting issues is intended to provide a structure for broader consideration of questions of ethics and of ethics versus policy.

PROBLEMS CREATE MORE PROBLEMS

The first cross-cutting theme is complexity itself—the difficulty of isolating a single ethical issue. Each of the case studies was designed to bring out one distinct issue. But one problem begets another, and several of the scenarios, short as they are, raise three or more questions of ethics and policy. Table 2 lists some of those by way of illustration. Scenario F, for example, deals with the withdrawal by authors of an accepted paper, but also presents matters of multiple simultaneous submissions of a manuscript, copyright transfer, and serious delays in publication, each with its own separate issues of ethics and policy.

Or consider Scenario I, which describes possible deviations from a "first in, first out" sequence of publication policy. It also elucidates the conflicting responsibilities of editors, the combined ethical and policy implications of a

TABLE 1. Some Cross-Cutting Issues

Separation of ethics and policy

Responsibilities of a journal

Locus and nature of editorial responsibilities and authorities; strong and weak editors

Concerns of "fairness" (to whom? why?), including anonymity

Stability of decisions

Publish or perish—it applies to journals, too

Ownership of, access to, and uses of data

Costs and benefits of decision processes, including peer review

Enforcement of editorial policies, including sanctions

Research quality and the role of scientific and technical merit in decisions to publish (should every perfect study be published?)

Impact of journal policies, processes, and decisions on scientific inference and progress

Role of disclosure

Scientific inference: pressures and precedents for data-dredging, selective publication, multiple publication, etc.

---

large backlog of accepted but unpublished papers, and the ugly issue of buying one's way into earlier publication by paying optional page charges.

We have tried to identify and comment on each major additional issue in our discussions, but the frequency of multiplicity of issues suggests that something more is at work—that, as in many other human endeavors, attempts to deal with one problem often lead to others, so that a matter small in itself can have large and far-reaching effects.

The lesson we draw is that there is a need for constant attention to basic matters of ethics and policy and their interaction. Prevention is better than treatment, especially when treatment is not likely to be fully effective.

MULTIPLE RESPONSIBILITIES

Both editors and journals have multiple responsibilities—to authors, reviewers, readers, publication owners or sponsors, members of scientific disciplines, and advertisers and printers. Those factions often have conflicting priorities, and there is generally no set hierarchy for consideration of the priorities or resolution of conflicts among them.

Perhaps there should be none. Giving a little on something of high value might sometimes be better and sometimes worse than giving a lot on something of low value. Nor is there reason to think that values, or even their rankings, would or should be the same for all journals and editors or in all circumstances. The editor of a for-profit journal and the editor of an association-owned journal

TABLE 2. Examples of Scenarios with Multiple Issues

Scenario D

Primary issue:	Undisclosed data-dredging
Other issue:	Extra information about an author or paper
	Abuse of statistical concepts and procedures, against a background of the limited statistical sophistication of most editors, reviewers, and readers
	Bias against "negative" reports

Scenario F

Primary issue:	Withdrawal of an accepted paper
Other issues:	Willful breach of journal policies
	Copyright transfer (also a legal matter)
	Delays in publication
	Multiple simultaneous submissions

Scenario I

Primary issues:	Sequence of publication
Other issues:	Conflicting responsibilities
	Buying one's way into earlier publication
	Effects of backlog

might properly have different obligations to their publishers. A very long delay in reviewing a manuscript increases the responsibility of an editor for a prompt decision once all reviews have been received and can diminish the responsibility of an author to complete requested revisions rapidly as a convenience to the journal. Acceptance of a paper for publication is ordinarily binding on a journal—a high responsibility to authors, who necessarily depend on the word of the editor—but can sometimes properly be reversed if the editor discovers that (for example) an author was remiss in not citing a prior publication with essentially the same findings.

Editorial responsibilities cannot be arranged in priority order; there is often no "right" solution. Conflicting responsibilities must be balanced on the basis of a whole situation, including the nature and strength of prior commitments and the type and extent of damage likely to be incurred by one or another party.

Scenario B deals with the ownership and sharing of research data. The hypothetical participants, including the public, have values that conflict—the proprietary interest of the original investigators, the public interest in both a strong research enterprise and a timely return on its investment, and the secondary investigator's interest in promoting his or her career (legally and openly) by using materials that are in the public domain but of decreasing value as time passes. In our view, no set of values is dominant. Many respondents to the survey clearly supported one or another of those positions, but few seemed to recognize the different priorities of the investigators, editors, and the public.

The committee believes that the highest responsibility of editors must be to preserve scientific integrity—to publish valid data and objective analysis in a context that facilitates fair and unbiased interpretation by all readers likely to see the paper or use its findings. Closely linked to that is the need to protect the integrity of inferences drawn from the data. Readers—the basic target of scientific communication—can make or be led to make mistakes, and authors, reviewers, and editors jointly have a high responsibility to ensure that serious mistakes of interpretation are rare. That requires constant, explicit attention to the message received (by readers), as well as to the message sent (by authors).

The editor, representing the journal, must require that the highest standards of scientific integrity be met in each item published. That is the original source of concern about such matters as conflicts of interest, allegations of fraud, and undisclosed data-dredging (which distorts the apparent statistical and substantive significance of findings). It is also related to concerns about the effect of open review on reviewers and the initial interpretation of data by someone not directly involved in their production (Scenario B). Questions about scientific integrity do not always have clear answers, but the committee believes that there is no satisfactory reason for an editor to settle for anything less than the highest attainable standards determined for his or her journal. The angry author, the advertiser who threatens withdrawal, the board of directors that threatens to end a journal or replace an editor—all must be directly and vigorously opposed when the scientific integrity of the publication is at issue.

The responsibility of editors to safeguard scientific integrity through publication must rest on editors' authority. An editor must be able to exercise authority, and authors, reviewers, journal owners, and boards of directors must recognize and accept that authority as necessary for achieving the timely publication of the best possible scientific data. They must also recognize that editors must balance many elusive and competing priorities in maintaining scientific integrity and that their own perceptions of problems or possible errors in the editorial process might be incomplete. For example, disappointed authors commonly believe that they have been mistreated (as do others who disagree with specific decisions or policies), but the responsibility to protect scientific integrity requires authority in editors, who are sometimes fallible. That is not an excuse for editorial arrogance, avoidable error, or failure to make a reasonable response when error has occurred.

Scenario I raised several possibilities regarding the sequence of publication of accepted manuscripts in the face of a backlog. Does the editor's responsibility to individual authors—which might be translated as "first in, first out"—override the responsibility to help to develop new investigators, or to inform those who need to know about critical developments as soon as possible, or to provide a balanced range of topics in each volume or issue of a journal for a broader readership (and possibly a sponsoring society or publisher)? Survey respondents held quite firmly to a range of incompatible positions, with little indication of any sympathy for, or even recognition of, the legitimacy of other opinions.

How does the concept of fairness enter into the picture? Will an editor make a conscious effort to treat all authors alike, regardless of friendship or professional affiliation? Will the editor send a paper buttressing his or her own points of view to a reviewer known to be sympathetic to that point of view? Will the editor save the the the best reviewers (in both quality and timeliness) for "favorite" authors? Will the editor accept a disproportionate number of papers reflecting his or her own scientific or clinical interests—interests that the editor might even have been charged to promote? Will the editorial staff be instructed to spend more time polishing the manuscripts of favored authors, or will equal care be given to all accepted papers? As is suggested by those questions, the committee believes that the editor has a responsibility to be fair, but that the concept of fairness can be elusive.

A general lesson we draw from the responses to the 19 scenarios is that there is need for more discussion and, we hope, consensus about the multiple responsibilities of editors and about the resolution of conflicts among responsibilities. Such discussion might be especially helpful for new editors who have not yet come to understand the divergences among their colleagues, the pressures that can be developed by one or another constituency that feels aggrieved, or the need to work out their own priorities and stick with them. The only school for editors of scientific journals is the school of hard knocks, but some of the knocks might be softened by more effective efforts to reach consensus on the conceptual bases of editing. Pending such resolution, we suggest that the interests of readers be rated somewhat higher than now seems to be common and that the interests of sponsors, publishers, and owners be rated somewhat lower than is suggested by anecdotes and "horror stories" about the effects on journal contents of pressures for or against specific papers, as well as pressures to increase circulation and profits.

DISCLOSURE, CONFIDENTIALITY, AND RELATED MATTERS

The committee has become convinced that the best tool for preventing most problems regarding ethics and policy in scientific publishing is disclosure—by editors, authors, reviewers, and other concerned parties. Many problems would not arise or would present no ethical conflicts if all the parties knew and understood all the relevant facts and policies. However, disclosure is not a panacea. It is not an appropriate tool when there is a legitimate need to protect confidentiality, it has distinctly less scope in the resolution of problems than in their prevention, and it might have no role at all in some kinds of difficult and intense problems (such as that of Scenario B, on ownership of data).

Consider how disclosure might help. Potential conflicts of interest, if they are known all around, can be considered in the overall assessment of the worth of a paper, a review, or a journal. Sequence of publication does not seem to be an ethical concern (although it can remain a policy concern), if the rules are clearly communicated to authors before a paper is submitted and perhaps to readers before a subscription is entered. Data-dredging, if its nature and extent are known, should not present insuperable obstacles to scientific inference and hence is not an ethical problem. Some problems—such as fraud, plagiarism, and simultaneous submissions of a paper—would hardly arise if communication were open and complete all around.

But there is another side to the question, including the need to maintain the confidential status of information obtained by editors. Most editors seem convinced that the identity of reviewers should be kept confidential, but other kinds of information can also be considered privileged and not available to others under any circumstances. Should an editor ever be forced to disclose information about possible conflicts of interest of reviewers or authors (see Scenario E)? Similarly, if an editor has information about an author or reviewer gleaned during the peer-review process, should the information be used if the editor is asked to provide a recommendation for one of the authors (see Scenario H)? Can the information obtained in that way be separated from other information possessed by the editor?

The committee believes that editors should make every effort to be honest, open, and fair in their dealings with those involved in peer review. However, the information gathered during the process needs to be carefully protected, lest the system break down.

DECISION PROCESSES

Journal editors and staff members must make many decisions. Although they are often based on complex scientific data, decisions are usually straightforward, because the collection of relevant information—primarily in the form of reviews—is largely routine. And a routine operation is absolutely essential for effective operation; very few manuscripts can be handled as exceptional cases.

Journals vary widely in the number of people involved in the decision process. Many journals usually send a submitted manuscript to two reviewers; the editor than makes a decision by adding a final critique of the work to those of the reviewers. Other journals vary the decision process according to the subject matter of the paper. Are the data highly controversial? Are only a few people qualified to critique the work? Sometimes a paper will be sent to five or six reviewers, sometimes to the entire editorial board. When reviewers disagree, an editor may ask an editorial-board member to serve as arbiter—to study the earlier reviews, then to make a recommendation to the editor.

The committee understands the need for journal-to-journal variations in the decision process. It recommends, however, that each journal specify as fully as possible its scope of content, its criteria for acceptability, and its decision process in its instructions for authors. To the extent that the process is well specified and well known, the likelihood and perception of arbitrariness will be reduced.

RESEARCH QUALITY

Many of the problems that journal editors face involve questions of research quality. Research quality, however, is an elusive concept. There are fundamental problems in classifying papers on a scale (even a multidimensional scale) from low to high priority or as reporting a good or bad study. Such classifications are not objective and can vary from editor to editor, journal to journal, reader to reader, and of course reviewer to reviewer. Moreover, many aspects must be addressed: whether the basic idea was good, whether current techniques were used, whether the results are interpretable, whether the findings open new scientific areas, and so on. The committee notes that work at the cutting edge of science is likely to be less precise than later work that fills in fourth decimals, but adds no new concepts. Which is of higher "quality"?[1]

We know of few journals that attempt to assess the quality of research reported in papers that they have already published. One journal has tried identifying papers judged by at least two members of the editorial board to have been of poor research quality and discussing the course of the review process for the papers in depth at an editorial-board meeting. The editor hopes that that process will eventually help the journal to detect and correct weaknesses in its reviewing system. Routine feedback from editorial-board members to the editor about papers that the board members thought to be of poor quality is also used by some journals.

PROTECTING SCIENTIFIC INFERENCE

Some common practices are potentially (and sometimes deliberately) deceptive; these include data-dredging (Scenario D), fragmentation of reports, selective reporting of findings, post hoc hypotheses, inappropriate statistical tests, and undisclosed repetition of "unsatisfactory" experiments. The committee believes that those and similar practices can seriously distort the processes of scientific inference and should therefore be objects of concern. If any use of such practices has a legitimate application, it should be fully disclosed by the investigator, justified in detail, and accepted with caution by readers. Full disclosure means more than a few words buried in the fine print of a methods section; it means that the author must work to send a message and work to ensure that the message is received and correctly interpreted by readers.

Pressures to publish might account for many of the abuses. Scientists are evaluated for promotion and funding in large part according to the number of their publications. A research investigator might also choose work that yields rapid and, if possible, "positive" results, rather than long-term but uncertain studies that could ultimately be more important. The committee believes that deceptive practices will continue to be a major problem until the issue of "publish or perish" is addressed.

REFERENCE

1. Bailar JC, III. Research quality, methodologic rigor, citation counts, and impact. Amer J Pub Health 1982; 72:1103-4.

Other Issues of Ethics and Policy

One part of the first CBE survey asked respondents to check one of three cells for each of 22 issues not included in the scenarios: whether the respondent had ever had a particular problem, whether it should have high priority among CBE concerns, and whether it was a problem for editors to solve. This section of the questionnaire was included in the survey mainly to guide the committee in deciding whether to develop another survey with a new set of scenarios and, if so, to help in determining their content. Thus it is partially subsumed by the second survey, but retains some value in showing how experienced persons rank some important practical issues. Some quantitative results are included in our discussion, but they should be noted only as rough indicators of ill-defined opinions; small summary differences might have no meaning. We have not calculated t tests, confidence limits, and the like, because we think that random variation in results (the only feature of data captured in the usual statistical measures of variability) is likely to be dwarfed by other sources of error and variability, including the selective membership of CBE, nonrepresentative nonresponse, and variations in how survey respondents interpreted the brief statements.

We had to make many assumptions. First, as to whether respondents had ever had a particular problem, the committee did not collate replies with notes on other pages, so a statement like "As I said in responding to Scenario A . . ." or "I marked 'no' to all questions that don't apply" was lost, except for the page on which it appeared. All responses left blank or marked "NA" were coded as unknown. Where check marks wandered a bit, we did our best to interpret the proper row and column. A response "Yes and No" was generally taken as "Yes." Many respondents added notes of explanation; these are ignored in this analysis, although they will be a rich source of ideas for any future surveys.

A total of 212 persons returned questionnaires; of those, 17 left Part III entirely blank. In response to the first question, "Have you had problems related to this?" "No" was more common than "Yes," except for issues of

- Multiple publication.
- Delays in publication.
- Abuses of citations.
- Coauthorship.

Second, as to whether a particular issue should have high priority among CBE concerns, except for "citations," respondents marked "high" more often than "low" for the items listed above *plus*

- Copyright infringement by another journal.
- Confirmed fabrication of data.
- Plagiarism.
- Reviewers' abuse of privileged material.
- Reviewers' failure to reveal conflicts of interest.

On the matter of whether a particular issue is a problem for editors to solve, CBE members are activists; answers of "Yes" dominated answers of "No," *except* for:

- Failure to retain records.
- Failure to make data available to others.
- Photocopying outside the present legal limits.
- Disputes about ownership of data.

The response to the photocopying question surprised the committee. This issue could be seen as one for owners of scientific journals, rather than for editors, but the strong expression of opinion that it is not a matter to concern editors suggests that many people have given the issue too much weight.

Our survey is not to be used to calculate quantitative estimates, but we have used it to derive, very roughly, an index of priorities for future study. We first calculated the following differences:

- (Yes minus No) for "Have you had problems related to this?"
- (High minus Low) for "Priority among CBE concerns?"
- (Yes minus No) for "A problem for editors to solve?"

We then added the three differences to get a single overall index. This method of scoring effectively ignores all responses coded to unknown, or coded to "medium" for the question about priority. With 212 responses, the sum must lie in the range -636 to $+636$ or, if we look only at the 195 questionnaires with one or more responses in Part III, -585 to $+585$. The actual range was

TABLE 3. Assessment by Respondents of Issues Not Covered in the First CBE Survey

+ 365 Multiple publication
  252 Very long delays in publication
  154 Plagiarism
  124 High multiplicity of authors
  121 Listing authors who have not contributed to intellectual content
  109 Abuses (overuse or underuse) of citations
   95 Reviewer abuse of privileged material
   92 Reviewers who do not reveal conflicts of interest
   82 Confirmed fabrication of data
   21 Pressures from VIPs in the subject
   15 Refusal by authors or editors to correct unintentional errors (errata)
− 18 Copyright infringement by another journal
− 22 Insufficient funds to publish all worthy material
− 47 Anonymous review (names of authors not disclosed to reviewers)
− 70 Inappropriate pressures related to commercial interests (owners, advertisers)
− 84 Unnecessarily sex-specific language in publications
− 117 Amount and location of advertising
− 131 Publishing work that might damage legitimate nonscientific interests of society
− 232 Photocopying outside the present legal limits
− 235 Authors' disputes over ownership of data from a cooperative (multi-institution) project
− 316 Failure to make preserved data available to other investigators when problems arise
− 385 Failure to retain laboratory notebooks and other basic records for a "sufficient" period

---

−385 to +365, with a substantial spread between the extremes. Table 3 shows the scores in rank order.

Responses suggested that many persons did not understand some of the items. One problem came from a typographic error: We asked about "anonymous review (names of *authors* not disclosed to *authors*)" (italic added). Many respondents answered without comment, and many corrected the second "authors" to "reviewers" (as was the committee's intention). Some just left the item blank or said that they did not understand it.

We linked two issues of coauthorship with "and/or." Many respondents gave one set of responses for the pair. Those who answered twice generally gave the same answer for both, and we arbitrarily used the single sets as though they had been entered twice. That accounts in part for the similarity in counts between the two items (124 and 121).

The question about damage to legitimate nonscientific interests seems to have been confusing and widely misunderstood, as reflected in part by the high (our highest) number of "?" responses.

Many respondents wrote notes to explain their answers—some quite extensive, revealing, and possibly important. For example, the question about amount and location of advertising, which came at the very end, was generally marked low for both occurrence of the problem and CBE priority, but a few respondents expressed a strong feeling that this was a major problem.

The issues that were not given a high priority in response to the questions about priority among CBE concerns and whether respondents had had problems related to them involve situations that might be considered inhouse issues for a journal or that an editor should be able to resolve without outside consultation. For example, lack of sufficient funds, which might hinder publication of worthy material, might be considered an administrative problem of a journal and publisher. Refusal by authors (or editors) to correct errors by publishing an erratum, anonymous review of manuscripts, use of unnecessarily sex-specific language, and the amount and location of advertising are policy or style issues. Pressures on editors to publish particular material or work that might damage legitimate nonscientific interests of society are not unlike other issues that editors must consider when deciding the content and source of material for publication.

The four issues given the lowest ranking—photocopying outside legal limits, disputes over ownership of data, authors' failure to make data available, and authors' failure to retain basic research records—are also included in the latter category. Most respondents said that the resolution of those issues was not the responsibility of editors.

All the issues that many respondents had faced in their own editorial work were, in addition, listed as issues of major concern, with the exception of plagiarism. They involve situations that occur outside the control or knowledge of the editor initially, but can be resolved only by the combined efforts and actions of the editor and relevant outside parties, such as authors, reviewers, and perhaps other journals. The issue of long delays in publication is the only exception here.

Although short-term solutions can be applied to individual occurrences of multiple publication, plagiarism, multiplicity of authors, fabrication of data, etc., a long-term and more global resolution of each of these problems can be achieved only when all segments of the scientific publishing community—authors, reviewers, editors, and readers—understand that the problems and their solutions are the responsibility of every member individually, as well as of the group as a whole.

Part II

Conference Proceedings

Accountability and Authorship: Where Does the Responsibility Lie?

DONALD KENNEDY*

I am president of a research university that is active over the full spectrum of scientific disciplines. The daily diet of a person in my position includes an array of difficult problems related to responsibility for, and ownership of, intellectual property. The scope and variety can be indicated by a few examples:

- An abstract submitted by a faculty member contains the name of a graduate student as second author. Such communications are not refereed in the usual way, but this abstract has been cited in several papers. The authenticity of some of the work on which the abstract was based is challenged. The graduate student complains that her name was placed on the abstract without consultation by the professor, who responds that he was trying to do the student a "favor."

- A faculty member at University X is charged by members of a research group at another institution with having made unauthorized use of ideas and preliminary data that were part of an unpublished manuscript he had been sent for review. The faculty member denies the charge and declines a request from the complainants that the data books be made available for an examination intended to determine whether notes were made about the material in question. The provost of University X, concerned about public attention being given to the charge, asks that the faculty committee responsible for reviewing questions of this kind be allowed to look at the data books. That request, too, is declined by the faculty member on the grounds that the data books are private property and that the request for access to them violates fundamental principles of academic freedom.

- A former postdoctoral fellow, now at University Y, has been found to have falsified data in work done there. A scientific colleague has complained that earlier papers done with Professor A at University X are tainted as well. Professor A asserts that, although his name is on the paper, he was only the

---

*Because of airplane delays, Dr. Kennedy's keynote address was presented by Robert Rosenzweig, president of the Association of American Universities.

115

third author, in effect providing support and space for the work. The data books with the data in question, he says, were taken by the postdoctoral fellow when he left.

• A professor has published a paper demonstrating an important new experimental result. A former graduate student in the professor's laboratory, now elsewhere, asserts that she performed a substantial part of the experimental work herself, but was not given appropriate credit. The matter is brought before a university review committee; the faculty member asserts that the experiments were unimportant and only marginally related to the main point of the paper. The review committee finds in favor of the faculty member, but the former graduate student, still unsatisfied, presses her claim with the federal agency that supported the research and obtains the help of an influential member of the House Subcommittee on Investigations and Oversight. The representative promises hearings on the matter.

KINDS OF MISCONDUCT

None of these cases represents an actual instance at Stanford or—as far as I know—elsewhere. But their elements have been features of incidents at major research universities in the United States within the last several years. These scenarios will serve, I hope, to illuminate some of the issues that we must confront as we try to assign institutional responsibility for the concerns we examine here. Of these there are two. First is the validity of scientific work—whether a publication represents what was actually found, or was based on misrepresentation or falsification. Second is its provenance—whether the work is fairly represented as being that of the author or authors and *only* theirs.

In what follows, I shall discuss mainly the first kind of scientific misconduct—the presentation of fraudulent or misrepresented data—rather than disputes over the ownership of intellectual property. That does not mean, however, that I think cases of fraudulence are more in need of resolution. On the contrary, I suspect that ownership disputes are much more abundant, but see the light of day less often, because they are settled quietly (and often unsatisfactorily) or because they are so complex and ambiguous that they cannot be resolved at all.

In the university setting, disagreements concerning misrepresented data are especially troubling, because they sweep up *both* functions of university scientists: teaching *and* research. Complaints about misrepresented data are most frequently lodged against senior researchers by junior investigators who claim they have been deprived of rightful credit by senior colleagues who have published the ideas of the junior colleagues as their own, independently used junior colleagues' experimental data in publications, or deprived junior colleagues of rightful seniority of authorship. When valid, as they all too often are, these claims strike at the very heart of the relationship that makes a graduate research university the kind of institution it is. The development of a scientific career depends on receiving full recognition for work done; and senior scientists in the university ought to be eager, rather than reluctant, to allocate that credit fully and fairly to junior associates. When credit is unfairly withheld, the consequences are serious. To be sure, nothing "wrong" gets into the literature, and thus there is no stimulus for the misallocation of resources. In that limited sense, scientific plagiarism is a misdemeanor, whereas fraud is a felony.

There is a harsher, although less visible, injury. It afflicts unknown numbers of young scientists who are disillusioned, disaffected, or embittered by such experiences. Because the results threaten the very essence of their purposes, universities must pay serious attention to scientific misconduct, and they must heed carefully charges raised by the less powerful against the more powerful. Although principles of conduct cannot be fully codified, some guidelines can be developed and should be part of the disclosure in any research university.

Let us return to the kind of scientific misconduct that involves falsification. The issue with which we have to grapple is responsibility: What persons or institutions have the duty of detecting, investigating, sanctioning, and ultimately informing the scientific community about questionable work? There is an important relationship between ownership and responsibility, and we might begin with an examination of that linkage.

Recently I was asked, "What is your institution's policy as to who owns the data books of a faculty member?"

I replied that, although I had not checked, I was certain that no policy would have been thought necessary at Stanford in this connection, because no one would have entertained the possibility that anyone other than the faculty member would claim ownership.

The matter is, as I might have guessed, deeper than that. The basic law of copyright is that the person who puts pen to paper owns the work. There is a well-understood exception, commonly called "work for hire," but it applies mainly to work done under fairly close direction. It is not likely that it would apply to a scientist working freely on a project of his or her own design, even in a university laboratory on university time.

The copyright policies of many universities vest the royalties from textbooks, novels, works of art, or (these days) software with the author and do *not* lay claim to these works on the grounds of having heated the buildings and provided salary support.

But university policies have reflected a different view with respect to patents that result from scientific and technical work. Most universities retain those rights by contract of employment; only about one-third (including Stanford) treat material subject to patent and material subject to copyright identically and permit faculty scientists the primary rights to both. Whichever policy obtains, however, it would be a dubious claim on the university's part that it has any ownership rights to scientific information in data books.

Of course, most research projects also have sponsors, most commonly the federal government. The government has not asserted its own rights, if any, to the intellectual property generated by university faculty members; instead, the patent law adopted in 1981 gave universities the rights to ideas generated in the course of federally sponsored research. When private companies underwrite university research, they often make advance contract arrangements that give the sponsors substantial intellectual property rights. How these rights would be asserted in cases like the ones described is unclear; the problem seems not to have arisen.

The scientific journal in which material is published is also an important institution in this domain, and journals have important responsibilities with respect to the veracity and the provenance of what they publish. Many publishers automatically grant permission to reproduce material as long as the author consents, and in other ways they exert only minimal control over articles once they have been published. Publishers of journals that emphasize timely release of especially significant results often exercise their ownership rights with extreme vigor in the period just *before* publication, refusing to permit even general statements to be made about the results.

Journal publishers regularly display a strong sense of their responsibility for the veracity of what is published. The best of them provide for extensive peer review of articles to be published, and editors sometimes go beyond these ordinary mechanisms to assure themselves that the data are sound and that the conclusions based on the data are valid. Editors are clearly concerned about the problem of fraudulent data, but I suspect that few believe that the ordinary methods of review can catch an even moderately intelligent, determined cheater. Some of you might recall an earlier time when fraud was a major issue in the scientific community; it was in the 1950s when J. B. Rhine and his colleagues at Duke University published extraordinary results purporting to demonstrate "parapsychological" phenomena—results that many scientists doubted. At the height of that controversy, the chemist George Price wrote that scientists know exactly how to control experiments against chance, but have never found it necessary to control them against fraud. That is as true now as it was in the 1950s.

Journals and their editors are not in a good position, however, to take much responsibility for provenance. Ordinary peer review might catch the occasional case of blatant plagiarism ("This is a fine analysis; I thought so when I read it, and I thought so when I wrote it"), but peer review is unlikely to pick up the much more common instance in which a graduate student or fellow believes that an important contribution to a piece of work has been slighted by his or her absence from the list of authors. Nor have most journals been careful to ensure that each listed author contributed meaningfully to the publication or even that all authors are aware that their names have been attached to the work. Those and other matters have, sensibly I believe, been taken for granted. But that could be changing; and when we are no longer able to take them for granted, the task of journal publication and editorship will take on a great deal of added viscosity.

SCIENTIFIC FRAUD: ROLES IN DETECTION, INVESTIGATION, SANCTIONING, AND CORRECTION

Now we turn to the roles played by individual and institutional participants in the system. In examining those roles, we should look at various stages in the history of a case of scientific misconduct:

- Detection—an instance of misconduct is perceived by someone, and a question is raised.
- Investigation—an analysis is undertaken to determine whether misconduct has occurred.
- Sanctioning—some action is taken against the responsible persons.
- Correction—notification is given to the scientific community that a published work, or a widely circulated manuscript, if one has resulted, is not reliable.

Woolf's analysis of 26 publicly reported cases of alleged misconduct for the period from 1980 to 1987 showed that in 14 of the cases co-workers detected suspicious irregularities; six others were detected because scientists in other laboratories had their suspicions raised by data incongruent with their own. Editorial peer review on the part of journalists detected only three of the cases; that supports my earlier contention that peer review is not likely to uncover fraud.

In nearly all cases, the reports challenging the scientists' work were directed to the universities that employed them. Although most agencies that sponsor research maintain offices dedicated to dealing with scientific fraud (sometimes at congressional insistence), they are rarely the first port of call for a complainant. A university is expected to inform the sponsoring agency, undertake the investigation and report in full detail, and—on occasion—permit or invite the sponsoring agency to perform its own audit as well.

The university is expected to deliver the primary sanctions. Supporting agencies on occasion have declared individual scientists ineligible to receive further research support for a period. Journals can refuse to accept manuscripts; that is a serious penalty and has not been used often, perhaps because it is obviously supererogatory when other institutions have already imposed sanctions.

Correcting the record is perhaps the most important part of the process from the point of view of the scientific community. It is obviously best if the correction comes from the scientist, and the requirement for such correction has recently become part of a package of institutional sanctions. But it is still natural for university administrators to want to keep proceedings of this kind confidential, both because they guard their institutions' reputations jealously and because they might expose themselves and their institutions to lawsuits if their determination is found faulty in a later legal proceeding.

Correcting the record is not as easy as it sounds. In one recent case, a correction signed by all the coauthors and involving a clear retraction of specified data and conclusions was returned by the journal editor with the demand that the retraction be modified extensively according to his own view of the case.

Writers on scientific misconduct have assumed, almost without analysis, that the university is the appropriate institution to investigate and then impose sanction upon a finding of scientific fraud. That is probably the right conclusion, but one must also recognize a number of problems, some of them carrying serious consequences for the university's relationship to its faculty.

That relationship is, to begin with, festooned with legitimate restraints. It was shaped by the relatively new but nonetheless powerful tradition of academic freedom, which holds that faculty members require protection from political interference to permit the free development and exchange of unpopular ideas. The tradition accords faculty members charged with professional misconduct a great deal of due process. At Stanford, for example, if the president wishes to impose a sanction that entails loss of tenure, punitive reduction in salary, or any form of censure, the penalty must first be proposed to the faculty member charged. That faculty member can then either accept the penalty or request a hearing before the Advisory Board—the university's elected faculty body responsible for deciding on appointments and promotions. That hearing is open or closed at the request of the faculty member charged, and the faculty member has the right to be represented by legal counsel.

In Stanford's recent history, the matter has gone that far only once. When it did, I was not the president of the university, but the chairman of the Advisory Board. I had to preside, with the responsibility but not the authority of a federal district judge, over a proceeding that lasted for 6 weeks, 6 days a week, 6 hours a day, and produced more than a million words of testimony. The result, in which the Advisory Board upheld the president's proposal to discharge a faculty member, was challenged in a lawsuit that wound its way through the courts for more than 15 years before the final verdict was registered in favor of the university. The American Association of University Professors, which sent observers to the hearing, as well as every judge who heard the case thereafter, found that the university had provided adequate due process and a fair and reasonable result. But the cost of providing it was heavy.

Beyond formal, written provisions, there is an unwritten web of restraint as powerful as the British "constitution." Our instinct is to make the most favorable presumptions about faculty conduct and to intervene and investigate with the lightest touch possible. The university, as investigator and sanctioner of scientific misconduct, has what might be called an authority conflict. In undertaking its punitive role, the university moves directly against the weight of tradition and conviction that governs its other relationships with the members of its faculty.

Why, then, does the punitive role fall to the university?

Perhaps it is because the university has a better capacity to investigate. After all, the faculty member is there in the institution; and surely the persons closest to the alleged act are the ones most capable of untangling the facts. But the proposition does not hold up well under serious examination. In the first place, those most knowledgeable within the institution—department colleagues or others well acquainted with the faculty member and his or her laboratory—are apt to be too close to the case. They might therefore have conflicts of interest. Furthermore, these scientists are not apt to be the most expert in the discipline. Most universities try to spread appointments out by specialty and not to build heavy concentrations of faculty members in a particular subfield. The most knowledgeable group of people who could be gathered to investigate a case of putative fraud, therefore, would not come from the institution itself, but would be peers gathered from the invisible academy of the discipline. The university offers no particular advantage as convener; indeed, a journal or a sponsoring agency or almost any other institution would do as well. From the point of view of tradition and available personnel, the university is by no means the obvious candidate for investigator.

What the university does have, of course, is the greatest sanctioning capacity. A single journal can at best close off one avenue amid an array of alternatives. A sponsoring agency can bar a professor from receiving funds; but there might be other sources, or the faculty member could continue to work with reduced resources or even take a rest. But the university can deliver serious blows, if it is able to reach the judgment that professional misconduct is involved. I suggest that is why the university has been selected for this role. It has a great deal at stake; it has a severe authority conflict that would make it a dubious candidate on other grounds; but it alone among the candidate institutions possesses the requisite sanctioning power. Thus, the university is in the same position as the man in the small Texas town who was made sheriff because he had the only gun.

In addition to the entities whose roles have been discussed so far—the journal, the university, and the sponsoring agency—there is a fourth, the scientific community, represented in this context by a scientific society or by the collective views of peers taken more generally. That community has a good deal at stake and only a modest authority conflict; but, because it possesses no sanctioning power to speak of, it has not been made a candidate for the task of investigation and sanctioning. It is clear, I think, that the university's candidacy for responsibility is based on its capacity to deliver sanctions.

What changes, if any, can we expect in the future? The most obvious trend is an increase in what is expected of universities with respect to their role in investigation and punishment. The traditions of due process and institutional caution have made universities reluctant to accept this role, but they now recognize that they have it and must make the best of it. That will be difficult for them; they have much to lose, because the prestige of their faculties is their stock in trade and they desperately need to conserve public confidence. In particular, I think university administrators will feel more pressed than previously to give careful protection to those who bring charges and to require public correction by scientists who have published questionable material. Neither task will be easy.

In addition to the list of well-publicized cases of scientific misconduct, almost every institution has a list of phony charges brought by junior colleagues who have been disappointed, who have misunderstood the rules, or who have been treated badly but nonetheless lack grounds for the charges they bring. To treat these matters with gravity often requires the willing suspension of disbelief, a commodity hard to maintain in the offices of the dean, the president, or the provost.

As to correcting the literature, that requires overcoming an institutional reluctance, sometimes arising in the legal office, to say publicly (or require someone else to say publicly) even things of which you are very sure.

A second trend, and we are watching it unfold day by day, is a rapidly increasing appetite for federal intervention. The agencies that support university research also have much to lose from an apparent increase in the number of instances of scientific misconduct. They are, after all, accountable to Congress for public funds. Any agency head whose organization has had a misconduct case can be expected to be asked at the next hearing why proper mechanisms were not in place to prevent it and to promise more accountability the next time around. That spells new statutory requirements that will include formal mechanisms of followup and new reporting requirements for sponsoring agencies. There also might be assignment of federal investigators to the task of auditing programs about which questions are raised.

Scientists are understandably sensitive to the attitudes of those who observe their world from outside the scientific community. There might even be a tendency among scientists to view the current level of public concern with too much alarm. Although there has been more media attention than we are comfortable with, scientific fraud might not be as high on the list of public worries as we think. *Time* magazine, in the second week in August, published a major story in the "Economy" section entitled "Fraud, Fraud, Fraud." In a sampling of white-collar crime, it mentioned Pentagon procurement scandals, how Hertz repairs rental cars, Medicaid fraud in New York, stock parking and insider trading on Wall Street, and the fraud conviction of Mario Biaggi. Scientific misconduct, I am pleased to say, did not make the list.

Some within the scientific community have become sufficiently concerned about this problem to recommend solutions of their own. There are, for example, the independent investigations of Ned Feder and Walter Stewart of the National Institutes of Health—efforts that have produced one set of congressional hearings and attracted substantial public attention.

I do not believe that independent vigilante work, however high-minded it is made to sound, will be helpful in this situation. "Trop pas de ziel," said Talleyrand. I see far too much zeal in these activities, and I am dismayed when they are given quasiofficial status by being invoked in a journal, as they were recently by *Nature* in what surely must be the most perplexing exercise of post hoc editorial review ever taken.

Flailings of that kind will only make plainer the scientific community's uncertainty about how to deal with this difficult issue. Far better, it seems to me, is to intensify the scrutiny, to pay serious and responsible attention to charges when they arise, and to disclose fault even when it hurts to do so. Perhaps most important, we might need to reposition our enterprise as we present it to the public. In recent years, basic research has been sold, and sold heavily, to the public for its utilitarian value—we can cure cancer, we can improve international competitiveness, we can raise the productivity of our economy. We might have persuaded the public that it is procuring results, rather than supporting research. If that is true, is it so surprising that concern for scientific fraud is being played out against the background of Department of Defense procurement scandals?

I am afraid it is not surprising. And in that sense, we could be the victims of our own loss of innocence. It is both true and good that our society now seems to care very much about science. But by portraying it as an activity to be pursued for glory and for profit, and by seeming to behave as though these rewards were worth cheating for, we will surely destroy the public regard that has brought us this far. The task of our institutions is to change the incentives that encourage these abuses and to restore the sense of stewardship we all once had over the venture of science.

Open Discussion

Dr. Singer:

I am puzzled by references to the difficulty of getting retractions and corrections published. Perhaps that experience is not uncommon, but I have not had that experience—either as an editor or as a scientist. I have submitted a retraction of an experiment from work in my own laboratory that was promptly published. When I was editor of the *Proceedings of the National Academy of Sciences*, retractions or corrections were given immediate attention, and they were published. I think it is important that we balance the picture.

In addition, it has been mentioned that journals have no sanctions. Again, I don't know how the balance comes out, but at least some journals have punished authors. The *Proceedings*, for example, has banned the work of one author in response to evidence of double publication.

Dr. Woolf:

There are indeed journals and editors that have been very responsible in this regard. I think that there are pressures on journals that have not been mentioned, and some members of our audience have had experience with those kinds of problems.

Dr. Dan:

Let's say we have a paper that has seven authors. Two of the authors write a letter after the paper has been published, saying that they wish to retract it. This puts the editors in the role of policemen. We write to the other five authors; three say that they defend the paper and that it should not be retracted, and the other two say that they want nothing to do with the matter. In this case, it is not easy to print a retraction, because, unless you have the data—the evidence—to back up that letter in the journal or you make some sort of editorial comment, you really don't know the truth of the assertions. The problem then is in going back to the institution, the dean or the department head, and starting an investigation, which may lead to great expense in resolving a squabble between authors.

Dr. Nemiah:

There is another problem, at least from my point of view. It is not entirely clear when an editor can retract. We have been struggling with a paper that clearly contains false data; it is fraudulent. We were about to retract it when we received notice from the authors saying that their lawyers had advised that we could not retract it unless one of the authors or their institutions requested it. At this point, our legal counsel suggested that we defer making a decision. We are still trying to deal with this issue, and I am still unsure when an editor is allowed to retract a paper. One way around the problem may be to retract editorial support, but that is not a solution.

Dr. Relman:

I cannot agree with Dr. Kennedy's view that universities have been given the primary responsibility for investigating allegations of scientific fraud largely because they have the greatest sanctioning capacity. I think universities have been given that responsibility mainly because of the general view that it is properly theirs. It is certainly true that institutions have the greatest sanctioning capacity, but they are also the guardians and patrons of the scientific enterprise. They represent the collective morality and ethics of science. They teach young scientists, and they set standards. Therefore, they should have the primary responsibility for investigating alleged violations of those standards by their faculty, students, or staff. After full investigation, an institution should be responsible for deciding when work is fraudulent and whether it ought to be retracted. Ideally, the authors ought to agree with those conclusions, but it seems to me that the journal editor simply needs to know that the institution has carried out a full and fair investigation and has reached a conclusion through due process.

When the institution reaches the conclusion that work should be retracted, editors have a responsibility to publish the retraction promptly. They should not be dissuaded by lawyers' letters or other threats of legal action.

Dr. Woolf:

I do not wish to speak for Dr. Kennedy on this, but my own opinion is that moral responsibility is a responsibility that cannot be divided. By its very nature, it is shared in science, and I do not believe that there is such a thing as the division of moral labor.

Dr. Berkow:

I agree with Dr. Relman on the question of institutional responsibility, but take it maybe a step further. Institutions must practice some preventive medicine as well. If institutions accept responsibility, which I agree is theirs, then they ought to have policies that are clear, that faculty members are aware of and are reminded of, and in which there are no questions of who has responsibility for the correctness of data and what can be done when a complaint arises.

Custody and Responsibility for Research Data

RICHARD J. RISEBERG

In approaching the question of ownership of research data, it may help to bear in mind an admonition by Lewis Thomas, quoted in the *New York Times*:

> If there is any single influence that will take the life out of research, it will be secrecy and enforced confidentiality. [Telling the scientific world] the unprecedented observation made yesterday in your own laboratory is a large part of the fun of doing science. I am worried that something may be happening to interfere with this high privilege.[5]

I propose to consider this topic in three settings: one with which I am most familiar, the government; the private, commercial sector; and universities.

I will address a couple of cross-cutting issues as well. I will assume that we are discussing nonhuman, animal data, to remove any questions of access by human research subjects under, for example, the Privacy Act.

GOVERNMENT OWNERSHIP

The government context may superficially seem the simplest. What a government scientist produces on government time belongs to the government. This would seem the obvious conclusion to be drawn either directly or by implication from normal rules of employment, from the Freedom of Information Act, from various standards of employee conduct, and from copyright law. Try telling that to a National Institutes of Health fellow who has come to NIH after 10 years of training and employment at other medical and research institutions and who will likely move on to another research establishment outside the government after a short stint on the public payroll. Such researchers view themselves, and are largely viewed by their colleagues, simply as scientists—not as government employees. The Freedom of Information Act therefore comes as a rude shock to them when it is *their* data someone wants to see. The reaction is similar when long-time government scientists are the recipients of requests for information under the terms of the act.

Even leaving aside the technical requirements of the Freedom of Information Act, does anyone seriously doubt that employees' supervisors should be able to look at the data? What about the secretary of the department? What about members of the public? After all, the data were produced with public funds.

PRIVATE SECTOR

In the commercial sphere, I gather that in the context of a dispute, ownership of data produced by a business depends on whatever express or implied contracts are found to exist between employer and employee. Although I am not sure that there is a general practice—I have not read many employment agreements between commercial researchers and their employers—there have been a number of court cases in which businesses have prevented former employees and their current employers from using proprietary data developed during the terminated relationship. Moreover, the lack of a dispute between employer and employee about the ownership of the data does not guarantee that the parties will be totally free to determine who sees the data. For example, a company is presumably producing data for some commercial purpose. If the information is to be used to support an application to some government agency, or as a deliverable item under a government contract, in the end it will wind up in government hands and be subject to the same laws and rights of access guaranteed, for example, by the Freedom of Information Act, as though the data had been produced by the government agency itself.

Even if the data are not regularly transmitted to the government—environmental information, for example—such agencies as the Environmental Protection Agency and the Occupational Safety and Health Administration may have a statutory right of access to the data.

UNIVERSITIES

Let us move on to academe. My wife is a professor of mathematics, who constantly reminds me that there is an Eleventh Commandment, academic freedom, which accords university faculty protection from those who pay their salaries that the rest of us do not enjoy. I have seen this played out most recently in a case in which a researcher did his work while employed as a professor at one university and took his data with him when he left for another university. When queried, neither institution believed that it owned the data— the first because its policy allowed researchers to retain and transfer their own data to a new institution, and the second because the research had been carried out solely at the first institution.

My office at the Public Health Service has looked into the general issue of ownership of research data, and in the course of doing so we spoke informally with persons at several associations that represent academe. We learned that universities rarely assert a proprietary interest in research data that are developed by a sole investigator, but that do not appear to have intrinsic value to the institution. The data are considered the personal property of researchers, as are, for example, research and lecture notes. We learned that, even where data include tangible items, such as tissue cultures, researchers are generally free to remove the items from the university upon termination of employment.

When research data are developed by a team, all members of the team are considered to have rights of access to the data, although usually either the principal investigator or the university retains the original data or tangible items involved in the research.

Obviously, however, these generalizations are affected, even in academe, by any special terms and conditions that a particular university has with members of its faculty. For example, under the 1988 Harvard guidelines,[3] although investigators' rights of access to their data are clearly preserved, it appears that actual custody of the original primary data belongs to the laboratory unit in which the data were generated.

OWNERSHIP IN THE GENERAL LEGAL SENSE

Technical ownership, however, is perhaps less important than are the rights of control that derive from being the producer of the data. To the extent that the data are of no interest to anyone, it is inconsequential who owns them. The interesting questions, at least from a legal standpoint, arise when someone wants to see the data.

Even in academe, where the employer is normally less interested in controlling what researchers do with their own data, researchers are not totally free of outside constraints. The data might be of commercial value and subject to a university's patent policy. Or there might be some question about the data. If public funding is involved, an inspector general could appear on the scene and demand access, or someone from NIH might do so. Under applicable statutes and regulations, those investigations could have a right of access.

Let me turn finally to considerations that affect control of data, regardless of who owns or possesses them.

First, subpoenas. As you might know from recent attention the topic has received in the scientific media, federal and state legislative watchdog committees have the power to subpoena data—not just from government agencies, but from any member of the public—in connection with their oversight activities.

More commonly, however, the courts are the source of subpoenas. Sometimes, in the context of litigation, the data behind some piece of germane research become the object of a subpoena by one or both of the parties.

The Public Health Service has had experience with such subpoenas in connection with data collected on toxic shock syndrome.[2] We were ultimately successful in protecting the names and addresses of the subjects of the study, but in finding in our favor the court nevertheless emphasized that "the law's basic presumption is that the public is entitled to every person's evidence."

In a case in California in 1988, the state court compelled a researcher to provide the director of the state department of health services with the results of a medical study of residents living near a toxic-waste facility, because the director was responsible for controlling hazards associated with the waste.[4]

Perhaps the most exhaustive discussion of the access of litigants to research data, through the subpoena process, occurred in the context of a proceeding in 1982 in which the Environmental Protection Agency proposed to cancel Dow Chemical Company's permit to manufacture a herbicide on the basis of evidence developed by scientists at the University of Wisconsin from research conducted on animals.[1] Dow wanted access to the researchers' raw data, and the university and its scientists resisted. In deciding for the university, the U.S. Court of Appeals concluded that, in determining whether to enforce a subpoena for records, a court is obliged to decide whether doing so would place an unreasonable burden on the record-holder—in this case, the Wisconsin researchers.

In reaching its decision, the court indicated that several factors should be weighed: the probative value of the information in relation to the issues in the lawsuit, the extent of the requester's need for the information, and the burden of compliance, which takes into account the volume of materials involved and the danger to the record-holder from premature disclosure.

In light of those factors, the court refused to enforce Dow's subpoena, concluding that Dow's need for the information was clearly outweighed by the burden it posed for the researchers to provide it. The court also noted that

> academic freedom, though not a specifically enumerated constitutional right, long has been viewed as a special concern of the First Amendment. . . . The precise contours of the concepts of academic freedom are difficult to define. . . . [It] is not absolute and must on occasion be balanced against important competing interests. . . . [Nevertheless,] it may properly figure into the legal calculation of whether forced disclosure [of data] would be reasonable.

COPYRIGHT

Any author who is not an employee of the federal government is in general entitled to protection of the copyright law with respect to what is published. Under the law, the owner of the copyright has the exclusive right to control the reproduction and distribution of the copyrighted work. However, there are a number of exceptions to that exclusive right, including the "fair use" exception (which includes an exception for research) and the exception for reproduction by libraries.

As the Court of Claims observed in the *Williams & Wilkins* case:[6]

[The "fair use" doctrine] has been influenced by some tension between the direct aim of the copyright privilege to grant the owner a right from which he can reap a financial benefit and the more fundamental purpose of the protection [provided for in the Constitution] "to promote the Progress of Science and the useful Arts. . . . The copyright law, like the patent statutes, makes reward to the owner a secondary consideration . . . subordinate . . . to the greater public interest in the development of art, science and industry."

I conclude by reminding you of what Lewis Thomas said: "[Telling the scientific world] . . . is a large part of the fun of doing science." I think the court in *Williams & Wilkins* was attempting to say that telling the world is not only a large part of the fun, but also a large part of the mission of science.

REFERENCES

1. *Dow Chemical Co. v. Allen,* 672 F.2d. 1262 (7th Cir. 1982).
2. *Farnsworth v. Procter & Gamble Co.,* 758 F.2d 1545 (11th Cir. 1985).
3. Harvard Gazette, April 1, 1988.
4. *Kizer v. Sulnick,* Cal. App. 1988.
5. New York Times, July 10, 1988.
6. *Williams & Wilkins Co. v. United States,* 487 F.2d. 1345 (Ct. Cl. 1973), *aff'd* 95 S. Ct. 1344 (1975).

Who Owns What in Research Data?

MIRON L. STRAF

I would rephrase the question, "Who owns what in research data?" to "When should society require that a scientist who has collected, compiled, or produced data as a result of research make the data available as a public good, for the potential benefit of all, in whatever way?" Moreover, what special responsibility and role do editors have in this regard?

ROLE OF SOCIAL INSTITUTIONS

Scientists have created and maintained scientific institutions through which they receive rewards and other benefits from their work. Scholarly journals are a prime example of such an institution. Those institutions serve

Except as cited from the Committee on National Statistics report, the findings, recommendations, and opinions are those of the author and not necessarily those of the committee nor of the National Research Council.

to confer benefits not only from the scientist's own professional community, as through dissemination of research results, but also from the public, whether through public recognition, through government research funds, or simply through benefiting society by advancing scientific knowledge. That public benefit, and the fact that scientists who constitute the institutions are themselves members of society, places a special responsibility on the institutions.

My first thesis is that scientific institutions—scholarly journals in particular—have a responsibility to guide scientific efforts in ways that benefit society. In general, nonprofit institutions are collectively altruistic in this way, but responsibility can extend even to the boardrooms of profit-making concerns. When the interests of a discipline are favored over those which may better benefit the public, society can move to correct the situation, sometimes through scientific institutions. The creation of institutional review boards and committees for the protection of human subjects and laws to protect the confidentiality of medical records are examples.

Because scholarly publication is the essential element of scientific research, editors and editorial boards of scholarly journals are paramount in conveying the benefits of their institutions to their scientific constituents. Editors must then assume the responsibility of guiding scientific efforts in ways that benefit society. In many cases, editors can do so by encouraging scientists to make data available to others.

Sharing research data, to be sure, involves costs, as well as benefits. Although the costs sometimes outweigh the benefits, making research data available to others is one of the ways in which scientists benefit society.

BENEFITS OF SHARING DATA

For most of us, sharing research data, like sharing research results, is such an important part of scientific inquiry—which seeks to extend the work of others—that we don't stop to think of the benefits. The costs, however, are more obvious; and because costs must be compared with benefits, it is useful to list some of the benefits of sharing research data:

- It reinforces open scientific inquiry and encourages a diversity of analyses and conclusions.
- It permits reanalyses that verify or refute reported results or alternative analyses that refine results to determine whether conclusions remain valid when various assumptions in the analysis are changed in reasonable ways.
- It promotes new research and serves to test new theories and methods.
- It encourages the appropriate use of empirical studies in the formation and evaluation of public policy through independent analyses and critical review.
- It serves to improve methods of data collection and measurement through scrutiny by others.
- It encourages the perspectives of others, especially in other disciplines.

- It provides a resource for training in research.
- It avoids the expense of additional data collection.
- It respects the desires of respondents or those who study other subjects to contribute to society.
- It serves to protect against faulty data, whether inadvertently distorted or willfully fabricated.

Most of those benefits, as well as the costs, are discussed in the report of the National Research Council Committee on National Statistics, *Sharing Research Data,*[3] which has guidelines to foster the sharing of data (see Appendix). The emphasis of the report is on problems and practices in the social and behavioral sciences, but links and parallels to the natural and biomedial sciences are identified and discussed.

OWNERSHIP OF DATA

I will return to the costs of sharing data, but now I want to develop a thesis on the ownership of research data. Society benefits from granting exclusive rights to intellectual property to reward creativity and innovation. Recognition of the benefit is evident in the copyright and patent laws. But the rights are not inherent in the production or even discovery of data. A court, for example, can order scientists to produce their research data, even when they are not parties to a suit.[1,2,5] The principle that the public is entitled to every man's evidence was enunciated by the Supreme Court more than 50 years ago.

My second thesis is that, ultimately, society confers on scientists any rights of ownership of research data. If society does so, would it allow the owners to destroy the data, modify them, or retain exclusive use of them, as it allows owners of ordinary property? Not if the data were to have value to society—and that brings us to a consideration of the value of research data.

DATA AS PUBLIC GOODS

For the most part, research data are not commodities, but rather public goods; others can benefit from the research data without reducing the benefit to the person who develops them. There are exceptions, such as data that lead to marketable biomedical products. As we know from economic theory, market economies will not invest sufficient resources in public goods like research data. That fact is a rationale for the government's role in funding research. My third thesis is that it is also a rationale for society to foster sharing of research data.

If we consider data as public goods, then we are led to place special importance on data that provide information for public-policy decision-making because of the apparent value of those data to society. The Committee on

National Statistics specifically recommended that "data relevant to public policy should be shared as quickly and widely as possible."

It is often argued that scientists' rights to ownership of research data should be waived if the data are collected with public funds. I argue that whether the collection of research data is publicly or privately funded is irrelevant. When research data would, on balance, benefit society, they should be shared, because our scientific institutions have a responsibility to guide science so that it benefits society, because the question of ownership of research data rests ultimately with society, and because research data are public goods.

COSTS OF SHARING DATA

I restricted the research data that should be shared to data that would, in consideration of costs and benefits, benefit society. The costs of sharing data are many and include the costs of:

- Surmounting technical obstacles, such as incompatibilities in computer and software systems.
- Providing documentation and explanations to others, so that they can understand the data.
- Storing, reproducing, and transferring data.

Those costs, however burdensome, can be shared by the persons who request the data and by the institutions that provide research funds. Far more difficult to compare with benefits are the costs to the original investigators that are related to:

- Discovery of errors by others.
- Unwarranted criticism based on a poorly done reanalysis.
- The loss to society of future discoveries that others might make and receive credit for.
- Breaching the confidentiality of responses.

Discovery of errors, of course, is a benefit to society. The potential of unwarranted criticism can be reduced through careful review of critical reanalyses.

Forgoing future discoveries can inhibit scientific inquiry and impose a cost on society. A balance is needed to ensure the motivation of possible discoveries and to prevent the practice of withholding data until all possible analyses are exhausted. The Committee on National Statistics recommended that, except in compelling circumstances, "investigators should share their data by the time of publication of initial, major results of analyses of the data."

Breaching the confidentiality of responses in some cases can be prevented by removing information that identifies individuals. Some data are not amenable to this technique, for example, an anthropologist's notes from interviews with famous people or records from which one can infer the identity of a respondent. Too often, however, confidentiality is promised when it is not needed and even when it is not known that confidentiality can be maintained. A simple promise of confidentiality, for example, cannot be used to circumvent the Freedom of Information Act.[6]

WHAT CAN EDITORS DO?

The Committee on National Statistics recommended that editors of scholarly journals encourage data-sharing in a number of ways:

- They should require authors to provide access to data during the peer-review process.
- They should strongly encourage authors to make detailed data accessible to other researchers.
- They should emphasize reports of secondary analyses and replications.
- They should require full credit and appropriate citations of original data collections in reports based on secondary analyses.

Editors, of course, must be careful to encourage authors to make data available only in ways that preserve the confidentiality of responses.

Requiring access to data by reviewers is already a practice of some journals, and more can be done to encourage making data available generally on publication. The *Journal of Applied Econometrics,* for example, has the following policy:

> Authors will be expected to make available a complete set of data used as well as any specialized computer programs employed, preferably in a machine-readable form.

And *Science,* with several other journals, "has developed procedures to help ensure that any individual who publishes in these journals will send the appropriate information to data banks."[4] Funding institutions also have moved in this direction. The Division of Social and Economic Science at the National Science Foundation requires that data sets produced with the assistance of a foundation grant be archived at a data library approved by the foundation program officer no later than a year after the grant expires.

By giving emphasis to secondary analyses and replication, journals can foster secondary analyses and thus the practice of sharing data. Giving full credit and appropriate citations to investigators who originally produced the data encourages not only data-sharing, but also scientific honesty. It has been proposed that, for articles written by more than one person, journals should require an explanation of the contributions of each author. Consistent with this practice would be an acknowledgment of the source of data being analyzed.

Editors of scholarly journals are in an important position to fulfill the responsibility of their scientific institutions to guide scientific efforts in ways that benefit society by encouraging the sharing of research data. The development of data does not necessarily carry with it an exclusive right of ownership; ultimately, that right is granted by society. Because, like research itself, the data are public goods, it is proper for society to encourage the sharing of data, just as it is proper for the government to fund research.

Sharing research data involves costs, as well as benefits. Some costs can be shared by those who request data and the institutions that provide research funds. Important cost-related issues for editors to consider are mitigating unwarranted criticism by careful review of critical reanalyses, determining when data should be shared (one suggestion is at the time major results are published), and protecting the confidentiality of responses. With attention to those issues, editors can encourage data sharing in general and specifically by requiring authors to provide access to data during the review process, by giving emphasis to reports of secondary analyses and to replications, and by requiring that full credit and appropriate citations of original data collections be given in reports based on secondary analyses.

APPENDIX

**Recommendations from the
Committee on National Statistics Report, *Sharing Research Data*[3]**

Principal Recommendation

Sharing data should be a regular practice.

Recommendations for Initial Investigators

When to share data

Investigators should share their data by the time of publication of initial major results of analyses of the data except in compelling circumstances.

Data relevant to public policy

Data relevant to public policy should be shared as quickly and widely as possible.

Planning for data sharing as part of research

Plans for data sharing should be an integral part of a research plan whenever data sharing is feasible.

Keeping data available

Investigators should keep data available for a reasonable period after publication of results from analyses of the data.

Recommendations for Subsequent Analysts

Bearing the costs

Subsequent analysts who request data from others should bear the associated incremental costs.

Keeping burdens to a minimum

Subsequent analysts should endeavor to keep the burdens of data sharing on initial investigators to a minimum and explicitly acknowledge the contribution of the initial investigators.

Recommendations for Institutions that Fund Research

Reviewing plans in applications

Funding organizations should encourage data sharing by careful consideration and review of plans to do so in applications for research funds.

Encouraging data archives

Organizations funding large-scale, general-purpose data sets should be alert to the need for data archives and consider encouraging such archives where a significant need is not now being met.

Recommendations for Editors of Scientific Journals

Providing access to data for peer review

Journal editors should require authors to provide access to data during the peer review process.

Publishing reanalyses and secondary analyses

Journals should give more emphasis to reports of secondary analyses and to replications.

Journals should require full credit and appropriate citations to original data collections in reports based on secondary analyses.

Encouraging accessibility to data

Journals should strongly encourage authors to make detailed data accessible to other researchers.

Recommendations for Other Institutions

Providing training for sharing data

Opportunities to provide training on data sharing principles and practices should be pursued and expanded.

Developing a reference service
A comprehensive reference service for computer-readable social science data should be developed.

Providing recognition for data sharing
Institutions and organizations through which scientists are rewarded should recognize the contributions of appropriate data-sharing practices.

REFERENCES

1. *Andres v. Eli Lilly & Co., Inc.*, 97 F.R.D. 494 (1983).
2. *Farnsworth v. Procter & Gamble Co.*, 101 F.R.D. 355 (1984).
3. Fienberg SE, Martin ME, Straf ML, eds. Sharing Research Data. Washington, DC: National Academy Press; 1985.
4. Koshland DE. The price of progress. Science. 1988 241: 637.
5. *Richards of Rockford, Inc. v. Pacific Gas & Electric*, 71 F.R.D. 388 (1976).
6. Small MA, Tomkins AJ, Cecil JS. The unintended disclosure of data through freedom of information laws. Presented at the annual meeting of the American Association of Public Opinion Research, Toronto, 20-22 May 1988.

Open Discussion

Mr. Riseberg:

I could apply the worst-case analysis: the person who is a self-taught genius and finances his own work. Should society be able to demand those data? In most countries this would not be an issue, but in the United States we value individual rights to a great extent. As a practical matter we do not often face this situation, because usually the person was trained at a government-funded facility. He probably relied on research that was funded by the government, so that, whereas his particular contribution may have been driven by his own resources, it is likely that there also is a substantial investment by society.

The Freedom of Information Act applies to government data only, and there are exceptions to the disclosure requirements.

Dr. Straf:

To answer the question of whether society should be able to demand data: It depends on whether the data are really proprietary and have commercial value, in which case the person should have ownership rights, or whether the data have a value to society and provide a public good. If the data do have value to society, for example, in settling a court case, they can be subpoenaed. But I think at the time the data arrive at society's institutions—for example, when the data are submitted to a journal—society could request that the data be produced.

Mr. Riseberg:

One concern I have about the subpoena process is that there is no orderly procedure for dealing with requests from congressional committees or from courts. The other arms of government get so involved with the principle of separation of powers and the rights of the individual parts of government that we don't work out procedures that take into account everyone's interests and rights.

Dr. Straf:

Suppose the data have no commercial value to a business. What is a scientist's liability in releasing those data without permission?

Mr. Riseberg:

My reaction is that you have to show damages to make a meaningful recovery. In the usual situation, it is not going to be worth while to pursue ownership rights, or resist, unless money is involved. The costs of the lawyers and the costs of the process of either punishing someone or defending yourself from having to release the data are too high.

However, I suppose someone could go to court and get an injunction, even if there were no monetary damages.

Dr. Thier:

The question of who owns the property or the data would not be a big issue if people were not ascribing progressively greater value to that property. If the property were valueless, the principal debates would go on in the halls, and we would not have meetings at which we discussed ownership.

There is a great tendency for scientists to assume that they are producers of or contributors to what other people are disproportionately benefiting from, and that if it were not for their role, science would not go on. So all persons tend to give themselves a role that is more altruistic than that of any other persons in this process, and I suspect that that is not quite fair.

The investigators have ideas and create new knowledge. They also benefit in recognition, in advancement, and in the opportunity to pursue further knowledge. The institutions that house those investigators—whether the government, universities, or commercial concerns—draw a significant benefit from the productivity of scientists, and they do not trade lightly on it; they trade heavily on it in fund-raising and in the marketing of their products. In addition, funding agencies, whether the government or foundations, become critically involved in documenting the quality of their role as managers of funds, and they have a critical investment in how productive researchers are, in how that intellectual property is generated, and in what its value is.

Journals can be seen altruistically as the mechanism for disseminating the results to the public, but they depend absolutely on the data and on the growth of research for their own well-being. There is, in fact, a potential conflict of interest in the process: the public, which is supposed to be the ultimate beneficiary, is also in many cases the funding agency and it theoretically holds back the ability to confer ownership and decide how it wishes the enterprise to run.

Dr. Adams:

We seem to have gone from the researchers' creation of the data to publication without looking at the process in between. What does one do with the editors and referees in terms of whether this material gets published? What is the responsibility of a journal to maintain confidentiality? What about the publication of referees' names? What do the issues have to do with the Freedom of Information Act? What right do those whose work is not published have to know why their submissions are not published?

I am quite concerned about whether the referee is a positive or a negative influence in the transfer of data from a private laboratory to the public domain and about what the responsibility of a journal is to maintain the confidentiality of the information it obtains from a referee in making that judgment.

Dr. Straf:

Referees are ultimately responsible to editors and to editorial boards; it really is the boards that should determine policy. Editorial boards should encourage that the data be published or at least be made available, once the decision is made to publish the results of the research.

Dr. Relman:

Of course editors have a responsibility to tell authors why their papers are not accepted and to transmit the comments of the reviewers—unless a paper is clearly inappropriate for the journal. In that case, the editor owes the author no more than a courteous and prompt return of the manuscript.

Mr. Riseberg:

In the public sector (NIH), we do make available the name of everyone who is on a peer-review committee. What is not revealed is what individual persons on the committee said about a particular application.

Dr. Adams:

The background for my question is that the American Physical Society is facing a case in the U.S. Court of Appeals as a third party. We are being required to disclose the name of a referee on a paper that is actually 12 years old. We are facing a serious question about the process from creation of data to their publication.

Dr. Relman:

I wanted to ask three questions of the panelists and then make a brief statement. First, how do we define data? It seems to me that this is a deceptively simple question. After all, what authors submit in manuscripts includes what we call data—the numbers observed. I presume that that is not what Dr. Straf is referring to, because that is made available to anybody. If the paper is published, there are the more or less raw data from which conclusions are made.

I imagine you mean something more than that: information about what actually went on in the laboratory or in the research process. Some of this is almost noncommunicable. That is to say, you have to have been there to have seen what was done, and you can't really interpret the numbers unless you know, unless you see, how the experiments are done. I am not so sure that it would be a simple matter to make such information available, and I am not at all sure that it should be made available.

Second, who or what decides whether there is public interest in the data? You have said that you believe that data that have no public interest should not be shared; the public has a right only to data that have public interest. Well, that is a vague criterion, and I don't know how you would know where to draw the line.

Third, you apparently attribute more importance to commercial property rights than to intellectual property rights. If the data have economic value, have commercial value, then authors have a right to keep them. Authors should not have to share data, presumably even if there is public interest. But if the authors have tremendous intellectual property rights, if they have had brilliant insights that have enabled them to do something in a way of gathering data or making measurements that nobody has done before, then they should immediately have to give that up. I find it distressing that you apparently place money above intellect in this situation.

Now I want to make a comment. You said that data should not be shared until after publication, but you say that they should be shared during peer review. It is hard to see how referees can be privy to all kinds of background information about what goes on in the laboratory. Moreover, if referees were to have the background information there would be a greater risk of the loss of confidentiality, and the author's rights to their intellectual property, at least until publication, would be even more in jeopardy.

As it is now, editors have a tremendous problem protecting authors' rights to their ideas and data when the material is under review. Many referees make copies of manuscripts, put them in their files, consider them their property, and use them in their own work or in teaching. If referees in addition were handed the authors' data books and all the background information, that risk would be magnified further.

Dr. Straf:

The answers to all your questions are "It depends." First, how does one define data? They are more than just the numbers, and there have been cases in which scientists have taken publicly collected data and pored over them, giving an enormous effort to documenting the data, finding the errors, and editing the data. What they have produced becomes a new set of data that should be shared. So I would include in the definition not only the original observations and results of experiments, but any kind of documentation and edited data that can explain what the numbers are.

Second, who decides whether there is a public interest? All of us do, in a way.

Third, I drew a distinction between commercial data and data that serve a public good because it is easy for me to see how data that serve a public good should be shared. There is a rationale that appeals to me. I don't know the answer for commercial data.

Unidentified Speaker:

Couldn't you have commercially valuable data that also had public interest? And what would be overriding there?

Dr. Straf:

I think that must be handled on a case-by-case basis; there are no general rules. There are some situations in which it is difficult—just as the courts have not decided whether a survey can be subpoenaed, whether the identity of respondents can be made available, or whether the identity of reviewers should be made known. They will handle that case by case because there is no simple solution.

I am simply taking a case in which the data have no current commercial value, so that I can say that the data may be of value to society, even in the future. I presume that all data have a potential value.

Mr. Riseberg:

At least as far as the Freedom of Information Act applies, Congress has determined that for data generated outside the government, only proprietary, confidential, commercial, and financial information can be protected. In any attempt to include data that were strictly intellectual but that did not have value, if there is such a thing, we would have to go beyond the statutory language to offer protection.

Dr. Straf:

I know that journals are concerned about protecting the rights of individual investigators. The same problem arises in reviewing grants before any data have been collected; people can steal ideas. I don't think that theft of data is peculiar to publishing.

Dr. Yankauer:

You have said that among the costs of sharing data are unwarranted criticism and poor analysis. Let's take the second first. I know from personal experience that many federal data sets are very poorly analyzed, because I clear them with the agency that produces them. Should some be tagged—not just federal data sets, but any set—to give the owner some ability to look at the outcome of this reanalysis before it is submitted for publication?

The other issue is unwarranted criticism and, again, this is not speculation. Some "investigators" use data for their own biased ends. Should there be some screening mechanism before one releases data to anybody at all who wants them?

Dr. Bailar:

Some problems of quality of analysis, as well as fairness, can be solved if editors routinely ask the generators of data to serve as peer reviewers for any secondary analyses.

Dr. Straf:

There are people who believe that the qualifications of those who are requesting data should be considered. But if you view data as an economic public good, once you make them available to someone, they must be made available to all. It is not a good that has a particular cost, except the cost of transferring it.

As to unwarranted criticism: I think it is a common courtesy—and the Committee on National Statistics stated that in its report—for people who are doing reanalyses to submit them to the original data owners. But I think it is still a fact that anyone's work can be poorly criticized. It is a question of whether society's institutions are going to give credence to poor criticism. That is the protection.

Dr. Yankauer:

This places a great burden of cost on the investigator, who then must reply.

Dr. Straf:

It is a great cost, but it is not always necessary to reply.

Dr. Singer:

By starting off with the question of ownership, which is fundamentally a legal consideration, we have put an emphasis on data as a commodity; for most people who are editors of scientific journals, however, the questions of intellectual property and creativity are at least as important, if not more so. In that sense, scientific information is both a commodity, such as data, and a creative activity or the product of a creative activity, like a piece of art. So the commercial analogies are not necessarily the most appropriate. Perhaps analogies that come from the creative arts would do as well. This discussion focused on the ownership of data has given us an asymmetrical view of the whole problem. The most important property that scientists have is their ideas. New ideas, innovative ideas, new ways of looking at old problems are precious and important to all of us. It is those things that, as editors, we need to protect at the front line.

The question of who owns the data is a secondary one—secondary to whose idea it is.

Dr. Stossel:

I think I am returning to your mandate, which is, who owns the information? There are currently at least three biotechnology companies vying to produce what will probably be a good AIDS therapeutic agent. If this information were to become public, it would destroy that competition. There would be no way that any of the companies would want to disclose much information.

I would argue that our leaders are more interested in public health than in scientific creativity and that the ultimate mandate is to make scientific information public.

Ms. Mishkin:

In response to the question of what would happen to employees who shared data when their employers didn't want them to, the obvious point is that the employees are likely to lose their jobs, because somewhere in almost every employment contract there is a clause about checking through the hierarchy before giving out data. People who come from academe and the government into the industrial complex often do not notice this until too late.

I also want to pose a question: You suggested that someone's primary data should be available at the time of publication. What I suggest we consider more fully is what the time of publication is. Presumably, journal editors interpret publication as the time at which something is printed and released in a journal, but lawyers talk about publication as including reporting something at a scientific conference, for example, or presenting it to an assembly, or even just telling one colleague. If we are to discuss when data should be available, and one possible benchmark is publication, then we need to define what publication is and when that happens.

Dr. Straf:

In some situations, it is clear. It is when the journal article is published and printed, but keep in mind the purpose of that. We want to protect the creativity and innovation of a scientist, so we want to give that scientist a "short-term patent," so that all the results can be explored from the data, but we don't want to give the scientist exclusive rights in perpetuity. In a sense, society finds that wrong. So it is only a question of choosing a particular moment that achieves a balance between the two.

I was suggesting that we take as the time of publication the appearance in print of the major results from those data. Sometimes it could be the second or third article; sometimes it will be the first article or simply a letter to the editor.

Ms. Porcher:

What will be the effect of the Technology Transfer Act, which permits government scientists to benefit from their work, on the free exchange of ideas?

Mr. Riseberg:

Because government inventors are now able to obtain a share of the royalties from their inventions, the interest in filing invention reports, as well as in submitting articles to journals, has gone up astronomically, at least at the National Institutes of Health.

One major problem that the government had in protecting its commercial property before this law was in getting scientists to report discoveries to the patent lawyers before they told all their colleagues and published papers. That is now much less of a problem. I think enlightened self-interest has its place.

Dr. Koshland:

I wonder if we haven't made a very important problem more complicated than it is, particularly from the point of view of an editor. Our policy would be that anyone who submits a paper must provide whatever information we think is needed or the referees think is needed under highly controlled conditions; that is, the information is not to be disclosed to anyone. If an author does not provide that, whether it is coordinates, raw data, or whatever, then we have the privilege of not publishing the paper.

In an era in which fraud and misconduct have become more important, what happens to the notebooks? It is important that someone is responsible to keep those intact. That may be a gray area, but it is something that should be decided by the granting society. It is important that scientists cannot just destroy the notebooks—Harvard now has a policy about the preservation of notebooks. At the University of California, scientists can photocopy notebooks and so they have their own information, but the university keeps a copy as well.

As far as confidentiality is concerned, as a journal editor, I believe it is important to maintain the confidentiality of a reviewer, but we should all recognize that if it comes up in a court case—and it has come up—the court can rule that it is relevant to reveal the name of a reviewer. As a general policy, we should maintain the confidentiality of our reviewers, but just as in the case of a doctor who keeps patients' records confidential, if a patient is involved in an automobile accident, the question of whether he has epilepsy then becomes relevant, and the courts always have the power to demand that information. What you do in ordinary practice may be different from what you do in extreme cases.

Dr. Woolf:

I want to speak to the interesting and important point that Dr. Singer raised and to acknowledge with her that in formulating this session we did not mean to confuse data with knowledge, but to recognize that scientific editors do preside over some sort of transformation of raw data into what is considered knowledge. This session was chosen to begin the meeting because it is almost a classical example of a situation where traditions and values of many different professions that impinge on the scientific process and scientific information have come into conflict recently with laws and regulations.

Recently, I had a conversation with a congressional staff member who said, in defense of issuing a subpoena for raw data of an investigator, "It belongs to the public; they paid for it." Now, whether that staffer confused the public with the staff of the committee is one issue. But we do know that scientists traditionally regard the data that they generate as their own, and we also know that the institutions that receive the grants have a fiscal responsibility for maintaining the data and that usually—unlike Harvard, the University of California, and some scientific societies—they have not developed policies in this regard.

Dr. Thier:

Let me summarize a bit. Dr. Singer was asking us to consider why we are here, which is to discover our roles in the process of generating scientific information, in communicating that information, in having it evolve, and in having it become exploited, either as the basis of further knowledge or as the basis of something to serve the public. That is the goal.

You may have to say that the question of ownership of data as an abstract issue is not going to be useful. What you publish can be as diverse as numerical data, the product of biotechnology, or a unique, creative interpretation of data; any of those would qualify as an intellectual contribution.

Questions of ownership will get more complicated as you work backward from published paper to raw data, and you will have to figure out how you want to handle each step along the way. Different people are going to own different parts of this enterprise.

Then, you must remember what Dr. Stossel said about the public good. The public good doesn't operate in the ethereal sense unless we change the entire mechanism by which we exploit information and make it available. We are headed in exactly the opposite direction in the development of the biotechnology industry—we are creating a structure in which the ability to capitalize on new biologic information is going to come progressively more into the commercial arena in a shorter time. And decisions about the connection between commercial enterprises and the academic laboratory are going to become important; in the absence of figuring out how to make sure that these connections are appropriate, you could cut off the translation to public good.

I think we should not oversimplify the issue of ownership. Think about what it is that we as scientists are really trying to produce and, when you get to the end of it, then figure out who owns the various components of that product and that process.

Medical Misconduct: A Survey in Britain*

STEPHEN P. LOCK

Patricia Woolf has explained that all studies of deviance are plagued by the difficulty of estimating prevalence; the numerator is used by the accusers, and the denominator is used by the defenders.[16] After contacting the major federal granting agencies about the number of charges of misconduct in medical research they had investigated, she concluded that there was no evidence of an epidemic of fraudulent science, but that there was a persistent and growing concern about the conduct of science and its publication.

Any study of scientific or medical misconduct is more difficult in Britain than it would be in the United States. In particular, we have no Freedom of Information Act, and we do have stringent libel laws; the smallness of the country means that any accusation is likely to get to every medical school, with serious implications. On the other hand, the smallness means that there is a closely knit medical society whose members can be asked in strict confidence for their knowledge of cases of misconduct. I have used that positive feature to do a nonsystematic survey.

METHODS

I wrote to one professor of medicine and one of surgery in each of the 29 medical institutions in Britain, asking whether they could add any cases of fraud to the ones already documented in Britain; a second question was about any mechanism in their medical schools for dealing with future cases. I also wrote to anybody these respondents suggested might help, five other academics and physicians who I knew had experience or a special interest in the topic, two scientists and physicians concerned with the management of medical research, and the editors of 15 medical journals. I also obtained details of a few cases in Australia. Given, however, that I am not well acquainted with the Australian system, I relied on help from Kathy King, editor of the *Medical Journal of Australia,* and followed up a few of the retractions, undisputed cases, and so on.[3,5,9,10,14]

---

*A longer version of this paper has been published: Lock S. Br Med J 1988;297:1531-5.

RESULTS

Before my survey, I knew of a few cases of medical misconduct: Alsabti, who had started work in Britain;[12] Purves, a Bristol physiologist who resigned his academic post and retracted some fraudulent research findings;[8] an Oxford medical student who had sold an editorial printed in the *British Medical Journal* to a postgraduate review journal;[4] and a well-known but never-named pirate whose activities had earned the distinction of a mention in a book by Peter Medawar.[11] To those, earlier this year could be added a psychiatrist who had lost his medical license because he invented some data for a clinical trial on an antidepressant.[7]

The rate of response to my questionnaire was almost 100% (Table 1). More than half my correspondents knew of some instance of medical misconduct—in which I include plagiarism and misrepresentation, as well as outright fraud (whether falsification, fabrication, or forgery).[16] Most of these had been encountered first-hand, although a sizable minority were well-authenticated second-hand instances—and there were also a few rumors (Tables 2-6).

Most reports concerned episodes in Britain (Table 6). There was a surprising proportion of senior workers (18 of 43 cases in which the grade was reported [Table 4]). Other data show that they had usually committed plagiarism or misconduct, rather than fraud. In more than half the cases of misconduct described, the results had been published, but in only five cases had retractions appeared—all in terms too vague to indicate the nature of the misconduct. Only three of 20 institutions reported mechanisms for investigating misconduct, although one respondent thought that, if the possibility were raised, some sort of ad hoc committee would be set up to deal with an individual case.

Table 7 summarizes four documented episodes in Australia. In two cases, appeals about the administrative details had been used to delay the process of inquiry. But all these cases had been brought into the open with official inquiries; this also happened eventually in another, nonmedical instance of plagiarism at the University of Newcastle, New South Wales, Australia.

DISCUSSION

My small, nonsystematic survey found that misconduct in medical research certainly exists outside the United States, but again provides no data on its prevalence. What can be said, however, is that most of these cases seem to be known only to a few individuals, that little of the published work was retracted (and when it was so, only in the vaguest terms), and that in Britain few institutions have any formal mechanisms for dealing with misconduct.

Clearly, the informality of this survey might be criticized. There were few ways of checking many of the statements, and yet they ring true, for several reasons. First, I know most of the respondents; second, five of the cases were

Table 1. Knowledge of Misconduct

Discipline of Respondent	No Knowledge	Knowledge
Medicine	9	26
Surgery	17	10
Editing	6	8
Other	1	2
Total	33	46

Seventy-nine of 80 people approached replied.
The 46 with knowledge knew of 72 cases (including duplicates).

Table 2. Number of Cases by Discipline

| Discipline of Respondent | Number of Cases | | | |
	1	2	3	4
Medicine*	13	8	8	1
Surgery	8	—	1	1
Editing	5	1	—	2
Other	1	1	—	—
Total	27	20	27	16

*Two respondents with knowledge of multiple cases were excluded.

Table 3. Proximity of Knowledge

| Discipline of Respondent | Type of Knowledge of Each Case | | |
	First-hand	Authenticated Second-hand	Rumor
Medicine	20	16	3
Surgery	11	5	—
Editing	10	3	2
Other	—	2	—
Total	41	26	5

corroborated independently by other replies; and, third, given the circumstances of the inquiry, the respondents had nothing to gain or lose from their replies. If anything, the results underestimate the true number of cases, because total confidentiality was sometimes preserved: One respondent who had

Table 4. Discipline and Grade of Perpetrator

Discipline of Respondent	Grade of Perpetrator			
	Senior	Intermediate	Junior	Not Stated
Medicine	11	14	—	7
Surgery	5	1	—	4
Other	1	—	1	3
Not stated	1	8	1	15
Total	18	23	2	29

Table 5. Type of Misconduct

Discipline of Respondent	Type of Misconduct		
	Plagiarism	Misrepresentation	Fraud
Medicine	1	—	31
Surgery	2	—	8
Other	2	—	3
Not stated	4	2	19
Total	9	2	61

Table 6. Country in Which Misconduct Occurred

Country	Number of Cases
United Kindgom	41
United States	7
Australia	4
Other	7
Not stated	13

been involved in a case as an examiner did not tell me about it (although he gave details of another case), but another person concerned did. Another respondent told me of a well-authenticated case, but said that he had been sworn to secrecy about the details (hence it is classified in Table 3 as a rumor). Sometimes in discussing the problem with outsiders I was told about still other cases, which I added to the list if there were sufficient details. Finally, the survey did not cover other major disciplines, such as obstetrics and gynecology or pediatrics, and only one professor of surgery and one professor of medicine

Table 7. Reported Medical Misconduct in Australia

Name	Position or Role (Institution)	Nature of Misconduct
Michael Briggs (1981-1987)	Endocrinology (Deakin University)	Forged data on oral contraceptives challenged in 1981; moves for inquiry blocked by legal injunction and university visitor; second inquiry started in 1986; Briggs resigned
Ronald Wild (1985)	Professor and dean of social science (La Trobe University)	Fifth book contained large-scale plagiarism from 10 sources; resignation after difficulties with initial inquiry
Ashoka Prasad (1988)	Psychiatrist (Victoria Mental Health Insititute)	Fabricated data on 1,000 patients with schizophrenia, showing higher incidence of birth in winter; committee of inquiry reported to state parliament
William McBride (1988)	Director (Foundation 41)	Forged data on studies of action of a pharmacologic agent on fetal rabbits

in each school were asked to participate in the survey—again a feature that probably led to underestimation of the figures.

The pattern of misconduct resembles that of the substantiated cases in the United States discussed by Woolf.[16] Most of those implicated medically qualified persons, predominantly clinicians in departments of medicine of prestigious medical schools working in "hot" topics of research: cardiovascular disease, cell biology, endocrinology, immunology, and oncology. Even so, a definite problem in Britain, although proportionately small, was work done in district hospitals without any academic connections. I know of two such cases, both entailing nonexistent laboratory work in drug trials. In one, the whistleblower was a colleague of the perpetrator; he asked my advice on the disciplinary mechanism. Independently, both of us thought of the same two possibilities, but neither the regional medical officer nor the chairman of the local ethics committee that had sanctioned the research would have anything to do with the case. The colleague eventually convened an ad hoc committee to interview the malefactor and give a strong official warning not to repeat the abuse. In a second case, the consultant concerned was reported by the drug company to the Association of the British Pharmaceutical Industry and then to the General Medical Council, which deprived him of his license to practice.[7]

The problem is likely to be considerably larger than indicated by the survey. One of my informants told me that it is accepted in the industry that 5% of drug trials are untrustworthy, because of misconduct of some sort. Much of this work is done under contract in district general hospitals or in general practice, yet on legal advice the drug companies take no actions on suspicions, however cogent. (He added that in his view the amount of fraud is proportionately lower in Britain than in the rest of Europe.) Another expert knew of more than one major pharmaceutical company that had received reports that purported to measure drug effects when either the patients did not exist or the studies had been "completed" before the drug was available for study.

This situation may change with the publication of a report by the Association of the British Pharmaceutical Industry on the relationship between the medical profession and the drug industry.[2] The report states that companies have a responsibility to ensure adequate monitoring of all clinical trials. If an investigator is suspected of deception or fraud, the matter should be drawn to the attention of the association and through the association, if necessary, to the attention of the General Medical Council—the body responsible for licensing physicians in Britain—or dealt with in the courts. Nevertheless, action by the Association of the British Pharmaceutical Industry may be needed the other way around. I was told of a well-authenticated case in which a whistleblower working in a drug company resigned when the company persisted in suppressing data that challenged the efficacy of one of its products.

The problems of setting up an inquiry outside an academic framework have been well illustrated in Australia with the recent allegations that William McBride, the physician who first described the teratogenic effects of thalidomide, had deliberately altered data from an inconclusive experiment on the actions of a pharmacologic agent on fetal rats.[6] The work was done at Foundation 41, a private research organization, with two junior colleagues of McBride, both of whom had been unaware of the changes. (McBride is chairman of Foundation 41.) The work was published in the *Australian Journal of Biological Research*. In February 1988, scientists wrote to the Australian National Health and Medical Research Council, urging an inquiry; the council said that it was willing to undertake the study, but only if asked. In April 1988, Foundation 41 asked the Australian Academy of Science to nominate a committee, but the academy is said to have declined, fearing litigation. In July 1988, Foundation 41 set up its own committee, and it reported in early November that McBride was found guilty of fraud.[15]

All my findings in Britain echo those described in the United States by Marcia Angell,[1] who commented that initial responses to early cases of fraud were marked by confusion and a horror of going public; action also was slow. Woolf has suggested that, because cases of misconduct (particularly plagiarism) are often handled locally, the total number is likely to be underestimated.[16] She states that lawyers often have an important role in preventing the disclosure of information and examination of the circumstances. And not infrequently—particularly in the case of students found to have invented or plagiarized data for a thesis—a bargain is struck: The thesis is disallowed, and the student is permitted to resign with nothing said publicly on the other side.

Given all this, the next step should be for the British authorities to recognize the problem of misconduct and resolve to tackle it. So far as sloppy science is concerned, the solution must be with individual institutions—particularly the heads of departments—in tackling the problems of gift, or honorary, authorship (i.e., including as authors people who have made little contribution to the work), least publishable units, and duplicate publication. Concerted official action is needed against plagiarism and fraud. One way would be for the official bodies (including the General Medical Council, the Association of the British Pharmaceutical Industry, the Medical Research Council, and the medical royal colleges) to get together and follow the American practice of devising some uniform, fair mechanism whereby each institution could bring any suspected or proven case into the daylight and deal with it fully and fairly. Research bodies might consider following the example of the National Institutes of Health,[13] by insisting that a prerequisite for a research grant be that the institution have a mechanism for investigating fraud.

That said, however, the problems of medical misconduct outside academic institutions also need consideration. Possibly my proposed committee of the official bodies could assign this task to the local ethics committees responsible for approving research protocols. Nevertheless, these committees would often need to have their representations strengthened from the legal side and would also, I suspect, need some sort of audit of their performance to ensure that standards are maintained.

Whatever the answer, Britain should be reassured by the American experience: within the last decade, most of an entire process has been worked through. First, a form of scientific deviance was identified; second, it was studied; third, steps were taken to deal with existing cases and to try to prevent new ones. The final stage—which I hope is in progress—is some sort of audit to see whether all these measures have diminished a small but serious blot on the face of medical research.

Some might question these suggestions. Why do anything? After all, some might argue, some sort of action is taken eventually in most overt cases of fraud, even if the action is only neglect of the data or ostracism of the wrongdoer by the invisible college. Nevertheless, there are several reasons for an active stance of due process. First, fraud is a crime. As Medawar commented, "I do not find this crime bewildering and inexplicable; it strikes me as a straightforward felony of which scientists must be supposed no less capable than other professional men."[11] Next, too many such felonies have gone unprevented, uninvestigated, or undetected, and this will encourage others to attempt them—with a consequent unethical waste of materials, money, and time in the laboratory and in the journal office. And, finally, if medicine and science no longer carry the hallmark of a profession—self-correction—then official outside agencies are likely to do the correcting for them. There are signs that such mechanisms are emerging in Australia, with bringing the problem into the open and with recognizing that a properly constituted inquiry is needed to allay professional and scientific alarm. We in Britain should follow suit.

REFERENCES

1. Angell M. Fraud in science. Science 1983; 219:1418–19.
2. Association of the British Pharmaceutical Industry. Relationship Between the Medical Profession and the Drug Industry. London: ABPI; 1987.
3. Dawson C. Briggs: unanswered questions. Australian April 1, 1987:14.
4. Differential diagnosis of dementia. Br Med J 1987; 294:1236.
5. Duncan T. Unit standards threatened by PhD student scandal. The Bulletin September 25, 1986: 26–9.
6. Ewing T. Australian scientists differ on how to attack fraud. Nature 1988; 332: 671.
7. GMC professional conduct committee. Br Med J 1988; 296: 306.
8. In Bristol now. Nature 1981; 294: 509.
9. Maslen G, McIntosh D. Doubts took eight years to reveal the truth. The Age October 3, 1986: 50.
10. McAdam A. Professor resigns after barrage of plagiarism charges. The Bulletin July 1, 1986: 30.
11. Medawar PB. Advice to a Young Scientist. Cambridge, Massachusetts: Harper & Row; 1979.
12. Must plagiarism thrive? Br Med J 1980; 281: 41–2.
13. Powledge TM. NIH's Raub on misconduct. Scientist 1986;1(3):18–9.
14. Smith D. Renewed attack on pill researcher. The National Times July 25–31, 1986: 22.
15. Swan N. Science not always right but it can't be wrong. Sydney Morning Herald. November 3, 1988.
16. Woolf P. Deception in scientific research. Jurimetrics J 1988;29(1):67-95.

The Editor: Mark, Dupe, Patsy, Accessory, Weasel, and Flatfoot

DRUMMOND RENNIE

At the annual meeting of the Council of Biology Editors, Marcia Angell neatly categorized seven kinds of deception in science and in publication, from fragmentation of publication through loose authorship and duplicate publication, all the way to plagiarism and fabrication.[2] Her classification and several others like it are still being argued as we try to arrive at a satisfactory definition of misconduct in research and to define the nomenclature of fraud on the way to finding a solution.

On September 19, 1988, the *Federal Register* published an advance announcement of proposed regulations to protect against scientific fraud or misconduct.[4]* In the discussion of the definition, it is made clear that the term "scientific misconduct" is preferred to the term "fraud"; however, because "fraud" is customary I shall use it, recognizing that it is a legally improper, although convenient, term. By "fraud," I mean all serious departures from the established norms of science.

The point is made in the proposed regulations of the Department of Health and Human Services that, to establish common law fraud, we must prove that a defendant knowingly made a misrepresentation to induce a plaintiff to rely on it and that the plaintiff was damaged by justifiably relying on that misrepresentation. Finding it difficult to know whom the defendant intended to deceive, the lawyers who drafted this document, who noted how hard it would be to establish discernible damages, could name only one class of possible aggrieved parties—the editors of scholarly journals to which fabricated articles are sent for publication. Moreover, the argument goes on, it would be tough to establish justifiable reliance, because the readers of the false papers would be scientists—who are trained to be skeptical.

I believe we are skeptical—skeptical not merely of the science, but of scientists themselves. It is not a nice notion, but times have indeed changed. Back in 1979, Dr. Helena Wachslicht-Rodbard, a worker on insulin receptors at the National Institutes of Health, raised a complaint about a manuscript from Yale. One of its authors was Vijay Soman, and the complaint was of plagiarism. After a good look at the evidence, I, helped by the fact that the

---

*The final rule, "Responsibilities of Awardee and Applicant Institutions for Dealing with and Reporting Possible Misconduct in Science," was published by the Public Health Service on August 8, 1989 (Fed Reg 1989; 54:32446-51).

review of her paper and the plagiarizing document were typed on the same machine, concluded in a lengthy report that "there almost certainly was" plagiarism of phrases—that and no more. I now quote as evidence for my 1979-style naiveté my written aside in this report, in which I commented on the originality and scientific accuracy of the plagiarizing group. I wrote that their work was "better, cleaner, neater—but . . . not as original."

I could not possibly have proved, without a visit to Soman's laboratory, that the "better, cleaner, neater" results were entirely fabricated. Not even on-the-spot questioning by the paper's senior author had revealed that. My point is that early in 1979—before the egregious cases of scientific fraud provided by Long (1979), Darsee (1981), Slutsky (1985), and Spector (1981)—we were skeptical, but even when we had had our attention drawn to the paper because of one crime, we still were not skeptical enough to wonder whether all the data in the paper had been fabricated. Now, with these well-publicized examples, we have learned to keep "fraud" at the edge of our minds and have also learned that a plagiarist is a fabricator and a fabricator may be a thief.

After the Darsee revelations and the analysis of Darsee's papers by Stewart and Feder,[19] Heilemann[12] wrote to *Nature*, placing the responsibility for the publication of fraudulent material squarely on the editors. For some defensive reason, I know in my heart that Heilemann is unjust, and I have only to read the frequently expressed views of editors to see that most editors agree. It is true that editors must take responsibility for what appears in their journals, but they cannot endorse anything they did not do themselves, so the responsibility is qualified. Our editorial prejudice is that the fault lies with the fraudulent workers, with their coauthors, with their departments and institutions, with universities in general, with society and its system of rewards, and specifically with the publish-or-perish principle. Fault lies everywhere but with editors. According to this attractive hypothesis, blaming editors is as logical as blaming little old ladies for being gulled by con artists before being mugged in the streets.

But I am uneasy about this, and, as my frothy title suggests, I intend to examine this prejudice. Are editors "marks" (the intended victims of a swindle)? Are they "dupes" (a word that comes from the Latin *upupa,* a hoopoe or stupid bird) or "patsies" (these last being persons easily tricked, fooled, imposed on, or victimized)? In short, when a clever trickster appears, are editors as stupid, blind, deaf, doddery, demented, gullible, and little-old-lady-like as they seem to be?

The answer seems to be yes.

We think back on our own experience and we proudly remember all the cases of fragmented "salami" publication that we have caught. We do not dwell on the far greater number that we must have missed. Duplicate publication turns up quite often in review, but as often as not it is unmasked only after publication. I suspect that even then we hear about only a small fraction of cases. Even plagiarism, a crime that one would think in a peculiar way seems to involve the writing alone, is almost never caught by editors or reviewers, but must await discovery by the plagiarized author before detection.

The same goes for fabrication. Angell[2] seems to imply that, by applying specific rules, the review process will catch the criminal. I am less optimistic. She has reminded us to be skeptical when data fall too easily into place, when they are too startling, or when the work is done in isolation. True. But how useful is that? I have given an example, the Soman paper, of data that are too good, but expert reviewers looking at data in the Soman paper had no complaint. The same might be said, for example, of the perfect data of Deborah Spiva.[23] I submit that fraudulent scientists will tend to submit data that are sophisticatedly shaggy, which means not too shaggy, for I should also point out that editors are not noted for their enthusiasm for dirty-looking data, no matter how impeccable the provenance of the information. The astute faculty-committee member who had been asked by Slutsky to write a letter of support found the statistical errors that brought the whole house of cards down in two of Slutsky's papers, when they were placed side by side.[9] Can we expect reviewers to go through the previous publications of each author in this way, looking for the potential bad apple?

Arnold Relman, when he answers the question, "What kind of protection against fraud does peer review offer?" says it best: "The Darsee affair gives a clear answer: Little or none. Most of Darsee's fraudulent work was published in peer-reviewed journals, some with very exacting standards, and yet in none of the reviews was there enough suspicion to warrant rejection."[16]

Of course, we can all give examples of outright fraud detected during review. One review we received said:

> Unfortunately, while the paper is written convincingly, the data are highly suspect. First, the prevalence is inherently unlikely. Secondly, I have searched the author's hospital's autopsy file for the relevant five years. Only two of the 12 patients listed as having autopsies could be found to correspond in initials and sex to the patients in the file, and though the clinical diagnoses coincided, the lab values in these two patients' charts did not in any way correspond to the ones given by the authors.[18]

After horror, my *second* thought was to blame myself for selecting a reviewer who was too close to the authors and then to blame him for not having declared this conflict. But such a discovery is rare. The sort of thing that reviewers can pick up more easily and that therefore seems more common is this:

> The differences found in this paper are statistically significant, but entirely different from those found in their previous study, and all the values are entirely different, with no consistent differences and with no explanation or discussion. The authors *must* have known of the inconsistencies of absolute values between their 1977 and 1978 studies (using the same subject groups and the same analytic techniques) yet failed to discuss this grave matter.[19]

The fact remains, however, that there is no reason from their past performance to predict that editors and reviewers are able to weed out fraud, unless by the sort of coincidence I have quoted above. Reviewing is a hard enough task as it is. Although lapses in good scientific review have been demonstrated by Stewart and Feder,[19] it is my bias that reviewers are good at this. The peer-review system seems to work well when the questions being asked of it are the questions of science; but, when the questions have to do with whether there were any patients in the first place or whether the data points were entirely fabricated, editors and reviewers are helpless. In the unlikely event that they harbor suspicions, they do not even have the freedom to investigate (nor, perhaps, the detective skills) of the flattest flatfoot. Experience has shown us that a crafty fabricator can easily dupe us, turning us, his marks, into patsies who are then pointed out by others as, in effect, the criminal's accessories. (Perhaps that is why the embarrassed editor seems to use such weasel words when trying to avoid publishing retractions.)

In view of all that, should editors start from the hypothesis that what is in front of them must be assumed fraudulent until proved otherwise? The honesty of scientists as a class has been tested only once, by Wolins,[22] and he found that they are dishonest, a position backed up by St. James-Roberts.[20,21] Certainly, few would argue that the act of submitting a paper to a journal automatically confers the attribute of honesty.

How would that hypothesis play out? It would mean, as a start, that personal trust, without which it is scarcely possible to imagine the scientific enterprise continuing, would have to be jettisoned in favor of collegial suspicion. It would require the delivery to journals of masses of supporting material. Journals would have to expand their staffs enormously, and at the end of it all the editors would *still* not know whether the material provided was trustworthy. In short, the assumption of dishonesty would be impractical and ineffective and, because of the damage it would do to the community of science (as well as to the already delicate relations between editors and authors), would be harmful.

If we editors cannot do that, what should we do? Others have argued that editors announce that papers will be received for review on condition that, if asked, the authors are willing and able to produce all their data for inspection. That, of course, is no more than an extension of good laboratory practice. They have also strongly urged that editors define authorship and that authors be made to sign statements before publication designed to make them aware that they assume the responsibilities, as well as all the privileges, of authorship. Above all, they have urged the Angell approach[3]—that faculty promotion committees rate candidates on the quality of a few publications, rather than on the weight of many.

I have several proposals to put forward now for discussion. Behind all of them is my belief that, although we must do everything possible to stimulate creativity by preserving intellectual freedom, the public and political reputation of science is being degraded by the perception of fraud, and we must deal with it.

First, I believe that journal editors should, as at this conference and at meetings of the International Committee of Medical Journal Editors (ICMJE), set up policies and procedures for dealing with allegations of fraud, and these should include the setting up of sanctions[1] and the sharing of confidential information between journals. Although I like the idea of each journal's having a completely free hand in the way it responds to every problem, the fact is that, as parent institutions tighten up their procedures, journals, which have as much to lose, should cooperate. The ICMJE has already made a good start with policies for authorship and for retraction.[13] Editors will be grateful for such written procedures when the cheaters' lawyers, or those of the cheaters' co-workers, begin to harass the editors about retraction or when powerful interests move to protect the guilty. They will also help an editor to be less of a weasel.

My second proposal is an extension of the "produce all the data if we ask for them" idea. I am suggesting that we should *always* ask for them, but, because we have neither the time nor the inclination to read them, the raw data should be deposited in the form of a copy, in an archive specially set up for the purpose, like the National Auxiliary Publication Service, that would have other benefits. For reasons of space, journals must limit severely the amount of raw data they can publish, although such limitations can hamper the progress of research, which can, for example, include reanalysis of the data by someone else with the sort of agreement suggested by Layne et al.[14] Anyone with a legitimate interest in the data would have access to them; if any questions were raised about the legitimacy of the published work, it would be easy to refer to the archives. Naturally, the system would require protections to safeguard the intellectual property of the authors. The archives' existence, and the fact that journals would not accept a paper unless the raw data were deposited there, would deter theft on the one hand and contribute to good scientific practice on the other. Incidentally, the system would go a long way toward satisfying the recommendations of the Committee on National Statistics as to the sharing of data.[10]

My third proposal is for an audit under the control of the journal editors. Two weeks after I put forward this suggestion at the Institute of Medicine on Sept. 6, 1988, the legislative proposals to which I have referred were published in the *Federal Register* by the Department of Health and Human Services. These suggest that, to deter and detect scientific misconduct, the department might set up an office of scientific integrity, which would have investigative and adjudicative branches, and might conduct routine or random on-site audits of the research data collected in research projects funded by the Public Health Service.* The data audits could be conducted either by department staff or by

---

*The department has since set up the Office of Scientific Integrity and the Office of Scientific Integrity Review, which oversees the decisions of the first office.

independent contractors. The office would work closely with that of the department's inspector general.

Scientists will object. Davis calls the idea "too fantastic to get very far,"[8] but he also notes that the power of the purse is virtually unlimited, implying, I suppose, that we will all fall into line. I take the view that it will certainly happen, because, although many members of Congress are not scientists, most are lawyers who understand fraud and believe that it is rife in biomedicine. Anyone who doubts that has only to read the testimony of the witnesses and members of Congress at the April and September 1988 series of congressional hearings on the issue.[11] Because we have never done what as scientists we might have been expected to do, that is, a scientific survey, we are simply unable to assert that our critics are wrong. Surely, for political as well as for scientific reasons, we should know the extent of the problem. Editors are in an ideal position to throw their weight behind such an audit.

I should point out that I am not talking about the sort of after-the-fact audit that was done as a condition of *Nature's* publication of the incredible report from Benveniste's laboratory,[7,15] which has recently received so much publicity.

Would an audit be generally effective? It certainly can be. It was a Food and Drug Administration (FDA) audit in 1982 that caused Wilbert S. Aronow, a prominent researcher and a member of FDA's advisory committee on cardiology, suddenly to admit to falsification of data and resign. I had had a hand in publishing one of his papers, of which he was sole author, and had, before it was retracted, used it in lectures as an example of a well-designed and well-conducted study. I know he could not have been detected in any other way. Even the most cursory audit would have shown the world, as well as his co-worker, that Darsee's 46-member kindred with taurine-associated cardiomyopathy did not exist, despite the massive amount of data and the echocardiograms that were published.[6,19]

I am sure that there is a time when every editor wishes that it were possible to call on some outside expert to go into the author's workplace to conduct an audit—free. This is exactly what happened for me. In 1987, we published a paper from an important institution.[17] The article purported to show for the very first time that a patient during two admissions failed to respond to the FDA-approved generic version of a drug, but was well controlled on the proprietary equivalent. FDA followed up with an on-the-spot investigation, which soon showed that a few months earlier the patient had not responded to either drug. In addition, the audit showed that no other patient on the generic preparation had relapsed. Finally, investigation of two other cases, suspected by the authors of relapsing because of the generic drug, had proved that this was not the case. We had been given none of this information, although the manuscript reached us more than a year after the events.

We heard first from the manufacturers of the generic drug, who believed that they were harmed by our article and vindicated by the FDA report. Then one of our reviewers protested that he was not given relevant facts, which, had he known them, would have led him to recommend rejection of the manuscript. He demanded an investigation. Finally, FDA wrote to put the record straight. The authors replied that the events after the admissions they described were irrelevant and occurred after their manuscript was written (13 months before we saw it). They also stated that their paper "passed a critical peer review prior to publication," a remark that we were disposed to think of as disingenuous at best.

I am therefore impressed by my only experience of audit in the two cases just described: the revelation of misconduct in 1979 and of the failure to provide full data due to an error, 9 years later.

How would the experimental audit I am proposing work? This would be one way: First, cooperating journals would give authors two years' notice that manuscripts would be accepted for review on condition that authors agree to random audit. The journals would publish a list of the sort of documentation they would expect, and this would be in line with the rules for good clinical and laboratory practices being refined under the aegis of the Institute of Medicine. After review and revision, manuscripts provisionally accepted for publication would be available for audit. A random selection of original research papers and case histories would be made. For biomedical journals, the auditors could be retired scientists or postdoctoral fellows with training in biomedical research, and it would not be necessary for them to have a deep knowledge of every field, because they would be seeking answers to much simpler, more basic questions: Did the patient exist? Was the work done? Are the records preserved? Do the data in the charts correspond to those in the reports, and is the report fairly representative of these data? The auditors would not adjudicate the gray areas of scientific disagreement, but would check the relatively crude facts that would confirm whether what was reported had any resemblance to what had occurred.

I believe that the government would be particularly anxious to fund such an initiative. It could be done under contract to a group of journals, and I believe that the editors would be able to insist on complete independence and confidentiality. I also believe that, once the editorial committee charged with working out the rules had done its work, there would be no extra difficulty for editors. I can see no reasons why it should prevent editors from publishing heterodox science.

Why should editors volunteer to be involved with the distasteful business of policing the biomedical research industry? As I have already said, the audit is going to be part of our scientific, as well as our medical and tax-paying, lives, and I am proposing that we should seize the initiative to direct, rather than merely record, the events. That is an unfamiliar and uncomfortable idea to most editors, who might see a vague threat to their editorial freedom in being labeled government-appointed cops—the federal flat of foot. Well, I think we already *are* seen to have a policeman's lot, and one of the reasons we are unhappy about it is that we are ignorant of a problem that is ruining our reputations, and up to now we have been powerless to correct that ignorant impression.

I believe that editors are, and are seen to be, independent of research institutions. Although I urge institutions to conduct their own internal audits, these are bound to be viewed with suspicion by any outsider. The record that institutions have achieved in investigation—for example, in the Breuning affair[5]—has been truly terrible, presumably because it is the nature of institutions to circle the wagons when challenged. Editors are seen to have but one interest: the integrity of what they publish. Audits backed and supervised by the journals would be seen as disinterested, authoritative, and fair. The audit system would be scholarly and would not demand the setting up of a large federal bureaucracy that could not easily be dismantled. The time of submission of the results of research to a journal is the moment at which one may assume that that segment of work is completed and all the authors have signed off on it. It is therefore an ideal point for such an audit, because the auditor will have in hand the product that the author wants to disseminate as the truth.

What advantages would accrue? It would be interesting scientifically while providing a service to science. We would begin to get some crude idea about whether fraud is so common that it is destroying science. If it is, then with the research institutions we can set up serious procedures for policing it. If it is negligible, we can feel relieved. We can then reassure our congressional masters, and this time we might appear credible, instead of merely ludicrous, and we will all be able to stop having around-the-clock meetings about a subject on which there are absolutely no data. And if, as I suspect, we find that scientists are like the rest of mankind, we will uncover quite a lot of sloppiness and not much real crime, and we will be able to make recommendations for improving our practice that are based on facts.

I started by saying that the victims of scientific fraud had been identified by Department of Health and Human Services lawyers as us editors. There are others—the young patients whose therapy was (and is) based on Breuning's fabrications, for example. But I would also like you to ponder the fate of the fraudulent scientists' wretched co-workers, their professional lives ruined by such cheats. We editors, we victims, patsies. Do we want to stay mired as accessories without making any effort at all to protect our own reputations?

REFERENCES

1. Abelson P. Excessive zeal to publish. Science 1982;218:953.
2. Angell M. Editors and fraud. CBE Views 1983;6:3–8.
3. Angell M. Publish or perish: a proposal. Ann Intern Med 1986;104:261–2.
4. Announcement of development of regulations protecting against scientific fraud or misconduct. Fed Reg 1988;53:36344–50.

5. Are scientific misconduct and conflicts of interest hazardous to our health? 19th Report by the Committee on Government Operations. September 10, 1990. Washington, D.C.: U.S. Government Printing Office, 1990.
6. Darsee JR, Heymsfield SB. Decreased myocardial taurine levels and hypertaurinuria in a kindred with mitral-valve prolapse and congestive cardiomyopathy. N Engl J Med 1981;304:129–35.
7. Davenas E, Beauvais F, Amara J, Oberbaum M, Robinzon B, Miadonna A, Tedeschi A, Pomeranz B, Fortner P, Belon P, Sainte-Laudy J, Poitevin B, Benveniste J. Human basophil degranulation triggered by very dilute antiserum against IgE. Nature 1988;333:816–8.
8. Davis BD. Precinct NIH. Nature 1988;335:8.
9. Engler RL, Covell JW, Friedman PJ, Kitcher PS, Peters RM. Misrepresentation and responsibility in medical research. N Engl J Med 1987;317:1383–9.
10. Fienberg SE, Martin ME, Straf ML, eds. Sharing Research Data. Washington, D.C.: National Academy Press, 1985.
11. Greenberg DS. Fraud inquiry. Sci Gov Rep 1988 (Apr 15):1–6; (May 1):3,5–6.
12. Heilemann PP. Disinformation and fraud. Nature 1987;327:362.
13. International Committee of Medical Journal Editors. Uniform requirements for manuscripts submitted to biomedical journals. Ann Intern Med 1988;108:258–65.
14. Layne SP, Marr TG, Colgate SA, Hyman JM, Stanley EA. The need for national HIV databases. Nature 1988;333:511–2.
15. Maddox J, Randi J, Stewart WW. "High-dilution" experiments a delusion. Nature 1988;334:287–90.
16. Relman AS. Lessons from the Darsee affair. N Engl J Med 1983;308:1415–7.
17. Rennie D. Editors and auditors. JAMA 1989;261:2543–5.
18. Rennie D. The ethics of medical publication. Med J Aust 1979;2:409–12.
19. Stewart WW, Feder N. The integrity of the scientific literature. Nature 1987;325:207–14.
20. St. James-Roberts I. Are researchers trustworthy? New Scient 1976 (Sep 2):481–3.
21. St. James-Roberts I. Cheating in science. New Scient 1976 (Nov 25):466–9.
22. Wolins L. Amer Psychol 1975;17:657.
23. Yoffe E. The deadly doctor. Texas Monthly 1987 (Apr):104–82.

INVITED DISCUSSION
Maxine Singer

In an earlier discussion, the point was made that the responsibility for the veracity of scientific publications should be tied to the ownership of that information. Editors of journals represent one element in a complicated system of ownership, and I certainly agree with Dr. Lock and Dr. Rennie that journals, editors, editorial boards, and the societies that publish many of our journals can play important roles in dealing with the issues of scientific fraud.

American society, as Dr. Lock told us, is not British society, and, although we might not be as cynical as our British colleagues, we have a slavish attention to ephemeral fashion—and that goes in science and in science publications, as well as in how we deal with persons whose reputations have been called into public question. We don't have much control over the nature of official inquiries, and we cannot be certain that they will be fair, as Dr. Lock suggested is the case in Great Britain. I think it is important for us to keep that in mind, because it helps us to evaluate the reticence of many American scientists about proposals for official regulation, whether the proposals come from scientific societies or from the government.

I also think that it is worth asking to what extent other aspects of our university situation are influential. In the United States, the large research universities are now accepted as leaders in scholarly activities of all kinds. Although at one time they leavened their research activities by dedication to teaching, they do so less and less, and investigators are less and less challenged by students at any level. I think that it is an important aspect of the problem.

I am concerned about editors becoming policemen, primarily because I believe that editors' ability to maintain the quality of scientific publication depends mainly on the ability of authors to look at editors as colleagues. If we put aside the infrequent case of misconduct—and no matter what the numbers turn out to be, they are likely to be a small proportion of the papers that are submitted—our ability to improve those papers and our ability to challenge data that are not well reported or are reported in a confusing way or appear insufficient depends on authors seeing editors as colleagues. To the extent that we act as policemen, we diminish that collegial aspect, and our role as editors becomes something of a problem. Whatever kind of structure we devise or whatever kind of guidelines we develop for editors, it is important that we keep in mind the problems engendered when one tries to be both colleague and policeman.

INVITED DISCUSSION
Paul J. Friedman*

When an investigative committee of the School of Medicine at the University of California, San Diego, determined that Robert Slutsky had fabricated data in three manuscripts, two of which had been published, it confirmed a suspicion of fraud and fulfilled its initial charge. The committee then addressed the problem of the rest of his published work, all of which had originated at UCSD. This was not covered by the school's policy on responding to charges of unethical research practices. The committee recommended a review of all his 135 other publications. The committee recognized an institutional responsibility to minimize the inevitable uncertainty that would attach to any paper bearing his name. One motive was to caution readers about papers that might

*The views represented herein are those of the author and do not necessarily reflect those of the University of California or the author's colleagues at UCSD.

not be valid; another, to reassure readers as to which papers could still be regarded as sound, and thereby to offer support for the younger faculty and students who had been coauthors with Slutsky on many papers. A new committee was convened to undertake this enormous task and then to report its results publicly.

The committee had barely started work when a journal reported to us that Slutsky's personal attorney had submitted a letter retracting two papers. We contacted the attorney and were sent the citations of 15 papers retracted from eight journals. The committee nevertheless proceeded with its charge.

As previously reported,[1,2] it was impossible to find raw data for papers that Slutsky had written, but it would have been impossibly time-consuming to review data for over 130 papers if they had been available. If any coauthor (usually the first author) had the data or had participated in each experiment, had been personally involved in the analysis and reporting, and could vouch for the accuracy of the final paper—methods and results—then we accepted the paper as valid. We also classified the four review papers as valid, because they contained no original data. If there was testimony or documentary evidence that experiments had not been done as reported, we classified the papers as fraudulent. The remainder were papers in which no coauthor of Slutsky's had been fully involved in some step—experiment, analysis, writing—and therefore there was no assurance that the manuscript had been valid; these were classified as questionable. Papers in which the published data did not match the statistical analysis were classified as questionable, because it is sometimes not possible to distinguish deception from error when it comes to statistics. When statistical tests were claimed that we knew had not been performed, we classified the paper as fraudulent.

After 15 months of analysis, we addressed letters to 30 of the 32 journals that had published papers with Slutsky's name, excluding the two that had each published only one review paper. We requested publication of a general statement that briefly described the criteria of the classification and a list of the papers in each category. We did not use the word "retraction" in our letter or statement. We later sent one or two followup letters to 14 of the journals and received written or telephone responses from 13 of these.

Of the eight journals that were addressed by Slutsky's attorney: two published his letter in full, four others conveyed the retraction message in different words or an edited version of the letter, and two took no action in print for over a year, eventually responding to the UCSD statement with a notice that included reference to the earlier retraction letter. The response to our letter was complicated by the prior publication of these earlier notices. Three of these journals would not also publish the later UCSD statement, despite its listing of questionable or fraudulent papers in addition to those covered by the Slutsky retraction. Three others published the UCSD statement as a second notice; the other two, as mentioned above, have not yet published any statement.

We classified 12 papers as fraudulent.[1] Eventually, statements covering eight of them were published. One of the missing citations was discovered during this review to have been an error in failing to include the citation with the 16 others reported to the journal. One fraudulent paper was in a journal that had a firm policy to accept retractions only from authors, but had not received a retraction notice from Slutsky or any coauthor. The other two were omitted from the lists published by the journal editor.

There were 48 questionable papers, of which 31 have been reported by published notices. The missing papers include another error in our correspondence: one questionable paper was reported as valid. Several were included in the refusals to publish a second notice. Another was in a journal with which we have failed to establish communication (it had undergone a change in name and editorship). One journal has apparently failed to follow up on its early assurance that it would publish the statement. Another journal recently decided to require a coauthor-initiated retraction.

In terms of effectiveness of the UCSD effort, only nine of the 17 journals with any nonvalid papers have published statements that listed all papers about which we sent them information. Published statements now cover 39 of 60 such papers. In terms of access to this information, electronic retrieval of only 18 references includes the information that they had been retracted.

We classified 75 of the 135 papers as valid. Eventually, statements covering 18 of those were published. Five journals that had only valid papers published the information under a variety of headings, of which the most informative was "validation of a study." The other eight such journals declined to publish any statement, either considering it unnecessary or, as a result of legal opinion, deciding that printing UCSD's claim of fraud in other papers was unwise.

The facts presented appear to show marked nonuniformity in response to a major effort by a university to correct the literature. Furthermore, the initial lack of written response by fully half the journals to which we wrote was deplorable. Although three of the silent editors had in fact published a statement in response to our letter, they failed to inform us of that fact, and regular electronic retrieval attempts failed to pick it up. It was impossible for the university to close the books on this investigation in the absence of knowledge of the actions taken by the journals.

Current attempts to improve how universities respond to allegations of fraud should address journals' similar problem; we received the kind of response that has drawn criticism to the universities. The terminology of and responsibility for "retraction" must be defined and recognized more uniformly by all parties. The standards for what kind of correction should be published are not widely accepted, and it is obvious that the standard of responsiveness of journals in their dialogue with universities must be improved.

REFERENCES

1. Engler RL, Covell JW, Friedman PJ, Kitcher PS, Peters RM. Misrepresentation and responsibility in medical research. N Engl J Med 1987; 317:1383–9.
2. Friedman PJ. Fraud in radiologic research. Editorial. Am J Roentgenol 1988; 150:27–30.

Open Discussion

Dr. Angell:

I have some concerns about Dr. Rennie's notion of random audits by government agencies, by journals, or by anyone else. We can consider the conduct of research in two stages. One is the generation and recording of the data, and the other is analysis—the interpretation and the translation of the study into a manuscript.

The data themselves usually are messy, not because of misconduct on the part of researchers, but because that is the way science is. There can be outlying data points; there are things that are surprising or at least unexpected. These must be gone over in preparing a paper for publication.

In earlier times, when there was no expectation of a random audit, you might find misconduct by looking at the primary data. But setting in place a system of random audits will merely change the stage at which wrong-doing occurs. After all, you can fudge primary data as well as you can fudge the manuscript.

This also is going to have a chilling effect on honest researchers, who will fear unexpected pieces of data or surprising findings. What you might end up with is a system in which what should be an honest recording of data to be looked at later in a creative, positive, innovative process becomes a process of second-guessing, even before data are recorded. And instead of looking ahead creatively, researchers will be looking over their shoulder at what you called the "flatfoots."

Dr. Rennie:

The sort of audit I am talking about is crude and has very little to do with things like the analysis. Auditing is going to be demanded. It is going to be the law, the regulation, and so on. We should live with it. I was recommending that editors have some controlling influence over it, because they are in an excellent moral position to do so.

I quoted one review that I received at the *New England Journal of Medicine,* which stated that the reviewers knew that the data were false and that most of the patients listed in the paper did not exist. I have a file of reviews just like it. Moreover, reviewing the paper before submission does not work. The institutions are not going to conduct audits, although that would be the most desirable thing. Their record is poor, and the granting agencies are not going to believe them. Will this destroy relationships that the editors have with authors? I think that the editors in some senses are already seen a little bit as policemen. In any case, we spend a great deal of our time working with authors to try to achieve some higher good.

Editors can also distance themselves from the audit process. They should provide the material that would flow into the audit and set up the system for the audit, but editors themselves would not actually be doing it.

Dr. Dan:

Rather than talk about the philosophic issues here, I will get down to some pragmatic aspects of your proposal.

Researchers who fabricate data do so not because it is better to do so, but because it is quicker and easier to write numbers down than to do experiments and make observations. I think editors will also be enamored of the idea of doing things more efficiently and faster. We think about turnaround time constantly. There are about 20,000 medical journals; with approximately 10 original articles per journal, about a quarter of a million articles come out each month in the scientific literature. I will leave it to those with a statistical bent to give the actual numbers. Even if you propose a prevalence rate of fabrication, what sort of sampling must we have to uncover the problems that we suspect? Do you really think that there are problems that we can solve with these sorts of numbers?

In mathematical sciences, some problems that are soluble are called computationally insoluble, because they cannot be solved in feasible time. If it is going to take us 300 years to find the fabrication, I suspect that we will be able to disprove the reported findings way before that and show that they are invalid by their very nature, rather than by having "flatfoots" out there trying to find the small number of articles with a few fabrications and cases of sloppiness.

Dr. Rennie:

We are interested in producing data to respond to a perception—not on the part of scientists, but on the part of the public and their elected officials— that fraud is rife. I do not believe that it is, but an audit is going to be demanded.

Now, I would go to the statisticians for numbers, but I think that, if one audited 1,000 papers and found that in 30% there was no correlation whatsoever between the very crudest figures—no patient charts were available, because the patients were invented—then we would all be brought up short and say that we have a major problem on our hands.

If none of the papers was found fraudulent, we would say, let's quit all this. Let's dismantle the audit. Let's stop having meetings. Let's go home and say that we have dealt with fraud, and it is an unimportant problem—but we would have figures. We would have some sort of response to the public, which is skeptical and distrustful of us for good reasons.

Dr. Lock:

I think Dr. Rennie's idea of an audit is superficially attractive, but, like Dr. Dan, I am worried about the statistical aspects. I would be much happier if it concentrated on the entire spectrum. We are dealing with something that all of us believe to be rare.

If the audit were to address the spectrum of sloppy science, of gift authorship, of duplicate publication, of fragmented publication, I would go along with the suggestion. But I really do not think it is going to detect the problems associated, for example, with the case of Slutsky, as presented by Dr. Friedman. I know that Slutsky was actually detected by a very percipient referee when he applied for a senior post. That was perhaps happenstance and the only time it has occurred.

Dr. Bailar:

Dr. Dan asked a question that has a very neat, clean, precise answer, which can be given in terms of what I call the "rule of three": If the incidence of fraud is one in 1,000 papers, it takes a strictly random sample of about 3,000 papers to have a 95% chance of finding at least one that is fraudulent. If the incidence is one in 100, it would take a random sample of about 300 papers to be 95% sure of getting at least one. If the incidence is one in 10, it takes about 30 papers. These examples are for the true incidence of fraud in the population studied. I do not believe that an audit could catch all the fraudulent papers. We would have to build in a factor for the detection rate, so sample sizes would need to be larger.

Furthermore, if we want to learn something about the characteristics of fraudulent papers and their authors—the circumstances in which they come to journals and so forth—finding one fraudulent paper would not be enough. We would need still larger samples. I suspect that we are talking about a very large operation here. However, it need not all be carried out by one journal. Journals could cooperate to assemble a sample of whatever size was deemed necessary.

Dr. Friedman:

From your perspective as editors, you are worried about detecting fraud and misconduct. All my experience is that there is someone else who already knows. These events are usually not limited to one person absolutely keeping it to himself or herself. In today's busy laboratories, someone else knows. It is usually a junior person, who is afraid to tell anyone or is compromised. It is a colleague who wishes that it would stop, but does not want to cause trouble.

There are many reasons that fraud is not reported. One is that it is not traditional to do so. We do not have an honor code in science that requires those who observe cheating to report it. Until we do devise an honor system—and I think that must come—we must recognize that detection is a waste of resources, because we are not going to find anything that other people do not know about already.

I am not sure who is going to do these audits, because you would have to hire people to do them. Editorial staff members will not conduct audits, and, once you have people earning a salary for doing this, they will find something to justify their existence.

If Dr. Rennie is correct that we will be required to have an audit, it will be done by someone who is approved and regular. It will be set up probably in the institutions or maybe by the inspector general, but it will not be hit or miss, and it will not be under the control of the editors. It will be under the control of either the institution or the inspector general's office.

My final point is that, in fact, the government and regulators have trusted the institutions in other, equally touchy issues to regulate themselves, after they set in place a framework within which the institutions must operate. I am thinking, in particular, of the regulation of research on humans and animals. The institutions were driven to it, to be sure, but then they put something in place; and now the level of oversight from the government is negligible.

Dr. Singer:

I would like to say that this is the first time that I heard Dr. Rennie's proposal, and I think it is an interesting idea that requires serious consideration. It stands a chance of accomplishing something important, if its motivation as a means to acquire data is kept in mind.

Dr. Friedman just mentioned that there have been various incidents in the last 10 or 15 years that have raised public concern about matters in science and particularly in biology, but, when the scientific community did assume responsibility in a serious way, it was given a chance to proceed. We have models in human-experimentation committees, recombinant-DNA-experimentation committees, and animal-experimentation committees. So there is a precedent for the scientific community to regulate itself. In fact, this has meant that more formal arrangements by the government—with all their possibilities for stifling the creative process—have been avoided to a large extent.

With respect to Dr. Rennie's idea of an audit, one possibility is to reduce it to a checklist. We would not ask for fine value judgments. We would ask whether the notebooks are on the shelves and whether the notebooks have experiments that are in some way related to what is being published.

However, I do share Dr. Friedman's concern about a professional group of auditors, and, in thinking through the proposal, we would want to see whether work would be audited without some sort of professional cadre, which might be poorly informed and unproductive.

Finally, I am interested in the idea, at least at first look, because it deals with issues besides the very rare instances of out-and-out fraud. It deals with issues that are more pervasive and more serious for everyday science. It deals with issues of authorship. Who are the authors? Did each of those people really have something to do with this paper? Is each of the people responsible for what is in the paper? Do the references give reasonable credit to past workers? How many other papers on the same subject have the authors submitted to other journals in the same period, and will their submissions result in multiple publication?

I think these issues can be dealt with on a checklist. As an editor, I have often wished that I had such a list. A random sampling of papers for this information could teach us a lot about the culture of research.

Dr. Last:

Who will conduct this auditing? Will it be something that could be applied to all journals, including small, low-budget operations, like the one I run, or will it be something that is done primarily by the large and widely circulated mainstream scientific journals?

Dr. Rennie:

Journals would cooperate. The idea would be that journals, perhaps the International Committee of Medical Journal Editors (the Vancouver group) or an expansion thereof, would agree to do this together.

Dr. Koshland:

My own instinct is that the way to solve the problem of fraud or misconduct is to require thorough investigations and severe penalties. There was one mention about recovery of damages.

The greatest damage is to other research workers who spend months or years thinking that some result is true, only to find that their time has been wasted. Some kind of civil action or actual damages, in addition to the loss of a career, is not inappropriate.

But Dr. Rennie's idea of an audit is a good one, as long as it is an experiment. That is, we do need the data, and we must have some credibility with the people who are questioning us. I presume that this would be something like a National Science Foundation grant, where you do a random sample that would justify it, not put it in the federal bureaucracy.

Dr. Rennie:

I would want very much to keep it out of the federal bureaucracy, so that we can all respect this as a matter of science and learn something from it. We do not want to set up a great machine that will merely grind forward heartlessly.

Dr. Koshland:

Dr. Bailar's statistics, I think, are good; if it turns out that only a small number of authors are producing fraudulent work, you do not want to set up a large, expensive bureaucracy to go after them.

The statement about maintaining the credibility of the scientific institutions is absolutely correct. We have lived a rather charmed life, and I do not think there are many cases of fraud; there are more cases of other kinds of misconduct. But we are going to have to develop fair and thorough procedures.

One of the delusions is to have some outside group conduct the audit in a highly technical manner. It has never worked. The Nuclear Regulatory Commission is always made up of nuclear engineers; scientists don't want to serve on those committees. I think the best institution to do audits is the university, because it can require people in departments outside science, if needed, to serve, just as they serve on animal regulatory committees.

For the recent fraud investigations at the National Institutes of Health, it was hard to get scientists within the community even to participate, but if the alternative is to start asking lawyers to serve on scientific committees, to acquire the expertise and do all the things that are needed for a thorough investigation, my instincts are that the institutions will be better suited than editors to conduct a thorough investigation.

Aren't we editors equally suspect because we are part of the scientific community and therefore will be no more exempt from criticism than, say, departments of biology?

Dr. Relman:

I do not share the enthusiasm for the idea of an audit. I take the view, as Dr. Angell has, that an audit would not prevent fraud. Once there is a checklist, if that is what we set up, then scientists who are going to commit fraud will just see to it that they have the evidence to meet the checklist.

The only way to be sure is to be there to see what was done. The adroit malefactor will have the record that is necessary to pass the checklist. The checklist is not going to be a reliable way of detecting fraud. It seems to me that, no matter how simple the design, audits would be a nightmare of confusion, misunderstanding, and misapprehension. I think they would erode the whole fabric of trust and collegiality in science. I think it is a very bad idea.

I suggest, instead, a simple and more acceptable way to prevent fraud: Almost no work nowadays is published by one person; virtually everything has at least two authors, but when fraud is committed, it is rarely a conspiracy among several people. It is usually the work of one person, who somehow gets the others to go along without knowing it, just by putting their names on the paper.

If, as part of the process of accepting papers, we made all the authors certify not only that they have read and approved the paper, but that they are prepared to stand behind the validity of the data and accept full responsibility for the honesty of the work, the situation would change immediately. All the cases of fraud that I know of have involved ignorant authors, who accepted their inclusion as authors without the responsibility of knowing that the work had been done.

Dr. Rennie:

I could not agree more. This is not a good idea for the prevention of fraud. It would be more a way of finding out about the crudest forms of Darsee's sort of fraud, the fraud that Congress has questioned and that will influence research findings. First, I think the plan about getting coauthors to sign off is wise; then the coauthors cannot claim to be surprised to find their names on papers they know nothing about. But it would be encouraging not to have a paper that listed large numbers of patients who turned out not to exist. And you could show that pretty quickly. I am not saying that this will prevent fraud. I am not saying that it will scare people. But it will yield some sort of rate of prevalence of the crudest sort of malfeasance.

Dr. Singer:

I think that we scientists are sometimes worse than the lawyers. Lawyers understand that laws do not stop everything. I agree with you that this proposal would not prevent fraud; it might not even stop most of it. But it is a step that can be taken. It has the advantage of providing data, as Dr. Rennie has emphasized, and that part of it appeals to me a great deal.

Dr. Relman:

But we have never, until now anyway, asked coauthors to assume publicly, on the record, that kind of responsibility.

Dr. Singer:

I understand that, but at least when I trained, we were taught to assume that each author had contributed to a paper and knew what was in it. I think that the random experimental audit notion—actually we need to call it by another name, not "audit"—has the advantage of generating data, which could help us to understand the extent of the problem.

Editors and the Problems of Authorship: Rulemakers or Gatekeepers?

EDWARD J. HUTH

An invitation to discuss authorship implies that current practices in authorship are presenting us with questions for which some of us would like to find answers. What does need our attention? What can we do to prevent or change what we see and do not like?

THE PREMISES UNDERLYING CRITERIA FOR AUTHORSHIP

A judgment, or even a vague sense, that not all is well with authorship implies that we are judging it against standards, that we are looking at authorship with some premises in mind. These must be made explicit, lest I suggest solutions that might be unacceptable to editors and authors with differing premises. The central premise was stated succinctly by Bentley Glass, an eminent biologist and former chairman of the Council of Biology Editors, in his 1965 essay[5] in *Science* on the ethical basis of science: We must be able to trust others. That need for trust was amplified in Chapter 1 of the fifth edition of the *CBE Style Manual:*[4]

> Scientists can proceed with confidence only if they can assume that the previously reported facts on which their work is based are indeed correct. Thus all scientists have an unwritten contract with their contemporaries and those whose work will follow to provide observations honestly obtained, recorded, and published.

The first premise that follows from that position is that the only persons who can be and should be called authors are those who report their own work and have been closely enough engaged with it to defend what they report as work that has been "honestly obtained, recorded, and published." Authors are those who are accountable to the scientific community for what they say in a paper and who can and will respond to questions about content. A second premise is that authors are those who take public responsibility for what is *not* in a paper; scientific papers are necessarily short accounts of the work actually carried out, and we must be willing to accept that some omissions of what was actually done do not keep a paper from being a fully adequate scientific document.

CRITERIA FOR AUTHORSHIP AND COAUTHORSHIP

Those premises are central in criteria for authorship developed and published by several scientific and professional bodies. Among the criteria of the American Chemical Society[1] for coauthorship is the judgment that coauthorship can be given to "all those persons who have made significant contributions to the work reported and who share responsibility and accountability for the results." The American College Personnel Association notes that its "members who agree to cooperate with another individual in . . . publication must cooperate . . . with equal regard for the completeness and accuracy of the information provided."[2] The American Psychological Association states that authorship is "for persons who . . . hold primary responsibility for a published work."[3] The Endocrine Society states that "a co-author's signature on the copyright release form submitted with the manuscript indicates that the co-author has had a part in the writing and final editing of the report, has been given a copy of the manuscript, and agrees to share responsibility and accountability for the results."[11] The criteria of the Council of Biology Editors[4] and the International Committee of Medical Journal Editors[9] likewise give responsibility for a published work the central place in their statements on authorship.

EVIDENCE OF IRRESPONSIBLE AUTHORSHIP

What is the evidence that some authors of published papers do not meet the central criterion of responsibility?

Number of authors

Many of us sense that we have been seeing a steady rise for a decade or two in the average number of authors per paper published. That perception is supported by calculation of the average number of authors per paper in a number of individual journals and groups of journals. The point is made adequately by some data that I gathered for a paper I prepared for a committee of the Institute of Medicine.[7] The data (Figure 1) show an exponential rise in the average number of authors per paper in the *New England Journal of Medicine* between 1915 and 1985; the rise was much the same for *Annals of Internal Medicine*. Data from *Science Citation Index* (SCI)[8] show a similar trend in a large group of journals. The SCI data show much smaller average numbers of authors per paper, but the data come from journals representing many disciplines; in some of them (as in mathematics and the history of science, for example), single authorship is characteristic, not exceptional. The rise in the average number of authors per paper in medical journals has been

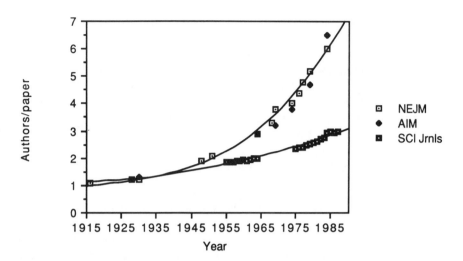

Figure 1. Average numbers of authors per paper. Upper curve, exponential fitted to data from number of years between 1915 and 1985 on average number of authors per paper published in *New England Journal of Medicine*; note that points for *Annals of Internal Medicine* lie close to this line. Lower curve, third-order polynomial curve fitted to data from *Science Citation Index*. *Science Citation Index* data represent journals in many disciplines, not just clinical medicine. Reprinted with permission of Institute of Medicine, copyright holder of paper for which it was prepared.[7]

judged occasionally to be a post-World War II phenomenon related to the great stimulus to medical research from National Institutes of Health funding, but the trend seems to have started many years before.

Number of authors and the work reported

Is the rising number of authors per paper evidence of irresponsible authorship? There is no clear answer. Biomedical science is more complex than it was 70 years ago. Rigorously conducted research might need more brains and hands. In some scientific fields, such as high-energy particle physics, research carried out with costly and complex accelerators and detectors is often reported in papers with 60-90 authors, and some papers have carried close to 200 authors. Two students of the scientific literature have suggested that there is a close link between the amount of money invested in a piece of research and the number of authors that its reports will carry.[6] But even if we can identify swelling authorship as a consequence of social pressure, should we accept this change? What should be our position when we judge the rising numbers against editors' standards for authorship[9] requiring that all authors of a paper have been sufficiently involved in the design of a study, in the collection and analysis of its data, and in the writing or revision of the paper to be able to take public responsibility for the paper? Such standards suggest that a typical research report in the biomedical sciences can legitimately have no more than three or four authors. For some papers, such as case reports, even that appears excessive; the intellectual contribution of substance surely comes from only one or two persons.

Objections to the rising number of authors

Observers of biomedical literature other than editors can properly ask what is objectionable about large numbers of authors per paper. I suggest that those who raise that question probably base their standards for authorship on the premise that immediate credit is the proper basis for authorship, rather than the capacity, as judged by editors' standards, to take responsibility. The number of authors per paper in excess of a number that represents true capacity to be responsible for the paper's content does debase the currency of authorship, if one might coin a Gresham's law of authorship. But such debasement is not the leading concern of editors. We are asked to ensure as far as we can that what we publish is reliable information. If we publish papers by authors who cannot truly be responsible for what appears under their names, we might be irresponsible ourselves. But how far can editors go toward guaranteeing that authorship is legitimate by our standards? The most striking example of this problem in recent years came out of the Darsee affair. When Darsee's failures as an author were uncovered, some of his coauthors did not admit that they had not been close enough to the reported work to be able to defend it; they simply washed off the dirt and did not explain how it had gotten onto their hands.[10] How could editors who published any of the Darsee papers have known the legitimacy of Darsee's coauthors when they accepted those papers?

WHAT CAN EDITORS DO?

If we conclude that editors must take some responsibility for the legitimacy of authorship of papers that they publish, what can we editors do, if anything, to assure ourselves that we have gone as far as we can to act responsibly? I suggest that we have three options: We can do nothing; we can serve as rulemakers; or we can act as gatekeepers.

Editors as rulemakers

Do we know whether authors know our rules for conduct in authorship? I have said that clear standards for authorship have been published by some professional societies and associations of editors. But they are probably not widely known in authors' circles. In preparing the paper for a committee of the Institute of Medicine, I surveyed 14 medical schools with questions about authorship and other matters.[7] I found that few medical schools have explicit guidelines on authorship. In defense of authors' ignorance of our standards for authorship, I must point out that journals' information-for-authors pages generally lack explicit statements on authorship. If we are going to try to ensure responsible authorship, we must start by making our standards for authorship clear. Editors' associations could collaborate in providing academic administrators with copies of standards. We could go further and require that authors certify that they have adequately participated in the work they report and that they have taken part in preparing the report in accordance with our standards. Perhaps the social pressure that leads to the demands for authorship as credit would simply ride over such efforts to raise awareness and acceptance of authorship as responsibility, but I believe that we have not yet tried to make our standards well and widely known.

Editors as gatekeepers

Our alternative is to become gatekeepers. We could decide individually or collectively on the number of authors per paper that we believe to be the maximum that can function as a group in research so as to be able to take responsibility for a paper. Papers submitted with more than that number of authors could be accepted for publication only if the authorship were converted to a corporate or collective designation. We could then accept an appended acknowledgment of specific individual contributions by the contributors. The suggestion is not original with me. Already some papers arrive in journal offices with three or four named authors and an additional designation of a named collective research group; presumably, the persons named as authors are writers and the rest are contributors in a smaller way. Such papers often carry acknowledgments of the additional contributions.

My bias is for gatekeeping. It arises in part from my firm view that only smaller numbers of persons can truly serve as authors in the sense of being responsible for what they put on paper. But I also see gatekeeping as the simpler solution, the one more easily carried out. Certification of authorship would multiply the number of pieces of paper to be moved around among authors and to be filed in editorial offices. But I am not sure that gatekeeping would be agreed to by all journals. Unless a major fraction of journals were to agree on and enforce such a policy, the gatekeepers would run a high risk of losing papers to journals with less rigorous standards.

THE BEST SOLUTION?

Despite my bias, I believe that editors alone probably cannot enforce authentic authorship. A solution to irresponsible authorship will come only from consensus among authors, institutions, and editors on an acceptable definition of authorship. Editors cannot function by fiat.

We have little certain knowledge of the extent of irresponsible or gratuitous authorship. I believe that we know even less about authors' standards for authorship. The data I cite indicate to me that standards of authorship well known to editors are little known in the wider academic community. If my view is correct, our first step might be to find some means, perhaps through the Association of American Medical Colleges, to disseminate explicit standards for authorship agreed on by such organizations as the Council of Biology Editors. Such standards should be widely known in all schools and departments of biologic and medical sciences. The social pressures for distributed authorship might be too great to deflect with rational standards, but we cannot properly come to that conclusion until we have tried to plant our standards in the soil in which they might take root.

REFERENCES

1. American Chemical Society. Ethical guidelines to publication of chemical research. In: Dodd JS, ed. The ACS Style Guide. Washington, DC: American Chemical Society; 1986:217-22.
2. American College Personnel Association. Statement of ethical and professional standards. J Coll Student Personnel 1981; 22:184-9.
3. American Psychological Association. Authorship. In: Publication Manual of the American Psychological Association. 3rd ed. Washington, DC: American Psychological Association; 1983:20-1.
4. Council of Biology Editors Style Manual Committee. Ethical conduct in authorship and publication. In: CBE Style Manual: A Guide for Authors, Editors, and Publishers in the Biological Sciences. 5th ed. Bethesda, Maryland: Council of Biology Editors; 1983:1-6.
5. Glass B. The ethical basis of science. Science 1965; 150:1257-8.
6. Hirsch W, Singleton JF. Research support, multiple authorship and publication in sociological journals, 1936-1964. [Unpublished preprint, 1965.] Cited in Price, DJD, Beaver DD. Collaboration in an invisible college. Am Psychol; 1966; 21:1011-18.
7. Huth EJ. Scientific Authorship and Publication: Process, Standards, Problems, Suggestions. Washington DC: Institute of Medicine, National Academy of Sciences; 1988.
8. Institute for Scientific Information. SCI Science Citation Index 1986 Annual: Guide and Lists of Source Publications. Philadelphia, PA: Institute for Scientific Information; 1987: 27-9.
9. International Committee of Medical Journal Editors. Uniform requirements for manuscripts submitted to biomedical journals. Ann Intern Med 1988;108:258-65.
10. Relman AS. Lessons from the Darsee affair. N Engl J Med 1983; 308:1415-17.
11. The Endocrine Society Publications Committee. Ethical guidelines for publication of research. J Clin Endocrinol Metab 1988; 66:1-2.

The Responsibilities of Authorship

VERNON N. HOUK
STEPHEN B. THACKER

The responsibilities of authorship in a collaborative study can be discussed from the standpoint of the principles involved. I will discuss these principles in general and the principles of primary authorship in particular. I am also going to touch on the time at which authors should be selected, and I will discuss briefly how disagreements about authorship should be handled and list some of the problems associated with writing a paper.

PRINCIPLES OF AUTHORSHIP

Authorship implies the contribution of thought and effort and an understanding of and professional responsibility for the work as published. It should be limited to persons who have contributed substantially and creatively to the investigation or study—that is, to those who originated the concept, designed the protocol, or were responsible for the conduct of the work. The routine performance of technical or management responsibilities should not be construed as a substantial contribution.

There is neither a single criterion nor any definitive algorithm for determining authorship. Each project presents a particular set of contributions, and decisions about authorship must be made on the basis of the collaborators' mix of skills and contributions. The point at which collaborators enter a study depends on their expertise. Authorship, therefore, is based on active participation throughout the study or in critical phases of the study. That participation consists, for example, of applying thought, expertise, experience, and appraisal creatively to further the progress of the collaborative study. Qualification for authorship is tied closely to the combined contribution of ideas, "hands-on" work, and responsibility for specific expertise.

In the selection of authors and primary authors, eight principles of authorship should be considered:

- Contribution of ideas.
- Design and writing of an approved protocol.
- Responsibility for observations and acquisition of data.
- Scientific leadership in execution of the study.
- Analysis and critical interpretation of data (including reviewing literature and evaluating evidence from previous studies).
- Writing (drafting, revising, and reviewing) of the manuscript.

- Responsibility for final manuscript.
- Ability to defend part of publication related to a professional discipline.

A minimal requirement for authorship is active participation in the conception and design of the work; measurement, analysis, or interpretation of data; drafting or revising of the manuscript or review of critical sections of it; and responsibility for the final version of the manuscript.

PRINCIPLES OF PRIMARY AUTHORSHIP

As with authorship, there is no criterion or set of criteria for selecting the primary or lead author, but those who meet the following criteria warrant consideration:

- *Outstanding contributions.* The primary author has shown continued interest—that is, has made positive, creative, and reliable contributions, has demonstrated leadership during the study, and is the person who "made it happen."
- *Major intellectual input.* Throughout the study, the primary author has generated ideas on the study design and modifications, on ensuring appropriate and eligible specimens, on productively conducting the study, on solving measurement problems, on analyzing and interpreting data in a particular way, and on preparing reports.
- *Active participation in work.* The primary author did the most work, made the study succeed, provided intellectual leadership, and tabulated and interpreted the data.
- *Key scientific leadership.* The primary author provided overall scientific guidance and direction.
- *Originality of contribution.* The primary author contributed an original technique or method that proved to be a highly important basis of the paper.
- *Major feature of manuscript.* In most scientific papers, one feature is of major importance: This author thought of that feature and actively developed it.
- *Subject matter.* The primary author participated actively by contributing positive ideas and doing productive "hands-on" work.

Primary authors should be chosen mainly through an assessment of their contributions to the conception, planning, and execution of the study. When two or more investigators have contributed equally to a project, the primary author should be the one who by mutual consent writes the paper. In rare cases, usually when the investigators have procrastinated, management might assign the primary author. No one has a right to primary authorship solely on the basis of expertise in a discipline or subject.

WHEN SHOULD AUTHORS BE SELECTED?

The committed collaborators should openly discuss authorship and select the authors as soon as responsibilities, workload, and staff assignments for the project are determined.

The committed collaborators, having agreed on a design, should tentatively decide on the authors and keep management informed of the decisions. During the study, the collaboraters might need to revise the tentative decisions on authorship. In any case, they should make a final decision before the first draft of the article is begun.

WHEN SHOULD THE PRIMARY AUTHOR BE SELECTED?

Primary authorship should be associated with natural leadership, the willing assumption of responsibilities in a major professional aspect of the work, and the demonstrated ability to ensure that the study objectives are met. The committed collaborators should select a coordinating leader and select leaders in distinct sectors of expertise, each of whom might qualify as the primary author. The primary author should be selected through negotiation among collaborators. Primary authorship depends more on a person's ability, expertise, and contributions than on the importance of the person's discipline in relation to the proposed publication.

In some circumstances, authorship may be assumed by a group, such as an expert committee, or by an institution, such as a university or a federal agency. In 1987 and 1988, the Centers for Disease Control (CDC) published a series of papers based on studies of Vietnam veterans. A unit of more than 50 persons was formed to conduct the so-called Agent Orange studies. One, the Vietnam Experience Study, included a cohort of about 18,000 men and was designed to assess morbidity and mortality among Vietnam and non-Vietnam veterans. Authorship of the initial papers published from the study was given to the Vietnam Experience Study group, rather than to individual investigators. CDC assumed primary responsibility for the design, analysis, and interpretation of study results.

APPEAL

Disagreements about authorship are difficult to deal with under any circumstances. If arbitration is required to determine authorship or primary authorship in a collaborative study, an effort should be made first to settle the matter among the collaborators. At no level of arbitration should authorship be determined on the basis of organizational or bureaucratic exigencies. It is unacceptable and unethical, for example, to decide that the first author of a paper should be a person in a specified organization because it is that organization's "turn" to have a primary author. Management is responsible for ensuring that such organizational balancing is done in accord with the principles of authorship.

WRITING THE PAPER

Problems can arise if participation in writing the paper is assumed to be the major or only basis for authorship. "Authorship" assumes responsibility for the content of a proposed publication in the author's area of expertise. In collaborative studies, collaborators should write the portions of the paper that concern their own expertise. The primary author should provide leadership and should coordinate the contributions of the collaborators. "Primary authorship" assumes leadership in writing, knowledge of and active participation in the creative phases of most of the study, and recognition by collaborating peers that the primary author deserves to be in that position.

The responsible author understands the purpose, methods, analysis, and results of a manuscript and can interpret the findings effectively. That person knows the context in which a scientific investigation is undertaken. The responsible author knows why a particular study was done, why a given scientific problem was addressed instead of others, and why the investigation was conducted in a particular way. The primary author understands the roles of investigators and obtains agreement on authorship and on issues of scientific dispute.

Ultimately, each responsible author must be able to defend the conduct of the study and its results.

Authorship, Acknowledgment, and Other Credits

CONSTANCE C. CONRAD

It has taken me a long time to recognize that, in talking about authorship, and in particular about authors, we are not using the first definition given in the dictionary—the author as the person who writes. Writing is probably the least valued of all the skills that bring an article into print. A piece of evidence for that is how often we hear debated whether statisticians who contribute to papers should be authors, compared with how seldom we hear discussed whether technical writers or editors should be offered authorship. That should have been a clue to me.

Writing *was* what authorship and being an author meant. That is no longer true. Getting the ideas and concepts into words and sentences and getting those onto paper (or onto disks and video screens) *was* authorship. That was what authorship meant for most of history since writing became possible, and that is what authorship means for many people today. In the worlds of fiction, poetry, journalism, and the humanities, authors are writers. It is in science that authorship has come to have a different meaning. It is in science that the second definition of author—the originator, beginner, or creator—is the prevailing and emphasized meaning.

Authorship in science emphasizes creation, not writing. And the complexity of authorship reflects the complexity of creation, the complexity of doing science today. That complexity derives from advances in knowledge and technology and from the vastness of the connections, resources, and skills required, which are no longer controlled by or belong to one person or even to a few persons. The growth and proliferation of science and technology, our growing interdependence, the processes, techniques, and methods for finding answers and solving problems—these all mandate an interdisciplinary approach, a condition that a single person can rarely meet in its fullest demands.

Even if the renaissance person existed, the difficulty would remain, for in public health that person must work where the problems are. The would-be problem-solver and author must gain access to the cases, to the data, to the geographic area. The would-be author must gain access to technical resources, to the persons who possess the skills that the author does not have. That is one way in which authorship is used as an incentive, as an inducement for cooperation. It becomes a trading chip in an economic game. I will bargain for what you have that I want, and what I have to offer is authorship. I hope its value to you will be high enough that it will buy what I want and need from you—whether that is permission to come into your hospital, an invitation to your state to investigate an epidemic, or your technical skill in analyzing data or running highly sophisticated equipment.

The utilitarian ethic is at work; the end justifies the means. The important thing is to finish the work, solve the problem, and get the information out to the public to decrease disease, halt epidemics, and make the world a healthier place. The calculus of utility balances out in favor of results, not in favor of preservation of honesty in authorship or in the prevention of deception of the public as to responsibility for the article.

The pressures to expand authorship come from other sources as well. These are the common and familiar ones: the superior who demands it, unwritten rules that give authorship to those who make the primary author's facilities available, and the needs of fellow climbers in the academic hierarchy to publish. All those pressures create the opportunity for future reciprocity in the extension of authorship benefits. Auctorial inflation has many parents.

The question of authorship can be seen as a question of distributive justice. What is fair? How should authorship be distributed for fairness to be achieved? Entitlement theory as voiced by John Locke says that we develop ownership of previously unowned property as we mix our labor with it. We own our labor; as it permeates the other property, our rights to that property grow. The reverse can happen, however. One's labor can be mixed with a property and with others' labor; instead of gaining the property, one loses one's labor. These guidelines from philosophy might help to explain our general instincts about authorship's rights and wrongs, but they are not at all helpful in the specifics.

Authors, technical editors, journal editors, and professional groups have been wrestling with the problem of authorship for some time, and progress has been made in developing definitions and guidelines. One helpful and significant contribution has been the publication of "Uniform Requirements for Manuscripts Submitted to Biomedical Journals,"[2] developed by the International Committee of Medical Journal Editors. The third edition of the requirements appeared in 1988. Clarity is being gained about the contributions required to justify authorship. Concomitantly, clarity is being gained about what does *not* justify authorship. Authorship has evolved in the definition put forward. The identity of the necessary components has been refined, and the formula to be applied has been stated. Authorship, according to those guidelines,[2] requires sufficient participation in the work to take public responsibility for its content, as well as substantial contributions to *all* the following:

- "Conception and design, or analysis and interpretation of data."
- "Drafting the article or revising it critically for important intellectual content."
- "Final approval of the version to be published."

In 1984, Nicholas G. Fotion and I published an article in the *Annals of Internal Medicine,* "Authorship and Other Credits,"[1] in which we noted that the current system of giving credit is unsatisfactory and could be partly to blame for auctorial inflation. There might be persons associated with an article who do not fully meet the criteria for authorship, but who make important and perhaps indispensable contributions that deserve more than an acknowledgment. We propose that credit be given to such persons, but not as authors.

Our model comes from the television and film industries. When the credits roll, persons are credited for what they have done. Producers, directors, and specialists in makeup, costume, and lighting each receive credit. British films seem to provide especially creative titles for contributors—or maybe they are just more faithful in giving credit where credit is due to the second boom lifter-uppers and the title-board clappers.

For credit to be given for contributions that are less than full authorship, proper titles would have to be devised and the location for this credit in the publication determined. However, more than that will be necessary. The credit must come to be recognized as having value in the world that now rewards authorship alone. Contributions for which persons have received credit should be listed on their curricula vitae. Professional societies can rethink their practices, and members can exert their influence in their work settings.

The third edition of the uniform requirements not only addresses the issue of what determines authorship, but also says what does not. Participation only in the acquisition of funding, in the collection of data, or in the general supervision of a research group is not sufficient for authorship. The requirements say that, when it is appropriate, papers should contain acknowledgments of general support, of technical help, and of financial and material support. They move toward creating categories of credit by suggesting that the functions of contributions that do not meet the criteria for justifying authorship should be named. Examples are given: "scientific adviser," "critical review of study proposal," "data collection," and "participation in clinical trial."[1] The requirements further suggest that acknowledgments of technical help be placed in a paragraph separate from the other contributions. That movement is in the right direction. But will it be enough?

Most probably not. The credits need to be given increased status. A middle category between the byline and the acknowledgment is needed. Also, databases do not list acknowledgments, let alone this new proposed category of credits. Until the credits can receive their proper value and be recognized as a coin of the realm in exchange for a proper portion of the benefits of power, prestige, position, and promotion that now accrue solely to authorship, we will be peddling Confederate money.

Professional groups can standardize the categories in which contributions should be recognized, develop guidelines for their use, stimulate their inclusion on curricula vitae, promote their use in professional assessment, and find a resolution to the database problem. Authorship could then be restored to its original meanings.

REFERENCES

1. Fotion N, Conrad CC. Authorship and other credits. Ann Intern Med. 1984;100: 592-4.
2. International Committee of Medical Journal Editors. Uniform requirements for manuscripts submitted to biomedical journals. Ann Intern Med 1988;108:258-65.

Pressure to Publish:
Tenure and Promotion Considerations

ROBERT G. PETERSDORF*

In May 1985, a charge of research fraud was made against Dr. Robert Slutsky, a former member of the Departments of Medicine and Radiology at the University of California, San Diego, where I was dean of the medical school.[3] Following established procedures of the medical school, I appointed an ad hoc committee to investigate the merits of the charge. I instituted those procedures in the wake of the Darsee case. They were based on guidelines issued by the Association of American Medical Colleges.[1] The committee examined Slutsky's papers and other records and concluded that fabricated research findings had been submitted and published. Those fabrications included the following:

• Stating the use of procedures that were not used.
• Inflating the number of animals studied.
• Using data obtained from one research protocol and claiming that the data had been obtained from animal or human subjects studied under an incompatible protocol.
• Adding clinical data to a paper on patients who could not be identified and for whom no human-subjects committee protocol was on file.
• Altering levels of statistical significance.
• Using previously reported figures and data, particularly in the methods-validation sections, without reference to where they had been published.
• Using the names of various coauthors without their knowledge or permission and identifying this practice as granting a favor.

Slutsky had also falsified some of his qualifications and bibliography when he submitted them in application for a faculty appointment in the Department of Radiology.

After the committee submitted its report detailing fraudulent statements in three manuscripts, the three papers were withdrawn. In accordance with procedures previously approved by the faculty of the school of medicine, I appointed a second investigating committee to review all of Slutsky's publications in an attempt to decide whether any others were invalid and to determine the role, if any, of the coauthors and supervisors in the fraud. The second

---

*Because Dr. Petersdorf was unable to attend, his paper was presented by John F. Sherman, executive vice president of the Association of American Medical Colleges.

committee was also to determine the genesis of the research fraud and make recommendations to prevent future occurrences or at least to detect them earlier.

Acting through his attorney, Slutsky withdrew 15 published papers, apparently in response to a letter of retraction sent by the ad hoc committee to the journal that had published two of the three papers investigated previously.

The members of the committee agreed that in scientific research authors must be prepared to prove the validity of their published results. In view of the proven unreliability of some of Slutsky's statements uncovered by the prior ad hoc committee, the investigating committee took the position that the work that only Slutsky could support could not be accepted as valid. The committee accepted as fact the basic honesty of Slutsky's coauthors and agreed to accept their statements of personal knowledge of the data from collection to publication as sufficient evidence of validity. In such instances, the committee did not require re-examination of the original data. However, if the coauthors could not vouch for the validity of the collected data, were unfamiliar with the analysis of the data, or had no knowledge of the accuracy of the final publication in recording actual methods and results, the paper was considered questionable.

The committee sent a response form to nearly all the 93 coauthors, asking them to explain their roles in the research and writing of each publication.

A second form was developed to determine whether anyone other than Slutsky had examined or collected the data from the original experiments. If a coauthor was confident of the reported data and methods, was familiar with the data analysis, and could assure the committee that there were no invalid changes in the final publications, the paper was considered valid. Eventually, all coauthors were consulted.

After the final round of consultation, the committee classified each paper as valid, questionable, or fraudulent. Classifying a paper as valid required reliable testimony on the availability of documentary proof that data had been collected and analyzed by someone other than Slutsky and that the publications reflected the actual results. The results were reviewed by the committee: 77 of the 137 papers (including reviews) were deemed valid, and 12 were deemed fraudulent. Forty-eight papers remained in the "questionable" category, because no coauthor could guarantee each step of the process. It was impossible to determine whether those papers were valid, because the original data and records had been lost or destroyed.

Committee interviews with a number of coauthors revealed a consistent story of how Slutsky fabricated data but managed to escape detection for so long. The factors that culminated in extensive research fraud can be grouped in three categories: those related to the investigator's psychologic drives, those associated with the academic environment, and those dealing with the attitudes and actions of the investigator's supervisors.

Slutsky asserted independence early in his training by assuming complete responsibility for putting projects together and for writing the reports. He avoided review of his writing or his data by others. Although he showed his supervisors summaries of the data, he hid the original data and destroyed the records. He would not produce lists of patient names from clinical studies for other investigators. He eschewed sharing research protocols and avoided supervision. He encouraged others to share responsibility for his research, whether valid or invalid, by putting their names on papers to which they had contributed little or nothing. In some cases, he forged his coauthors' signatures on copyright-permission forms.

Many of his coauthors were embarrassed to ask him to remove their names from his papers. Some encouraged coauthorship by insisting that they have their names on papers if their laboratory space had been used, even though they had made no substantive contributions to the work. Publications were rarely reviewed by colleagues or senior division or department members.

It is likely that Slutsky fabricated data from the beginning of his career at the university. His habits of keeping original data to himself and of not permitting review of manuscripts by coauthors even when such review was possible were important elements in his attitude toward manipulation of data and descriptions to suit a preconceived conclusion. For many years, he added the names of various colleagues to his papers as a "gift" unrelated to their contributions to the work. He sometimes added names without advising the persons to whom he presented such a gift and without giving them an opportunity to review manuscripts before publication.

The committee was satisfied that none of the coauthors had participated in or had knowledge of fraudulent practices; some were trainees and were simply unable to check the work of their superior. In some cases, their names were used on manuscripts without their knowledge or permission. Slutsky's unwillingness to share raw data or to allow others to perform analyses or to participate in manuscript preparation and revision inhibited detection of invalid statements before publication. The committee concluded that, if the coauthors had exercised their rights and responsibilities, fraud would have been readily detected.

Initially, there was considerable resistance on the part of some of the coauthors, but eventually most of them accepted as essential the committee's demand to review their work. That response was heartening, but at the same time it was disappointing that none of the coauthors came forward to say, "This paper is one that I am not sure is valid, and I think it should be withdrawn."

We need to ask how this situation could develop. It might have begun with the painfully familiar "premed syndrome," which begins with fierce competition in college, emphasis on grades, and people who become 22-hour-a-day study machines. The syndrome was analyzed in detail in the May 1985 issue of *Washington Monthly*.[2] Some quotes from the article are instructive:

> A recent study of 400 medical students by doctors at two Chicago medical schools revealed that *88 percent* of the subjects had cheated at least once while they were premeds. The researchers found widespread cynicism among their subjects, as demonstrated by frequent agreements with statements such as, "people have to cheat in this 'dog-eat-dog' world."

The majority of students continue to cheat in medical school.

> The most disturbing finding . . . was that "there was a continuum from cheating in college, to cheating in medical school in didactic areas, to cheating in clerkships and patient care. . . . Cheating in medical school may be a predictor of cheating in medical practice."

The culture in which we train our young promotes cheating.

> From crib notes in organic chemistry to Medicaid fraud and fudged results of medical research: the connection may be there.

A second factor in the pathogenesis of scientific fraud is big science itself. Faculties of medicine serve as an example. From 1965 to 1985, research funds available to medical schools quintupled. That increase was accompanied by a substantial increase in the size of training programs. The number of house staff tripled, the numbers of graduate students and postdoctoral fellows increased markedly, and the number of clinical fellows increased perhaps most of all.

It is not unusual to have as many as 18 fellows in fellowship training groups in internal medicine. I am not convinced that we need that many—either in the academy or in practice. The penchant for procreation not only among program directors of clinical programs, but also among trainers of basic scientists, knows no bounds. They maintain the right to train the progeny of the future, whether or not that results in overpopulation.

What are the consequences of big science? First, the inability to say grace over the large research groups that now exist results in an intermediate layer of junior faculty, many of whom are relatively inexperienced in training others or in supervising research. It also results in group projects. There are not enough ideas; because everyone must be kept busy, everyone works in groups. One consequence is the multiple-author paper. In a randomly chosen issue of one medical journal, the first paper had three authors, the second five, the third 10, the fourth seven, and the fifth five. One consequence is that no paper is ever completely reviewed; almost no paper is reviewed by all its authors. In the old days, the department head read every paper. That is clearly no longer possible, but nowadays even division heads do not read papers, as some in whose divisions fraud occurred now ruefully admit.

A third factor in the pathogenesis of fraud is competition itself. There is the competition to stay alive in science, which means competition for grants. Progressively better priority scores do not mean that science is necessarily better—they only mean that competition for research funds is greater. The necessity for getting a new grant or a competitive renewal requires productivity, and productivity, in turn, requires training of new people who can then publish more papers.

Then there is competition for position; our system of academic promotion is a prime example. Academic promotion committees count and weigh papers, but do not read them. The narrowness of the field in which people work and write naturally makes promotion committees unable to understand the nature of the work. It is much easier, therefore, to judge quantity, not quality. And it is far easier to judge quantity or quality of research than excellence in teaching and in clinical care.

Tenure appointments are guarded jealously, are made with a sense of elitism, and exacerbate competition. Competition among several young faculty members for one tenured slot returns us to the premed syndrome. Tenure is after all only a personnel policy, which in medical schools ensures only a small fraction of a faculty member's income. The good do not need it; because the mediocre use it as a shield, it tends to perpetuate mediocrity.

What should be done to treat and prevent research fraud? I have listed 11 points as follows:

- Peer review of faculty should focus on the quality, and not on the quantity, of work published.
- Each department should develop a procedure to identify the type and degree of participation of every faculty member in each published work. Coauthors must review manuscripts and approve final manuscripts. In fact, journals should require that as a matter of course.
- Peer review, particularly statistical review, should be improved.
- The writing of short papers that encourage fragmentation and republication should be discouraged.
- Although the independence of an investigator is a virtue, it must be granted only after a long period of careful supervision.
- Original data need to be checked by workers at several levels: graduate students, postdoctoral fellows, and junior and senior faculty members. Graphs or figures are often an intermediate product of research and should be retained. Although data books might clutter up the laboratory, they must be retained for review in case of doubt. That practice should be mandated by universities.
- Faculty members and trainees should be clearly informed of the expectations of the laboratory and the department. Realistic expectations of productivity should be included.
- In this era of big science, principal investigators must be more careful in screening their associates. All too often, researchers are invited to join a laboratory because funds are available to support them or because they

provide extra hands to do the work. Principal investigators must learn to contain the size of their laboratories. From time to time, I have seen the size of a laboratory equated with the quality of work emanating from it. In science, as in all else, big is sometimes beautiful, but often is not.

- Most universities' faculty are required to review all the material submitted for an appointment or promotion before voting on such a promotion. That review is rarely carried out, but it needs to be. The Harvard Medical School has issued a series of guidelines for investigators in scientific research.[4] To encourage review by appointment and promotion committees and at the same time to discourage excessively prolific writing for the sake of getting promoted, the Harvard guidelines suggest limits on the number of papers that can be submitted to a promotion committee: no more than five papers can be submitted for review for appointment as assistant professor, no more than seven for associate professor, and no more than 10 for professor.
- Heads of subdivisions, departments, institutes, and schools should be sufficiently familiar with the laboratories under their administrative purview to be able to make a preliminary investigation when fraud is alleged.
- Each school should have procedures for investigating cases of suspected fraud.

REFERENCES

1. Association of American Medical Colleges. The maintenance of high ethical standards in the conduct of research. J Med Educ 1982; 57:895-902.
2. Barrett PM. The premed machine. Washington Monthly 1985; (May): 40-51.
3. Engler RL, Covell JW, Friedman PJ, Kitcher PS, Peters RM. Misrepresentation and responsibility in medical research. N Engl J Med 1987; 317:1383–9.
4. Harvard University Faculty of Medicine. Guidelines for Investigators in Scientific Research. Cambridge, Mass.: Harvard University; 1988.

Open Discussion

Dr. Koshland:

I agree with all the speakers that authorship is extremely important and that we cannot afford to have it diminished in quality and responsibility. But defining it and its degrees is difficult.

Dr. Huth:

I don't think Dr. Conrad and I disagree as much as we might seem to, but I do have some reservations about some of the points she makes.

First, I agree with the general proposition that important or pressing social motives account for much of what goes on in determining authorship. Unless there is a substantial change in ethical judgments about the nature of authorship in the academic community, we will continue to see the rising curve I have demonstrated.

Dr. Conrad may have gone too far when she pointed to the simplistic definition in the dictionary about writing papers. I agree that in important research you can't have six persons sitting down at a table and writing a paper together. But there are examples of papers with large numbers of authors in which a rigorous process of reviewing successive drafts of papers has been carried out and in which all parties take responsibility for content.

Dr. Houk:

I am from an institution where number of papers does not determine rank, promotion, or salary. But there is something to being the author of a good paper; authorship is a matter of pride.

One of the most significant public-health papers published in years was on the association between gasoline production and lead in children in the United States.* That work was done principally by Lee Annest and Jim Pirkle, and they should have been listed as the only authors of the paper. Unfortunately, a large group of researchers insisted that their names be added to the paper because of their institutional organization. The citation is now "Annest et al.," instead of "Annest and Pirkle"; that is unfair.

Dr. Koshland:

I have been involved with tenure decisions in four institutions, and in not one case has the number of papers been an issue. Someone who publishes a lot in poor journals never gets promoted over someone who has four or five outstanding papers. As an editor, I dislike salami tactics—dividing one good piece of work into five or six papers. But the tenure matter is not germane.

Dr. Stossel:

Let me describe it from a user's perspective. Suppose that I am an associate professor in a university, and I have just cloned and crystallized a protein that can be used in urinalysis to detect fraud. I am going to collaborate with an x-ray crystallographer in another university. I carefully prepare a sample, and he carries out the x-ray work. There is no way I can understand exactly what he did to obtain the data. However, we have to work together to interpret them. So, I take his numbers and interpret them, and he takes my numbers and interprets them, and together we come out with a package. Now, we are

---

*Annest JL, Pirkle, JL, Makuc D, Neese JW, Bayse DD, Kovar MG. Chronological trend in blood lead levels between 1976 and 1980. N Engl J Med 1983; 308:1373-7.

supposed to sign an oath saying that we are fully familiar with the paper and the techniques involved. That is impossible and meaningless.

A second example: I am an associate professor at Pay and Play University, where my survival depends on grants and I supervise a number of postdoctoral fellows and technicians. We have several projects, and we are competing with Grasp for a Quick Buck University. There are some not-so-good postdoctoral fellows and some great technicians; sometimes the technicians make greater contributions to the work than do the fellows—and vice versa. How we eventually package this and divide it up gets complicated. I have a vision of a great machine. At the end of the day, all these people would go and punch a button, and we would have six creativity units and 13 technical units and five looked-up-article units. Somehow this wisdom would come out the bottom.

I think that the idea of numbers is way overblown, and what really counts is what each person does.

Dr. Koshland:

Let's say there is a professor—I will call him Sherlock Holmes—who is the head of a laboratory, maybe a big one. He has a faithful technician named Watson, who carries out his research. Holmes is interested in specific medical problems. Watson carries out the bioassays, perhaps hemoglobin measurements, faithfully working for him for years, so Holmes knows he can depend on those assays. Watson really doesn't keep up with the literature and couldn't write the paper, but what he is assigned to do is important. Would it be inappropriate to list both Watson and Holmes as authors on a paper, according to our definitions?

Dr. Huth:

My answer would be yes and no. At the Fermi Laboratory, expensive, large-scale research is being carried out. The critical part of the observations has to do with the design and construction of a huge detector, a ring, that extends from the floor to the ceiling and is slid into the beam line on a railroad track. The design and supervision of the construction of the ring are absolutely critical. The quality of the observations depends on it. Here we have a large group, approximately 190 persons, and many of them will probably have their names on a paper published as a result of their technical contributions. Those people are indispensable.

Dr. Koshland:

Would they understand? It really seems unlikely to me that all those people would understand the details of the work. They probably understand what it is in the same way that Dr. Stossel understands what the crystallographer did in his example.

Dr. Huth:

But Dr. Stossel is correct. I agree with him that we could get ourselves into a labyrinth of definitions of authorship down to the last period, but I don't think we should do that.

We need to get some central principles about authorship into the consciousness of the scientific community. I have the sense that, although we believe that there are standards for authorship, they are not generally known in the scientific community. As a start, we ought to try to plant standards as Dr. Houk has done at the Centers for Disease Control.

Dr. Houk:

By no means should you chalk up six points for this and four points for that to arrive at a mathematical score that decides who the authors will be. Since we put together the ground rules in my organization (incidentally, they were put together by the scientists and represent a consensus), these problems have rarely come to me for adjudication. Before that, much of my time involved settling disputes on authorship. If the consideration of authorship is brought up as part of the design and implementation of a study, the issues resolve themselves. When people from different institutions collaborate, the issues can be arranged beforehand without difficulty and without having each paper have 500 authors.

Dr. Conrad:

I am perfectly happy to live by the standards and definitions of authorship that the group has arrived at collectively. My only concern would be that Watson gets proper credit of one kind or another—credit that is worth something.

Dr. Yankauer:

Most papers—virtually all papers that are published in good journals— are revised at least once, and sometimes three times or more. Should all authors approve every revision? If they are scattered in different institutions, how will that delay publication?

Dr. Huth:

All authors listed on the version that is published should have approved that version. That can cause practical difficulties; but, if we are going to adopt the principle, we should try to stick to it.

Dr. Bracker:

Violations of authorship—honorary authorship and gratuitous authorship—represent fraud, because they involve taking credit for minimal or no contribution. A short article appeared in *Science* explaining that a member of Congress from Oregon intended to introduce legislation that would curb honorary authorship. That sounds ominous to me. I think we should consider whether that would be in our best interest or in the country's best interest.

I would like to see a wide spectrum of journals work with the universities to develop criteria about what constitutes authorship. The peer pressure across the nation that would result from having these criteria would have a good effect. It might not eliminate every abuse and misuse of authorship, but it could help head off threats of federal legislation.

Dr. Huth:

There is a simpler, more practical maneuver that we editors could launch ourselves. I have looked at my own "Information for Authors" page. We do not make a very detailed statement about what we regard as authorship. It would be simple for me, when I send a paper back for revision, to include a detailed statement about what we regard as authorship, even if it does nothing more than raise consciousness in the community. That would be a step forward and is cheap and easy.

Dr. Bracker:

I hope that we would not wind up with 50 detailed definitions of what constitutes authorship; rather, we should promote some kind of agreement that would be acceptable to most people.

Dr. Relman:

I agree that it is desirable to define authorship. The suggestion about editors' doing more than just making a recommendation is sensible; it would go a long way toward solving the problem.

As for the question about Watson and Holmes: If Watson used a technique that was already in the literature and did nothing more—made no other contribution to the work, but simply provided essential technical help—he is not an author by my definition or that of the International Committee of Medical Journal Editors. He should certainly be recognized, but not as an author. However, if Watson had done something creative and original in designing a technique that was particularly valuable in helping to solve the problem, and nothing more, then the question is legitimate. If Watson participated in the conception and design of the experiment and in the analysis of the data, he certainly ought to be an author. I would draw a distinction between routine work that has already been published and described and something original and imaginative that was done for the first time.

The crystallographer at the other institution qualifies as a coauthor, because he has done more than use a well-established technique. He has interacted with the other author in a more substantial way than if he had simply received the material for analysis and sent back the results of his tests. He should have been involved in the design and analysis of the experiment. The authors should have met, and each should know what the other is doing; there should be a shared responsibility.

I see nothing unreasonable, in that instance, about requiring that all coauthors take responsibility not just for their own contributions, but for the integrity and honesty of the work as a whole. There might be times when that criterion would be difficult to apply, but they would be rare. In most cases, all the coauthors know one another. Often, they are at the same institution or, if not, have collaborated. It is perfectly reasonable to expect every person who receives credit as a coauthor, and therefore by definition has done more than provide technical help, to take responsibility for the honesty and integrity of the work, not just to sign a statement agreeing to publication of the paper in its current form. This would dramatically reduce the publication of fraudulent information.

Dr. Koshland:

I find it upsetting when coauthors or administrators discover fraudulent or sloppy articles and say that they really didn't know about it. Heads of laboratories take credit for the work of their graduate students and others; if they are then caught being less than conscientious about the supervision, they shouldn't be allowed to say that they knew nothing about it. We have a responsibility to report these cases and not to let senior investigators off on that basis. If we did that, we would do a great deal to improve the dignity of authorship and the requirements for it.

But there is a second issue that is a little more complicated: The increase in the number of authors is a function of the complexity of science and of its compartmentalization. I want to pose this situation: Someone makes a recombinant-DNA material that is important in medicine. One group carries out the molecular biology, another tests the material in rats, and yet another carries out the clinical trials. These are three separate groups, all aware of one another, but not able to vouch for the integrity of the work. Would the definition of authorship require that all the researchers sit down to learn the other subjects so that they can vouch for them?

Dr. Stossel:

Of course, we should all understand everything and take full responsibility. I also argue that not signing a piece of paper doesn't ultimately absolve someone of responsibility. But Dr. Relman's criteria for Watson to be put on that paper would mean that half the molecular biology, the cloning that is being done by postdoctoral fellows today, would not justify authorship. This would revolutionize science.

Dr. Dan:

When I read a paper with eight names on it, I cannot tell whether someone has made an indispensable contribution, was the statistician, or held the test tube. I cannot tell who is the MD that solved the case and who is the branch chief. Obviously, we put some value on having our names on a paper. Part of our problem is that we have not stated the problem very well. Is there a problem of having many authors, other than that it takes up more space on the page?

Dr. Huth:

The primary reason that we are discussing authorship is the importance of maintaining intellectual honesty and responsibility. To dismiss the issue by saying, "What do those names really matter?" begs the important question about the sense of responsibility in the scientific community for what is in a paper.

I see many papers about which I cannot believe that every person can take responsibility for most of the content and the central conclusions.

Dr. Koshland:

We have many problems in science of how we are to cope with fraud. It is worrisome that honorary authorship is difficult to define and is not considered all that important. We depend on trust, and it is important that people take responsibility for authorship.

Dr. Relman:

Dr. Huth's point is well taken; one of the problems of honorary authorship is the identification of intellectual contributions and maintaining the value of authorship. In practical terms, honorary authorship poses problems in many spheres. First, it contributes to the likelihood of fraud. The nexus between the possibility of fraud and honorary authorship is clear; if you are concerned about fraud, you must be concerned about honorary authorship. I have sat on more than my share of promotion and tenure committees. It is difficult, in reviewing bibliographies that have many papers with many authors, to know whether a listed author made a substantial contribution to any of the articles. What is the significance of that, particularly when other coauthors on the same papers have already been promoted and received tenure on the basis of the same publications?

I have sat on the councils of honorary societies in internal medicine, and the same problem comes up all the time.

Finally, if those graduate students in molecular biology did not have anything to do with the conception of the work, with the interpretation of the results, or with the writing of the paper, and all they did was carry out some standard technique for cloning something at the direction of their superiors, they ought not to be authors.

Dr. Conrad:

It seems that we have greater sins and lesser sins, but all of them are sins, and we can deviate from ethical practice in any area—honesty of authorship or stealing other people's ideas. It becomes difficult to encourage ourselves to behave ethically, because often those who want to behave ethically meet with resistance. They are met with people who don't want to know that there is a problem—as though there were a right not to know. And defending ethics and honesty and trying to live up to the best standards becomes very costly in time and money and reputation. But it is the responsibility of each of us, and whether we duck our duty is a personal decision.

Dr. Angell:

Dr. Koshland has said that he disapproves of salami science; we have heard about the use of authorship as a bargaining tool; and we have touched on honorary authorship—not just the proliferation of authorship that is the result of increasing specialization, but truly gratuitous authorship. If the number of publications is not so important, why is authorship so prized? Is it merely vanity?

Dr. Houk:

It is more than pride. Particularly for young investigators, there is a great deal of satisfaction in the recognition by one's peers that one has been associated with and has been the author of a nice piece of work. It is more than vanity. However, one's feelings regarding the nice piece of work are diluted if, on the same piece of paper, everyone is included up and down the line, whether they contributed substantially or not.

Dr. Angell:

But why do they want to be included?

Dr. Houk:

I suspect that the old folks are more vain than some of the young folks. Why else would some department heads insist that their names go on every paper that leaves their departments?

Dr. Koshland:

Authorship is important, and honorary authorship is something we should all be against. But it is going to be difficult to draw a set of relevant instructions for a journal.

Dr. Huth:

Much of human behavior—perhaps most of it—hinges on economic matters. Authorship has economic value. There was a time in medicine—before, say, World War II—when research was not all that good a field to be in; it did not have the economic value that it does now. Part of the current problem is that there is a substantial economic value in being identified with research.

DAMN LIES AND STATISTICS:
MISREPRESENTATIONS OF HONEST DATA

Statistical Reporting in Scientific Journals*

STEPHEN E. FIENBERG

The use of statistics in technical manuscripts is concerned with the logic of the scientific method and with how we learn from data. Because high-quality measurements and data form the foundation of empirical science, statistical reporting in scientific journals should be and is ubiquitous. The biologic and health sciences include few empirical activities that do not involve the collection, analysis, and summary of data. Yet most scientific journals have relegated statistical reporting to the role of a barrier that authors must hurdle to reach the finish line of publication. As a consequence, "honest data" collected by well-meaning scientists often are misreported, misanalyzed, and misinterpreted. That is not peculiar to the biologic and health sciences. One need only scan a typical social-science journal or a broad-based scientific journal, such as *Nature* or *Science,* to find problems with statistics.

There are many reasons for this state of affairs. Limited space in journals, misconceptions of what constitutes adequate reporting, and mindless requirements of statistical significance have all helped to perpetuate the myth of lies, damned lies, and statistics. As a consequence, if we carefully examine and reanalyze the data that underlie many scientific publications, we can find misreporting or misguided use of statistical methods.

Here we discuss issues of data-sharing and statistical reporting, as well as alternative forms of statistical review that have been suggested to improve the quality of scientific journals. Implementation of the proposals will not eradicate misreporting or the poor use of statistics, but should facilitate the replication and verification of scientific advances.

REPLICATION AND THE SHARING OF RESEARCH DATA

The notion of replication is fundamental to scientific discovery. If we cannot replicate results reported in a scientific journal, we can have little trust

*Preparation of this paper was supported in part by National Science Foundation grant SES-8701606 to Carnegie Mellon University.

in the conclusions drawn by the authors. But replication means different things in different contexts.

In the basic laboratory sciences, replication typically means redoing an experiment by following a published description. Among the issues faced by those who replicate work are the quality of measurements and the uncertainty associated with them. If the experiment were reproduced in a different laboratory, how close would the results be?

In the clinical sciences and in the behavioral and social sciences, in which the experiment or the process of collecting data often involves enormous expense and considerable time and effort, replication would generally require the use of new subjects, new locations, and new measurements, each with its own sources of uncertainty. Asking a reviewer or a reader who is interested in building on published results to bear the burden of that kind of replication is unreasonable. In such circumstances, replication often means the ability to reproduce the conclusions from the raw data or from a basic summary of them. In this sense, replication requires the sharing of research data with reviewers as part of the review process, perhaps in the article itself, and with other investigators who request the data after publication. Professionally organized computer-based archives of the data that underlie published articles are crucial to data-sharing.

Rather than repeat the extensive commentary on the topic of sharing research data, we note that the benefits and costs, as well as the rights and responsibilities, associated with data-sharing have been summarized in a report of the National Research Council Committee on National Statistics.[5] Publications that have adopted data-sharing policies in recent years include the *Journal of the American Statistical Association,* the *Journal of the American Chemical Society,* the *Journal of Money, Credit, and Banking,* and the *Journal of Personality and Social Psychology.*[7]

Given that it is necessary to share data, it follows that data must be adequately reported, if data-sharing is to be as useful as it should be. Let us examine issues of bad data-reporting practice and what journals can do to promote good practice.

WHAT CONSTITUTES BAD PRACTICE IN STATISTICAL REPORTING?

Coupling basic principles of scientific reporting with the fundamental role of replication in science leads us to suggest the following standard for statistical reporting (suggested by John Bailar in a personal communication): *Any reporting practice that impedes proper inference is inappropriate.* As part of the publication process, we include such postpublication components as interpretation by journal readers and replication by secondary data analysts. The Committee on National Statistics recommendation about the sharing of research data[5] speaks to many features of good practice. Illustrations of bad practice include the following:

- Publishing a multiple-year study on the relationships among exposure to asbestos, smoking, and the occurrence of lung cancer based on a cohort of industrial workers and then informing others that, if they want to replicate the study, they should go out and gather their own data.
- Publishing a paper on the deterrent effect of capital punishment that draws on published government data without being explicit about the source of the data and then refusing to share the data with others, because they have access to the same source. This is especially critical if the conclusions of the study are sensitive to the choice of data used from the broader sources.
- Publishing the results of a laboratory biochemical experiment without providing sufficient experimental description to allow others to replicate the results in their laboratories. The concern will be even greater if reagents that are available primarily from the authors of the original study are denied to others trying to replicate and extend the results.

Each of those illustrations corresponds to an actual scientific publication and a related controversy in which the publication itself and the behavior of the authors were not in accord with the recommendations on sharing research data. To these we add references to three of the many papers that report on attempts to acquire data for reanalysis and to replicate reported statistical results.[3,4,6]

WHAT CAN JOURNALS DO?

To improve the quality of scientific journals, editors and publishers must change current reporting practices and reviewing processes. One way to do that is to involve statistical reviewers and editors in the review process. Two models that should be considered grew out of projects initiated jointly by an editor and a group of interested statisticians.

The first model comes from the *New England Journal of Medicine* and was begun in the late 1970s by Arnold Relman, Drummond Rennie, John Bailar, and Frederick Mosteller. Their project had two parts: a series of articles on statistical methods and reporting in medical journals[1] and a formal permanent working arrangement with a statistician who reviews all papers with substantive statistical content. Bailar has described a model for reporting and statistical review that is based in large part on his experience with the *New England Journal of Medicine*.[1 (pp. 261–71)] To discuss it in detail would require a separate paper. I merely note where I might disagree somewhat with an otherwise excellent approach. Bailar essentially opts for concise reporting of data, statistical methods, and the results of analyses. In doing so, he also argues against "accepting for review material that is not intended for publication," such as that which might allow direct verification of statistical calculations. Although it is true that there is a limited amount of space available in the *New England Journal of Medicine*, the pressure for conciseness and brevity seems to be in conflict with the requirements for replication outlined above. A personal experience with the *New England Journal of Medicine* review process, which ultimately led to the publication of a paper by Neutra et al.,[8] reinforces the concern over concise reporting and Spartan review materials. I believe, however, that the use of computer-based archives for related materials might alleviate this concern to a large extent.

The second model comes from *Science* and was begun in the early 1960s by editor Philip Abelson, Sylvia Eberhart, and statisticians active in Section U (Statistics) of the American Association for the Advancement of Science. The project began with a review of a sample of articles and reports published in *Science* in 1980 and 1981 and led to a revised editorial policy that included special screening of manuscripts for statistical content, revised instructions for contributors and reviewers regarding statistical material,[2] and the hiring of an editorial statistician. The process did not prevent the publication of statistically questionable material, but it did lead to a marked improvement in the quality of the statistical reporting. With the arrival of a new editor a few years ago, the process of statistical review changed somewhat, but the current instructions for authors contain a statement on "uncertainties and reproducibility."

SOME BASIC ISSUES FOR STATISTICAL REVIEWS

What kinds of issues are typically addressed in a statistical review of a scientific paper? Although it is difficult to make a generic list, the following examples will complement the perspective set forth by Stoto[9] (whose presentation follows).

- What are the original data? How have they been transformed for use in the statistical analyses?
- Are we given information on uncertainty and measurement error?
- How were the statistical analyses done, and is their description in the paper accurate?
- Are the statistical methods used appropriate for the data?
- Have the data or analyses been "selected," and does such selection distort the "facts"?
- What population do the data represent? Does the design for data collection allow for the inferences and generalizations made?
- Are there additional analyses that would be enlightening?
- Are the conclusions sensitive to the methodologic and substantive assumptions? If so, is this acknowledged? Do reported measures of uncertainty reflect this sensitivity?

Statisticians who regularly review papers for scientific journals ask questions like those when examining a manuscript. Their involvement in the review process adds an extra dimension that is related to a paper's scientific validity.

CONCLUSION

Changing the standards and practices of statistical review in scientific journals will not eradicate misreporting or poor use of statistics, but should facilitate the replication and verification of scientific advances. Authors must be trained to respect not only the quality of basic scientific data, but also the quality of analysis and reporting required for proper inference and interpretation. Only then can we as statisticians eradicate the myth of lies, damned lies, and statistics. Only then will editors of scientific journals have confidence that they are not perpetuating the misrepresentation of honest data.

REFERENCES

1. Bailar JC, III, Mosteller F, eds. Medical Uses of Statistics. Waltham, Mass.: New England Journal of Medicine Books; 1986.
2. Carey WD. 1981 annual report of the executive officer. Science 1982; 215:1063–9.
3. Dewald WG, Thursby JG, Anderson RG. Replication in empirical economics: the Journal of Money, Credit, and Banking project. Am Econ Rev 1986; 76:587–603.
4. Fienberg SE, Grambsch P. An assessment of the accuracy of "The Effectiveness of Correctional Treatment." In: Sechrest L, White SO, Brown ED, eds. The Rehabilitation of Criminal Offenders: Problems and Prospects. Washington, D.C.: National Academy of Sciences; 1979: 119–47.
5. Fienberg SE, Martin ME, Straf ML, eds. Sharing Research Data. Washington, D.C.: National Academy Press; 1985.
6. Hermalin A, Entwistle B, Myers LG. Some lessons from the attempt to retrieve early KAP and fertility surveys. Pop Ind 1985; 51(2):194–209.
7. Hushak LJ et al. Sharing agricultural data for research: benefits, costs, and legal and property issues. Paper prepared for Symposium on Sharing Agricultural Data for Research, American Agricultural Association Meetings, July 1986.
8. Neutra R, Fienberg SE, Greenland S, Friedman EA. Effect of fetal monitoring on neonatal death rates. N Engl J Med 1978; 299:324–6.
9. Stoto MA. From data to analysis to conclusions: a statistician's view, pp. 207–13. In: Council of Biology Editors. Ethics and Policy in Scientific Publication. Bethesda, Md.: Council of Biology Editors; 1990.

From Data to Analysis to Conclusions: A Statistician's View

MICHAEL A. STOTO

Discussions about the responsible conduct of research often concern outright cheating: fabricating data, misappropriating credit, and so on. Those problems are serious, but in one respect they are straightforward: Such behavior clearly contradicts the norms of science. Preventing and detecting deliberate misrepresentation are difficult, but there is no doubt that fraudulence is wrong and has no place in the conduct of responsible science.

I will address problems that arise in the analysis and reporting of honest data. Judgments about analytic methods and the strength and generality of conclusions are personal ones. Two analysts can legitimately come to different medical or policy conclusions from the same raw data. Although there are standards of good practice to help researchers make these judgments, there are no simple, unambiguous rules about what to do at each step. The result is that medical and health-policy conclusions arising out of biomedical research often involve a combination of scientific evidence and personal judgment that might not be apparent to readers of research reports. This kind of problem is probably much more prevalent than outright cheating, and it has a bigger effect on science.

There are at least two kinds of problems in the translation of data to conclusions: problems that arise in the analysis of data, and conclusions that go beyond the data and analysis. I believe that these are problems more of scientific communication than of scientific conduct. That suggests that journals and their peer-review process can play an important role in ensuring that readers have all the information they need to assess the validity of a report's conclusions.

ISSUES OF DATA ANALYSIS

Any research that draws conclusions from the aggregated experience of human patients or experimental animals, biologic samples, or experimental runs requires statistical analysis. Whether they are simple or complex, the conclusions of a study depend in many ways on details of the analysis. Although many unambiguous errors arise in statistical analysis, the issues discussed here mostly involve professional judgment.

One issue involves decisions about which data should be analyzed. At what point in bench or clinical research is it decided that the exploratory, hypothesis-generation phase of the research is over and that all further data will be used to test the hypothesis? In experimental work, when is one justified in discounting an observataion because the experimental conditions were not met? When is one justified in smoothing the output from a series of experimental runs because a few blips in an otherwise uniform data set are assumed to be caused by an unknown factor? Ideally, such decisions should be made without regard to their effect on the analysis and conclusions, but in practice this is difficult for even a well-meaning researcher.

The treatment of outliers is a related issue. Clinical and epidemiologic research data sets generally contain at least a few cases that are out of line with the rest of the sample, with respect to background factors or results. Investigators often are tempted to set the aberrant data points aside. It is statistically and scientifically appropriate to do that, and there are guidelines and techniques for identifying outliers.[11]

The statistical principle is that a small proportion of sample points should not have too much influence on the analysis and conclusions. Setting outlying points aside, however, is not the same as ignoring them. Scientific judgment is always needed to determine whether the outliers are the result of a failure of technique or an error in measurement or recording or whether they suggest an important relationship. Scientists need to consider carefully which data points to include in their analyses, and they should recognize that the choice can be critical for interpreting the results. If the outcome of an analysis depends on whether one or two data points are included, investigators have an obligation to disclose this fact and to discuss its implications.

Another issue arises in clinical trials, where the execution of a study plan can never be perfect.[5] For instance, sample selection and the allocation of subjects to treatment groups rarely go exactly as planned. Because of individual choice or logistical difficulties, some patients do not participate in an experiment, despite what the protocol says. Others do participate, but do not receive the treatment called for in the protocol. Despite vigorous efforts, followup of cases is rarely 100%.

Imperfect execution is a fact of life in clinical research; good practice seeks to limit errors, but it cannot eliminate them. The result is that statistical analysis must take the differences between plan and execution into account. There is, however, often more than one legitimate way to do that. For instance, treatment groups can be compared according to how the subjects were randomized to treatment or according to how subjects actually were treated. The first approach might tell us something about the real world, in which real patients don't always follow prescribed regimens, but less about the value of the treatment if faithfully applied. The second approach says more about the treatment, but suffers from potential biases resulting from how the subjects sorted themselves out. Because such matters can be critical to the conclusions of a study, authors should disclose the problem, their attempt to deal with it, and possible alternative interpretations.

The choice of statistical model used in the analysis of laboratory, clinical, and epidemiologic data also requires scientific judgment. For instance, if multiple regression or some related technique is used to control for differences between treatment and control groups in nonexperimental variables, the analyst must decide which variables to control for, and different choices can lead to different results.[8] The choice does and should depend on what variables are available, on the analyst's theoretically or empirically based judgment about what should be controlled, and on other factors.

A final set of issues arises in the calculation and interpretation of confidence intervals, P values, and related statistics. The usual interpretation of a P value, for instance, depends on the formulation of specific null and alternative hypotheses before the data are generated or collected. But the usual interpretation is not valid if the hypothesis was suggested (even in part) by the data in question. It also is not valid if multiple comparisons were made and only the "most significant" one is reported.[12] The use of confidence intervals avoids some of those problems, but other issues remain. For instance, when statistical models are being used, estimates of standard errors and deviations usually depend on the model chosen and do not reflect uncertainty about which model is best.[8,9]

In all those examples, the problem is not simply whether the researcher did the correct thing. Rather, it is whether the researcher has adequately disclosed what actually happened, so that readers can evaluate the author's choices for themselves.

CONCLUSIONS THAT GO BEYOND DATA AND ANALYSIS

Errors often arise when researchers misinterpret or exaggerate the implications of data and analytic results. That occurs in at least four ways.

First, some medical and health-policy conclusions are simply not supported by the data and analysis. That could be because of intentional or unintentional failures in logical analysis or because of the author's limited understanding of statistical techniques.

One common example is the acceptance of a null hypothesis despite the fact that a test has low power, i.e., that the data and procedures have little chance of detecting an effect even if it is present.[4,12] Standard statistical tests can say only whether the data are strong enough to permit one to reject the null hypothesis and thus to accept the alternative hypothesis. For instance, a positive test can tell us that a new drug treatment is better than the old, that some people are at higher risk for a disease, and so on. A negative test, however, could mean either that the old drug is at least as good or that there are too few observations to tell the difference. The difference between the two possibilities is critical.

Second, the conclusions of some studies are supported by the analysis presented, but could be reversed by other analyses. This is a complex issue. The author of a report cannot be expected to analyze the data in every possible way and to report all possible conclusions. Researchers should investigate the sensitivity of their conclusions to the method of analysis; but, because time, knowledge, and imagination are limited, other researchers need to have access to the original data, so that they can see whether a different mode of analysis would lead to different conclusions.

Third, the conclusions could be valid for the limited set of conditions under which an experiment was carried out, but invalid under other conditions.[7] This is called a problem of external validity. For instance, high-technology surgical interventions that work well at academic medical centers might not be transferable to community hospitals.

Screening tests afford a slightly more complex example. Even if laboratory procedures are well standardized, the performance characteristics of a test depend on the prevalence of the characteristic being screened for in the population being tested. A human immunodeficiency virus (HIV) testing procedure that works well for homosexual men in California might not be valid for testing marriage-license applicants in Illinois.

Fourth, some conclusions hinge on assumptions that go beyond the research in question that are not discussed or that are deliberately hidden. For instance, most conclusions about the value of a new technology rest on some assumptions about costs and benefits. An experiment can establish that a new treatment reduces mortality by some percentage, compared with the usual treatment, but a policy recommendation that the new technique should be used requires some assessment of its costs in relation to the estimated benefits.

Screening tests again provide an example. Assessments of the value of such tests require estimates of the relative utility of the various possible results.[6] Informal assessments that examine only the performance characteristics of a test lead to an implicit assumption about values. Formal analyses of such informal assessments often reveal implicit utilities that, on reflection, seem unreasonable.

When assumptions are explicit, other researchers can repeat the analysis with different values, if they believe that the original assumptions are not valid.[6] Trouble arises when hidden assumptions determine conclusions. Furthermore, in most cases, there is no single appropriate cost-benefit ratio, and good practice requires the analysis of several alternatives.[10]

COMPLETE AND ACCURATE REPORTING

Many of the diversions in the path from data to conclusions arise from the need to use statistical, scientific, and medical judgment. There are no simple rules to tell researchers and analysts what to do at each step, so different analysts can legitimately reach different conclusions from the same raw data.

The absence of absolute rules does not mean that "anything goes" in statistical analysis and the interpretation of results. Many outright errors crop up in statistical analyses in research. They include errors in arithmetic, misuse of experimental materials and methods, and misunderstanding of the assumptions of statistical tests.

It is often true that more than one method of analysis is acceptable (even though some statisticians would say that one method is preferable). In some cases, poor judgment can be corrected; even if it cannot, the results can still be valuable, if they are interpreted properly.

Statisticians have developed a collective but informal sense of what constitutes good practice. One principle, for instance, is that judgmental decisions should not be reached on the basis of their effect on the outcome of the analysis. Such professional norms and standards need to inform judgment. The absence of absolute rules does create opportunities for intentional and unintentional bias, and professional standards can help to counteract such biases.

Unlike the problems that arise from false or misleading data, the primary issue here is disclosure, rather than dishonesty. Readers need to know what was done in an analysis and how conclusions were drawn. Journals and the peer-review process can play an important role in ensuring that authors give readers all the information they need to assess the validity of a report's conclusions.

Research reports should disclose the choices made, in both handling the data and analysis, that could affect the conclusions.[1] That includes a discussion of how the sample was selected, of how randomization was performed (if it was), of whether all data are reported and used in the analysis (and if not, why some observations were not used), and of changes in the protocol as the study progressed. Although one might think that such matters would be disclosed as a matter of course, often they are not.[2]

Research reports also need to acknowledge uncertainties that arise from the choice of statistical models and methods of analysis. Some exploration of alternative models and methods is feasible and appropriate in original research reports, and there should at least be a discussion of how the conclusions might depend on such choices. Readers also need to know the precise assumptions under which confidence intervals and P values are calculated. Finally, authors need to disclose the assumptions that are necessary to draw medical or policy conclusions from analytic results.

The peer-review process can help to reduce the kinds of problems I have discussed. Peer reviewers cannot always tell whether disclosure is honest and complete, but they should be able to tell whether important items are missing from a manuscript. Reviewers should also be able to determine when alternative assumptions or methods of analysis could make a difference. Editors in turn can require full disclosure, and they can be precise about what that means. Editors and peer reviewers should be able to examine the logic behind conclusions, and they should look carefully for hidden assumptions. When statistical analysis is especially relevant to a report's conclusions, editors should consider using reviewers whose experience is primarily statistical to help to evaluate the analysis and conclusions.

DATA-SHARING

The exploration of alternative models and methods of analysis in a single paper can go a long way, but there is a limit to how many alternative methods an investigator can be expected to try before a paper is submitted for publication. Furthermore, investigators are experienced with only some analytic methods. They can't be expected to apply all methods that might be appropriate, or even to know which other methods might be appropriate. Those limitations suggest the importance of making data available for reanalysis by other investigators.

As the role of statistical judgment becomes more important in the translation of data to conclusions, journal readers can no longer assume that an author's conclusions are the only possible ones. But to move from suspicion about conclusions toward certainty, pro or con, readers must have access to original data. Journals have a responsibility to help their readers to evaluate conclusions found in their pages, and ensuring availability of data is an essential part of it. Although policies and procedures to ensure it are complex,[3] journals can help by recommending or even requiring that the original data behind published studies be made available to other investigators.

CONCLUSIONS

Biomedical research comes out of a tradition in which replication is the ultimate scientific test. Modern biomedical research is different, however, and replication can no longer be regarded as the only way to evaluate research results. Replication works well for small-scale laboratory research, but complete replication of data-gathering and analysis is not feasible for large clinical trials and epidemiologic surveys. Furthermore, good statistical analysis of clinical trials and epidemiologic studies requires professional judgment, and conclusions depend on that judgment. Therefore, opportunities for reanalysis with different statistical methods are essential to the integrity of conclusions. Journal editors need to be aware that statistical choices and assumptions can make a difference in conclusions. They should require authors to provide enough information in their papers so that readers can evaluate the effects of the choices and assumptions, and they should help to make data available for secondary analysis.

REFERENCES

1. Bailar JC, III. Reporting statistical studies in clinical journals. In: Bailar JC, III, Mosteller F, eds. Medical Uses of Statistics. Waltham, Massachusetts: New England Journal of Medicine Books; 1986: 261–71.
2. DerSimonian R, Charette LJ, McPeek B, Mosteller F. Reporting on methods in clinical trials. N Engl J Med 1982; 306:1332–7.
3. Fienberg SE, Martin ME, Straf ML, eds. Sharing Research Data. Washington, DC: National Academy Press; 1985.
4. Freiman JA, Chalmers TC, Smith HS, Kueblen RR. The importance of beta, the type II error, and sample size in the design and interpretation of the randomized controlled trial: survey of 71 "negative" trials. N Engl J Med 1978; 299:690–4.
5. Hoaglin DC, Light RJ, McPeek B, Mosteller F, Stoto MA. Data for Decisions. Cambridge, Massachusetts: Abt Books; 1982.
6. McNeil BJ, Pauker SG. Decision analysis for public health: principles and illustrations. Annu Rev Pub Health 1984; 5:135–61.
7. Moses LE. Statistical concepts fundamental to investigations. In: Bailar JC, III, Mosteller F, eds. Medical Uses of Statistics. Waltham, Massachusetts: New England Journal of Medicine Books; 1986: 3–26.
8. Mosteller F, Tukey JW. Data Analysis and Regression: A Second Course in Statistics. Reading, Massachusetts: Addison-Wesley; 1977.
9. Stoto, MA. Dealing with uncertainty: statistics for an aging population. Am Statist. 1988; 42:103–10.
10. Thompson MS. Benefit-Cost Analysis for Program Evaluation. Beverly Hills, California: Sage; 1980.
11. Tukey JW. Exploratory Data Analysis. Reading, Massachusetts: Addison-Wesley; 1977.
12. Ware JH, Mosteller F, Ingelfinger JA. P values. In: Bailar JC, III, Mosteller F, eds. Medical Uses of Statistics. Waltham, Massachusetts: New England Journal of Medicine Books; 1986: 149–69.

Open Discussion

Dr. Bailar:

My first point has to do with concise reporting. I believe that editors of journals tend to be faithful guardians of their readers' interests. It also seems to me that readers are not likely to read what they don't want to read; a 20-page paper is less likely to be read than is a 10-page paper. Conciseness in reporting can improve communication, but conciseness can have a cost: Important information can go unreported.

Another point is whether an editor should consider material that is submitted with a paper, but is not part of the paper and is not intended for publication. One purpose of such review, first by the editor and then by formal peer reviewers, is to validate the inferences, but it is a peculiar kind of validation.

Think about it. As a reader, you almost never know what additional material was submitted. You do not know who the reviewers were. You do not know what the reviewers said about the paper or about supplementary material. All you have is the editor's judgment about whether to publish what I think of as the rump part of the paper. I am unwilling to transfer full responsibility for conclusions to editors and reviewers, especially to unknown reviewers. I think that important information should be published, unimportant information should be left out. I recognize that this is not fully consistent with my views about conciseness, but we have to draw a balance.

Dr. Fienberg:

Both as an editor and as an author, I strive for conciseness. And I agree with Dr. Bailar that it is an issue of balance. I argue, however, that the role of supplementary material may really not be an issue, because if journals moved toward archiving material, then the role of supplementary material would be different and that material would be accessible to readers.

Mr. Whitney:

A practical problem occurs when our journal's statistician disagrees with the author's statistician. Sometimes, we send the paper to a third statistician, but then who is to say that that referee is any more correct than the other two?

Dr. Stoto:

The difficulty with that question is the assumption that there is a right answer. Statisticians certainly have strong feelings that some methods are better than others, but in many cases there simply is no one right answer. There needs to be some way to alert readers that some conclusion depends on whether one chooses one method of analysis or another and to help them to draw their own conclusions.

Dr. Fienberg:

Dr. Stoto says there are no right answers, but there probably are. The question is: Will you ever be able to find them, given the data set available in the study at hand? Probably not, and you are likely to get multiple answers—perhaps conflicting, perhaps similar.

My experience is that two reasonable analysts, even if they use somewhat different methods, may reach the same conclusions about the key issues. When they don't, if conclusions really seem to depend on the choice of method and there is no way around that, then the author must acknowledge that in the paper, even though the author might stress one method as appropriate.

Then the editor has to decide whether the substance of the paper is important enough to merit the conclusion. But don't make it the statisticians' responsibility to resolve that kind of uncertainty when it is probably the data themselves—the honest data—that bear the uncertainty, rather than the method.

Dr. Huth:

It may be time to look again at the question of making original data available. From an editor's point of view, the main constraint has been the problem of space and economical presentation. For economic reasons and because most readers do not want the data, we are reluctant to add appendix tables with a lot of original data.

But now, with on-line access and perhaps CD-ROM technology, it has become relatively easy to make those data available. An interesting innovation would be for journals to require the submission of original data and make them available in an on-line system at the same time that the full paper is published. The paper itself could carry instructions for the on-line system and how to get the data. That could be an important step forward, and we would not have to wait 2 or 3 years for someone to raise a question about interpretation, if the data were available as soon as the full paper is available.

Dr. Fienberg:

Then the question becomes: What are the data? What numbers do you want to see in that archive? I would not advocate putting the laboratory notebooks in the archive. Some form of derivation, some form of abstract, some form of organizing is needed. For example, in the case of the study that I mentioned earlier on fetal monitoring, you would need the whole CD-ROM to get access to the full range of data.

You don't want to have that. You want some reasonable summary. So, the issue is still using judgment, asking the kinds of questions that go beyond the current study and that others might want to ask to verify your judgments. That issue is different from taking the basic numbers that came popping out of a laboratory instrument or the full case record on every patient in a hospital.

Dr. Gallagher:

I want to raise some questions about the editor as the guardian of the readers' interests. I also want to mention the idea of science as an invisible college or communication among scientists. We think of publication as the be-all and end-all. We hear about how authorship is coveted, but the notion of the invisible college suggests that what is published is really just the tip of the iceberg; a lot of activity and communication go on otherwise. When you pick up a journal, even one of the main journals in your field, you are not really in a frame of mind to go through every article with a fine-tooth comb. One or two articles, the editor hopes, will interest you; others will be of interest to other people.

What wisdom, then, can guide the editor as the guardian of the readers' interests? I am speaking to this dilemma of the choice between compactness of presentation—that is, using space efficiently, keeping in mind the reader's attention span, and avoiding information overload—and presenting the important business of science that goes on in the invisible college. How does the editor choose?

There have been times when I have thought of banishing tables from my journal and simply letting the authors use words to describe what is important and what they found out. Tables are simply a form of guided, managed experience—allowing, almost requiring, the reader to agree with the author's conclusions.

Short of that radical step, one might leave out many numbers from the tables, but leave in an asterisk, a double asterisk, or a triple asterisk, depending on the level of significance to be attributed to the particular cell.

Dr. Fienberg:

I recognize the dilemma. Editors serve three groups or audiences. First, editors serve authors. The editorial process can do much to enhance the material to allow readers to draw conclusions better from the authors' honest data. I see editors as taking a major role in that regard, and they are the authors' friends in that sense. Second, editors work in behalf of journal readers. Third, and just as important, editors work in behalf of science. The dilemma arises in arbitration between the short-term interests of getting the material across to the readers when they pick up the journal and the long-term issues of protecting the validity of science, so that someone who wants to look at the results later can see enough detail to understand what went on.

Dr. Stoto:

The kind of publication suggested does exist. It is a publication of abstracts, a newspaper article, or a magazine that tells the results, but not the method. Certainly those publications have a place, and most people can learn quite a bit from them. But if we want to think of science as more than a collection of facts—as a method—we need the arguments as set out in the tables and in the detail of the paper.

Dr. Lock:

Has there been any audit of the statistical review described for both the *New England Journal of Medicine* and *Science?* It imposes an enormous load on the statisticians; and we don't necessarily have a gold standard for the end point. I am also interested in the ones that we don't let the statisticians see at all. Some of the worst articles may be the worst because of a defect of logic at the planning stage, rather than the multivariate analysis. Have you done any sort of audit to find out whether the statistical review improves the whole thing?

Dr. Fienberg:

There was some attempt to compare *Science* before and after initiation of statistical review. There was a sense that there had been an improvement.

Dr. Bailar:

There has been no audit of the effect of statistical review in the *New England Journal of Medicine*. The journal receives thousands of manuscripts each year, and perhaps 600 or 700 survive regular peer review. Half or two-thirds of those—perhaps 400 or 500 papers a year—are selected for statistical review, which is a review in a broad sense. The big problems we see are not in the kinds of things that many people think of as statistics.

In my own reviews, I don't look very hard to see how authors calculate, say, their confidence limits. I am much more concerned with the fundamental aspects of the processes of inference. Was this study designed in a way that could answer the questions that were asked? How and when were the hypotheses under investigation developed? In particular, did they come after someone looked at the data and said, "You know, that really looks kind of interesting"? Other questions have to do with the quality of the data, the general approach to the analysis, the construction of tables and figures, what is in them, and how they are presented. Still other questions in the statistical review have to do with problems of incomplete data, missing observations, and how those have been handled. Finally, they have to do with how the author makes inferences from the data at hand to some kind of larger population, extending beyond the data to generalize the results.

Now, you might wonder what all that has to do with statistics. In my view, that is the heart of statistics. The P values and confidence limits are out on the fringe somewhere. Often they are useful tools, but they are not at the center of what I think of as statistics and statistical thinking.

We have talked a lot here about the role of judgment. Perhaps we have not talked as much as we should about misjudgment, maljudgment, and deliberately distorted judgment. The pressure to publish interesting results, which I think we all recognize, might well be reinforced by how we educate our scientists, how we train them as new investigators, and what role models we present to them.

Our own interests in publishing from the standpoint of editors, scientists, or science administrators and our interests in authorship credit might be causing us to train future generations of investigators in ways that will sometimes undercut the validity of the scientific inference they make. Some of the worst practices are not generally considered misconduct, despite their destructive and fully avoidable effects.

Do we need to broaden our definition of "misconduct" to include deliberate or avoidable distortion of inferences? If so, what can we do about it?

Dr. Fienberg:

You lumped together two things as potential misconduct. One was deliberate and the other was avoidable. We need to educate scientists about many things in the way that you describe. Some errors of analysis and inference are avoidable. Many researchers will learn to avoid them; others will not.

At best, we can try to educate scientists from the beginning, and that is the role I take in the classroom when I talk about statistics and statistical methods.

Dr. Stoto:

But we must keep the approach positive. Repeatedly using the term "misconduct" for inadequate handling of data and saying that now we are going to study "misconduct" is not a good way to proceed. We need to stress the fact that judgment, and not simply cookbook formulas, is required. We need to construct opportunities for researchers to work to improve their judgment, rather than simply assume that they will learn enough in the course of their work. That can be done through examples, through reading published articles and trying to discern exactly where judgment comes in.

When Is Repetitive Publication Justified?

DONALD S. COFFEY

I do not think anyone would claim that duplicate publication is not a serious problem; it affects many of our journals and causes a lot of undue work. Why do researchers do it? Is it to increase the perception of productivity? Is it to increase communication to a new or wider audience or to diverse audiences? What about repetitive publication in reviews or to summarize a field of study? Is there justification for any of these?

I would also like to consider who decides the policy. Is it a legal policy? Is it the editors who decide? Is it the publishers? Should the authors decide? The scientific community? The government? Who is responsible, and who is harmed? Who is protected? When you make policy, the way you make it is as important as the policy itself. Who has input? Is the input properly weighed? What group makes the decision? How can the policy be changed?

Policy is like building walls, and the scientific community hates walls. We are a pampered bunch, and many of us believe that when you build walls you restrict our freedom of inquiry. When Robert Frost wrote about a wall, he said that when you build a wall you have to ask what you are walling in or walling out, because "something there is that doesn't love a wall." I think that also goes for policy; you have only to see some of the complications for the farmer, for the post office, for the railroads, when the government starts making policy.

My principal qualification in this matter is that I have dealt with repetitive publication as an administrator, as a scientist, and as an editor. In the last capacity, I had to solve a problem of duplicate publication. It was 20 years ago, when I was the assistant editor of *Molecular Pharmacology*, one of the Academic Press publications for the Society of Pharmacology. One day, I received a manuscript, logged it in, and got ready to process it. Next day, I received the exact same manuscript; every word, including the acknowledgments and grant credit, was exactly the same. It was from the same department in (let us call it) Duplicate University, and it was a single-author paper. One paper was from Jim Turner and the other was from Bob Jackson.

Wondering what I was going to do about this dilemma, I went to some of the wise heads at Johns Hopkins University. Where do you get policy when you are handling these things? Is there any book I can reach for, such as the legal profession has, that says, "In case 26B, you do the following"? I began to wonder what my ethics were and what my responsibility was. I spoke with a few senior editors around Hopkins, and one said, "Well, the first thing is, you are not God. You are not a rabbinical judge. You are trying to publish good papers, and you cannot get mixed up in university politics and the fight between these people. But you do have a responsibility in regard to fraud, and this a tough one. I don't know exactly how you should handle it without becoming immersed in what is obviously a very delicate matter at Duplicate University."

In the middle of the night, I got the solution. I sent Turner's paper to Jackson to review and Jackson's paper to Turner to review. I often wondered what those reviews were going to look like, but of course I never got to see either one of them: I never heard from Jackson or Turner again. A moment of hysteria and anger had no doubt been resolved at Duplicate University. But what is our role? What should an editor do when the situation is more subtle?

One reason I was asked to address you involves an important journal and a wonderful man—one of the great editors—whom I did not meet until today. He wrote an editorial about duplicate publication that affected one of our young people at the Johns Hopkins Oncology Center when I had just become the temporary deputy director. On my first day on the job, one of the fine young researchers in our department came in disturbed; her career had been ruined. I asked, "Who has ruined your career?" She handed me an editorial from this leading journal. I read it and went over each line with her. I said, "Bring me your files. Let's talk to the other authors." I wanted to see the complete record. She had evaluated a new, exciting drug in some clinical trials and had submitted a paper to the journal in question for peer review. Many months later, she received a request to go to a meeting of the American Association for Cancer Research to present a paper on the work, and she went. So the scientific community heard about the work at a meeting. Later, she was invited to give another talk on the same work, and this talk required a manuscript. The meeting organizers wanted all the details, and that meant that she had to include the tables and the charts. It turned out that the meeting proceedings were published as a supplement to a peer-reviewed journal before the first peer-reviewed paper came out. The editor of the first journal wrote a scathing editorial in which he appeared almost to equate this instance of repetitive publication with fraud.

The editorial set off a furor in our department. A few nights later, I was at a cocktail party, and everyone was talking about the editorial and whether it was right or wrong. The lawyer of a faculty member was there, and the legal aspect came up—not with a view to any legal action, but just to determine what the legal aspects were. The lawyer asked, "Who was harmed? What was the effect of this harm? What law or policy was broken? Who made the policy? What is the penalty if you violate the policy, and what are the due-process rights of those who are charged? Did they have an opportunity to tell their side of the story? What are the rights of those who are making the charges?"

He added, "It seems to me that this editorial represents a defamation of character. The act complained of has been equated with fraud. If this person did not receive the editorial to reply to before its publication, I would take that case in 2 minutes."

I checked and found that the editor is a wonderful person. We are a good university, and that is a great journal. So what do you do? I wrote a letter of rebuttal to the journal; the letter was seen by the editor before it was published. What was the result? I am sure the editor thought I was a jackass. I am sure I thought the editor was a jackass. A lot of people were hurt. The scientists had made some serious errors in regard to proper citations; and when the galleys were received, some action should have been taken. But I realize that the scientific community has a serious problem, and you, the editors, have a serious problem in how you respond to this sort of dilemma, especially because legal questions are raised.

Who makes ethics? Let me tell you something that helped me conceptualize the problem. I was invited by the National Institutes of Health to speak to some of its leaders: I was to put together a program as seen through the eyes of a principal investigator. From four major universities across the United States, I brought in a dean, a department head, an assistant professor, and a young postdoctoral research fellow. One speaker came in at the end of the meeting to speak about ethics and science. He said that ethics are described by the culture of the people and the fabric of the people. For instance, abortion is a major problem in the United States, but it is not a major problem in Germany or Japan. Don't people there love children? Don't they love life? Animal welfare was not always a major problem in the United States, although it was in England. Now, 10 years later it is a problem in the United States. There are 30 lawyers in the United States to every one lawyer in Japan. Doesn't Japan care about law?

He went on to show how the culture would guarantee that you will have 30 lawyers to one if the individual is more important than the university. He said that the individual no longer has castles; he has hired gunfighters, and those hired gunfighters are lawyers. The lawyers have been turned on the doctors, because when doctors were essentially people of the cloth, they helped us. But when they started driving expensive cars and making us wait for hours to see them and treating us like cordwood, the gunfighters were turned on them. The gunfighters have not been turned on the church yet, because we still believe that some church people are good; but if they abuse us, we'll turn the gunfighters on them, too. Gunfighters have not been turned on scientists yet, but it will happen, because we have become big-business people. We spun off from the culture of the church as people of the cloth, with very little money. Now the scientist's office is big business.

When I talk about pressure to publish, I should note that eight of the young people in my group at Hopkins are supported completely by "soft" money; 75% of my own salary comes from soft money—grants and the competitive world. You can see that the pressure to publish is fierce. It is big business, and the journals are big business. How do we handle that without getting too many lawers involved?

What is the purpose of a published work? We have to know whether it is to establish the source of a discovery or to increase the identity and fame of the author or to enhance the prestige of the journal and its publishers. We also have to inform the funding source of the results of its expenditures. We have to justify what we are doing to make money directly or indirectly for the publishers and all the systems underneath. If this is a business, there are laws and ethics. So we start talking money. Who pays? If you ask authors, they say, "I have got to write all those research proposals. It costs about $30,000 per paper. You get about three papers per grant, so it costs about $100,000 plus 50% or 60% overhead, to create, organize, and conduct the study. I have to pay for the drawings. I have to pay to get my paper reviewed. I have to pay page charges to publish it, and then I buy reprints and have to assume the costs of mailing them out. I am responsible for the study and the publication and the grant, and I have to sign off on all that."

There is a complicated interaction between the editor and the author. When is it all right to publish something again, in whole or in part? I have done both, and I don't consider myself dishonest. You say that a paper should not be published again in its entirety. I have had two of my papers published twice; they were published unchanged, the second time at the request of editors who said they were trying to pick the best, "hottest" papers in the field to highlight. They asked my permission to republish a *Cell* paper in a book and distribute it. A German group said to me, "We think one of your discoveries is a major breakthrough. We are collecting papers on major breakthroughs, and we wish to republish your paper in German." I said, "If it is all right with the publisher and the editors, it is all right with me, but you must get the right signoff."

Was it right to do that? Should I have said no? Was anyone harmed? I don't think so. What about republishing part of a paper? I have republished figures and tables from dozens of my papers in review articles. Of course, I cite the earlier sources. But should I do this at all? What about publication of an initial series in a continuing clinical study? If you are doing clinical research—say, cancer research—it usually takes 3 years before you get the results. So you don't get a lot of publications. Are you trying to expand your list of publications? No. But when you get enough information, you want the world to know. You have to tell your results, and your thinking changes. One person told me, "Yes, I published twice. I published these data again, because I changed my mind about what they mean, and I had to present the whole thing over again to get the work published."

As one approach to solving the problem, I believe there should be specific reference in the letter of submission to alert the editor regarding any previous publication. If any part of a submission is from a cumulative study, the authors should tell the editor that, and the editor should tell the reviewers. And you must have all the authors agree that the material can be published again as part of a continuing review. If the study is a long-term clinical trial of toxicity, for example, it might be hard to relocate everyone to get all the coauthors of a study to sign off, and, as we have noticed, lists of authors are getting longer and longer.

Another important consideration is to pick the right reviewers. If you have picked the right reviewers and they have been keeping up with the literature, they should know about a paper that has been published before. If they don't know, we probably need to send that paper to them. When I was an editor, I found that I was picking all the big names in the field to review papers. I found that they were the least qualified reviewers. The best reviewers are the young researchers who read every paper that comes out and go to every meeting and are not in the hall talking politics or in committee meetings. But as you know, there is good and bad to everything. You get the young reviewers, and what happens? You might get some nit-picking little kid who criticizes everything. Then the big person who has submitted the paper yells at you: "What kind of idiot did you choose to review my paper?" But if we had a balance, if we were charged with picking both a young researcher and an established investigator, things would improve. You might slip something by me, but you couldn't slip it by my staff. Choosing good reviewers is the first thing I suggest.

The next thing is to look at promotions. Professor Leslie Helleman was my mentor; he was associate editor of the *Journal of Biological Chemistry* and a consulting editor for some 20 years. One day when I was in his office, someone called about a recommendation for one of his students who had applied to work at a good school. He was giving the recommendation over the telephone, and the caller said, "How many papers has he published?" Dr. Helleman answered, "Am I supposed to count them or weigh them?" There was silence for a minute, and the caller understood.

In the Hopkins promotion system, a candidate's name is submitted through an executive committee of a department with a letter from the department director. We assume that the people in the department of oncology or medicine are keeping up with whether the candidate is worthy and they write detailed letters about the candidate's contributions, including a list of all publications. Then the matter comes to our 12-person promotion committee. The biochemist on the committee might send a series of biochemistry papers by the candidate to me for evaluation. I then appoint two other professors who are not on the promotion committee and who are in biochemistry, but not in the same department. The three of us look at the papers and give our evaluation; then we write, say, 15 letters of outside inquiry. The recipients of those letters don't get the publications; they don't get the curriculum vitae. We say, "What has been the contribution of this person to the field? How do you see this scientist?" We evaluate the scientific contribution, the clinical contribution, the administrative role, and the teaching ability. When responses to the 15 letters come in, we present our findings to the board, and then the board approves our sending the promotion recommendation to all the department heads in the school. The material has to lie there for a month to give people time to look at anything they want to. Then a vote is taken.

If you have that kind of rigorous scrutiny, will you uncover duplicate publication? The answer is, "Not in every case, but you should uncover most of it." I think that young people should understand that increasing productivity through duplicate publication works only when there are inadequate editorial policies, inadequate reviewers, inadequate promotion committees, and inadequate peers. We must tighten the system so that we stop bad practices at the scientific level, at the university level, and at the level of publishers, editors, and authors. I would rather that publishers and editors prepare guidelines for me than that the government do it. And I certainly don't want the lawyers doing it.

The Pressure to Publish: Considerations of Ontogeny

JAMES D. MARSH

Studies of developmental biology teach us not only about structural and functional changes that occur during the transition of an immature organism to a mature one, but about subtle control mechanisms that are important in the mature organism. Control mechanisms, which often are obvious by their absence and then appearance during development, may be more difficult to uncover in the more mature state. Such is the case for the ingrowth of autonomic nerves to the heart in concert with the new expression of receptors for sympathetic and parasympathetic neurotransmitters. It is also the case for the modulation of publication behavior by a scientist. In the formative years, the pressure to publish and the response to it may be obvious; later, it may be internalized and more subtle, although no less important. Accordingly, I will use the paradigm of developmental biology to examine the response of the scientist to environmental stress, particularly the pressure to publish. That will permit a brief examination of the mechanisms that control scientific and academic behavior as related to publishing.

ONTOGENY OF THE PRESSURE TO PUBLISH

Ontogeny is the study of the development of an organism. The organism to be considered here is the scientist-clinician-scholar-educator. It is evident from these broad descriptors that the mature form of this organism has considerable phenotypic diversity.

An examination of the earliest developmental stages of this organism reveals little evidence of significant pressure to publish before the age of 7 or 8 years, although some evidence suggests that the anlage of the writer may be evident as early as the developmental stage of 3 years (sometimes called the crayon stage). The first evidence of pressure to publish can be found during elementary school. Most members of the species experience the initial environmental pressure to write in about Grade 3 with the demand from a teacher that a student write full sentences, instead of brief phrases. By Grades 4-5, full paragraphs are required. Several environmental stimuli modulate the development of this writing (soon to be publishing) behavior. Among the positive effectors are a satisfactory report card, praise from the teacher and parents, and some peer recognition.

The next important stage in the developmental biology of the scientist occurs in junior high school. The developing organism first becomes involved with science projects that require written reports. The positive and negative environmental effectors are similar to those for earlier stages of development, but with some refinements, including opportunities to go to regional and state science fairs.

It is in high school that the pressure to write becomes more fully expressed as the pressure to publish. Although environmental stresses remain prominent, by this time there is some degree of internalization of the desire of developing scientists to produce written expression of their ideas or experimental results. At the high-school level, further opportunities for science projects in some cases can actually involve a degree of original investigation. It is also during this time that actual publication of written work at the local level occurs with some frequency. Students are encouraged to write for the high-school newspaper, and many high schools and preparatory schools have literary journals for which contributions are sought.

External review of scientific and nonscientific writing is introduced at the high-school stage and can become serious. In the competition for National Merit Scholarships and Westinghouse Science Scholarships, external review of developing scientists' and scholars' writing has a critical role in shaping their career development. Having one's writing well received can produce admission to a highly competitive university. Moreover, favorable outside reviews of writing can be crucial to obtaining scholarships that are necessary to open doors of elite institutions of higher education to students of ordinary means. By this stage of development (age 14-18), there is clear evidence of the pressure to write or publish and to have a satisfactory outcome from an external review process.

The pressure to publish begins to become deeply embedded at this point; a response often manifest at this stage of development is acquisition of a typewriter or computer. Moreover, there is nearly uniform development of complex neuronal synapses at the cortical and thalamic level that control a critical behavior known as typing.

The ontologic process of responding to the pressure to publish has now spanned 18 years and is still incomplete. This is an extraordinarily long maturation process. The process continues at the college level. In the early years of college, there is little perceived pressure to publish beyond that which has been internalized during high school. It is often manifest as a desire for "self-expression," whether in a laboratory notebook, in a local literary journal, or in the college newspaper. However, in later college years, there is a definite, although subtle and poorly perceived, pressure to publish. It is often during the senior year of college that it occurs to the developing scientist and scholar that an honors thesis related to original research work, with or without external publication, may have a substantial influence on acceptance to graduate school or medical school. That perception often occurs during April of the senior year and may produce concern more about the appearance than about the substance of the research report. In some cases, the emphasis on the appearance or the quantity of publication may persist for the next 20 years until the senior faculty level is approached.

INFLUENCE OF PUBLICATION ON MEDICAL-SCHOOL OR GRADUATE-SCHOOL ADMISSION

Admission committees of medical schools and graduate schools weigh a number of factors in the admission process. Coauthorship of a paper reporting an original investigation is neither necessary nor sufficient for an applicant to achieve admission to medical school or graduate school. However, it is unquestionably a strongly positive factor. At one research-oriented medical school, about 15% of students admitted to the regular program have a record of scientific publication and 75-80% of students admitted to the research-oriented track have been coauthors of at least one scientific paper.

Admission committees for medical schools receive hundreds of applications from earnest, well-motivated college students who have excellent academic records. A critical differentiating factor is sought in the application. Publication of research work is taken as strong evidence that the student has unusual initiative and is able to start and maintain a research program, bring it to completion, and participate in writing and publishing the results. A minority of applicants can actually achieve that. The quality of the research and ensuing publication is given little or no weight at this stage, in part because of the judgment that what is important and has predictive power is the process of research and publication and in part because of the sheer volume of the applications to be reviewed. Admission-committee members seldom have time to read a manuscript critically. Thus, the quantity and not the quality of the publication is of primary importance. During the college years, the developing scientist and scholar detects cues about the relative importance of the quantity and quality of publication.

PRESSURE FOR MEDICAL STUDENTS OR GRADUATE STUDENTS TO PUBLISH

It is in graduate or medical school that the developing scientist and scholar begins to interact in a repetitive fashion with editorial boards and editors of journals. The pressure to publish is real, although there is a wide spectrum of clarity in its perception. For some, pressure to publish becomes evident only when, at the conclusion of graduate school or medical school, the graduate can find no satisfactory job or postdoctoral position, and only a second- or third-tier residency is available. Thus, the pressure to publish, which may be only vaguely perceived during student years, in retrospect becomes perfectly clear.

Internship committees carefully weigh the record of publications. Having published an original investigation is neither absolutely necessary nor sufficient for acceptance into a first-line internship, but it can be of immense help. When a program director screens 1,000 applications for 30-35 internship positions, an application showing publication of an original investigation quickly sets the applicant apart. Given the volume of applications to be reviewed, it is again the presence or absence of publications—and not their quality—that is critical. One program director in a department of medicine estimates that more than 75% of applicants eventually chosen for internship in his department have published at least one paper in the biomedical literature; the mean number of publications is 3.2 for that program. Although the pressure to publish during medical school is felt keenly by some medical students, some otherwise bright and perceptive students are oblivious to it. Therefore, medical students may underestimate the importance of a record of publication as an aid in career development.

A record of publication is necessary and in some cases sufficient for the developing PhD scientist and scholar to obtain a satisfactory postdoctoral position or a job in industry. By the time the developing scientist and scholar has reached postdoctoral training, the imperative to publish has finally become uniformly perceived. The response to the perception is usually minimal during clinical training in physicians, but is substantial in research and postdoctoral fellows.

A record of publication has become an essential entry requirement for doctors who wish to pursue fellowship training in an academically oriented program. Applicants are not always aware of that. In the last 13 years of operation of the clinical and research training program in cardiovascular medicine at Brigham and Women's Hospital in Boston, a number of factors have been examined as predictors of which trainees will ultimately pursue full-time academic careers, an explicit goal of the program. The best predictor of a nonacademic career is the lack of any scientific publication by the time a candidate is midway through residency. That finding has led us to make a record of published research work an important criterion in consideration for a fellowship position.

Publication during a postdoctoral or research fellowship is crucial for obtaining the first faculty position and the first research award. The subtleties of the process are often poorly understood. For instance, the hierarchy of journal prestige and its effect on academic career development in a particular department often are not well recognized.

During the postdoctoral years, some unusual manifestations of the pressure to publish are expressed in a few developing investigators. It is as though publishing behavior on rare occasions undergoes malignant transformation. In particularly active fields, the pressure to achieve priority of publication leads some to extraordinary intensity and duration of labor in the laboratory, sometimes 16 hours a day, 7 days a week. In addition, there are rare instances of extreme phenotypic variation. Examples include a few well-known fabricators of experimental data and recurrent publishers of the same experiments.[3-5] Those extreme examples primarily reflect the maladaptive response to 25 years of internalized pressure to publish, rather than an acute response to a new environmental stress.[6]

VIEW FROM THE MIDDLE RUNGS OF THE ACADEMIC LADDER

To this point, I have considered the ontogeny of the biomedical scientist in relation to an environmental factor, the pressure to publish. What is the effect of that factor on relatively mature members of the species? One view is fairly simple: Continued publication of original research is necessary for academic advancement; at least a low level of publication is sufficient to achieve stasis in an academic position. At the Johns Hopkins University School of Medicine, faculty in clinical and basic-science departments who are promoted have about twice as many publications as those who are not promoted.[2] It must be acknowledged that there is considerable variation among universities in the expectations placed on part-time and full-time faculty in clinical and basic-science departments. The pressure to publish is probably most intense in departments in which time-dependent promotion or termination is based on scientific productivity.[2] A corollary question arises: Is publication sufficient for academic advancement? The answer: Probably. The response varies among departments, and ancillary contributions—such as teaching, administration, and clinical work—have some effect on promotion considerations. It is clear that junior faculty members perceive the number of publications to be the critical element for academic advancement.[2]

ACADEMIC CONTROL MECHANISMS

The foregoing consideration of the developmental biology of the physician-scientist proposes the existence of several kinds of control mechanisms.

- The pressure to publish is a career-long method of selection in academe. It is a process that not only impinges on junior faculty members, but becomes important in shaping careers by the age of 16 or 18 and might be manifest by the age of 7 or 8.
- During much of the long period of career development, there is more pressure to publish than is perceived by many developing scientists and scholars. Making the importance of publication more explicit in college, in graduate or medical school, and during postdoctoral training might be of advantage to all developing scientists and scholars. Trying to play a game without fully knowing the rules often is more anxiety-provoking and less productive than is participating in a tough game when all the rules are known.
- It is likely that only at the transition from junior to senior faculty does the quality of publication become as important as or more important than the quantity of publications. Measuring the quantity of publications often serves as a surrogate for critical evaluation of a scientist's level of scholarship.[1] A well-publicized situation demonstrates that. It was only when Robert Slutsky was being considered for academic tenure that his large opus of publications was critically reviewed and studied in its entirety.[4,5] It became evident that there was cause for concern about overlapping publications and about the veracity of some of the reported findings. Up to that point, screening procedures that shaped his academic development and advancement had relied more heavily on the quantity of publications than on a critical appraisal of their quality.
- The pressure to publish might produce many positive responses in the developing organism. There is no doubt that scientific curiosity is only one of the factors that motivate people. It is clear that the pressure to publish can produce academically desirable behavior much more frequently than it will produce undesirable behavior.
- The pressure to publish can produce less desirable responses. One response is to tilt the output of a researcher toward the quick and dirty, rather than the definitive study. There is an apparent advantage to producing multiple

fragmented publications ("least publishable units," or LPUs), instead of combining work into more comprehensive papers.[4] At some distinguished universities, it has been proposed that tenure decisions might include consideration of no more than 10 publications by a candidate. If that policy were adopted widely, there would be a considerable shift in the quantity-to-quality ratio of biomedical publications. Finally, pressure to publish leads to overt data falsification, although that is probably rare and likely reflects a long-term developmental aberration, rather than a response to acute stress.

- The pressure to publish has a substantial effect on journal editors, as well as on scientists. Editors and editorial boards of biomedical journals not only serve as gatekeepers for their journals, but also shape the scientist's approach to quality. Developing and mature members of the species have superegos, and they respond not only to directives (another series of experiments is needed), but also to the implicit question, "Is this really the best you can do?"

Editors and editorial boards have a substantial influence on the career development of scientists. At many stages along the way, acceptance or rejection of a paper can substantially change the direction of a scientist's career development. In a sense, journal editors have become highly influential members of academic promotion committees. It is difficult for senior faculty to evaluate the quality of scholarship of persons in different fields. To some degree, they must rely on the journal editors' appraisals of scholarship, as expressed by their decisions to publish manuscripts.

The timing of an editorial decision has a large effect on obtaining grants and promotions and on conferring status among peers. Not infrequently, whether an editorial decision is made next month or this month will have a critical effect on the success of a grant application. Study sections find a major difference between a manuscript submitted for publication and one already accepted by a critically reviewed journal. The timing of editorial decisions also can influence promotion considerations at important junctures and thus determine whether a scientist stays at the same institution or accepts a job elsewhere. Furthermore, status among one's peers is influenced by whether one publishes an important finding first or second. Not only whether but when a paper is accepted is important to individual career development. The pressure to publish involves the dimension of time.

CONCLUSIONS

The pressure to publish is an important effector for the developing and mature scientist and scholar. It is a critical mechanism for academic development. If properly modulated, the pressure to publish can be a positive force in research and scholarship. Repetitive and fragmented publication of research often appears to be rewarded; rarely is it scientifically justifiable. To alter that behavior, the complex system of academic rewards will need to be modified at several points.

REFERENCES

1. Angell M, Relman AS. Fraud in biomedical research: a time for Congressional restraint. N Engl J Med 1988; 318:1462–3.
2. Batshaw ML, Plotnick LP, Petty BC, Woolf PK, Mellits ED. Academic promotion at a medical school. N Engl J Med 1988; 318:741–7.
3. Culliton BJ. Coping with fraud: the Darsee case. Science 1983; 220:31–5.
4. Engler RL, Covell JW, Friedman PJ, Kitcher PS, Peters RM. Misrepresentation and responsibility in medical research. N Engl J Med 1987; 317:1383–9.
5. Marshall E. San Diego's tough stand on research fraud. Science 1986; 234:534–5.
6. Relman AS. Lessons from the Darsee affair. N Engl J Med 1983; 308:1415–7.

Open Discussion

Dr. Sherman:

How reasonable is the proposal for full disclosure, which was made by Drs. Coffey and Marsh, in the eyes of authors, reviewers, and editors? Do you believe that the current environment in academic institutions suggests a possibility for change, including changes in the attitudes of those who review for admission or promotion?

Dr. Marsh:

The issue of full disclosure is fairly simple: There needs to be truth in advertising by authors. If part of a paper has been submitted in a preliminary form elsewhere, if it has been published elsewhere in its entirety, or if it is going to be published as part of symposium proceedings, it is essential that that be stated in the letter of transmission to the editor. The editor and the editorial board can deal with it as they wish.

Dr. Coffey:

I don't have much to add, except that some of these things are hard to carry out. Let me give you an example. The American Urological Association says that it does not want abstracts with promissory notes in them; it wants data in the abstracts. It asks us to include tables, figures, and numbers in our abstracts. I do so, and the material is published by the society in its journal. Later, I submit a paper with the same data; I have done that many, many times. Should I indicate that this is duplicate publication? Should I not submit abstracts? The flagrant abuses are easy—we cannot stand having people publishing duplicate papers. And I think asking the author whether the material has been published previously will help. At least you will have documentation.

Dr. Marsh:

The proposal that universities base their consideration for promotion on a small number of publications is, in fact, just a proposal. At Harvard, that policy has not been accepted. Right now the number is the hoop one jumps through, although other considerations go into the decision. I will be interested to see whether the proposal to consider the best five or ten publications will be widely adopted. If it is, there is going to be a 180-degree turn in some of the problems that journal editors face. I think the backlog of papers to be published will shrink rapidly, and maybe the rate of increase in the number of journals will decline as well.

Dr. Coffey:

Dr. Huth, do you have any information on how widespread the problem of repetitive publication is? In the top 10 journals, how many times in a year do you have duplicate publication of a whole manuscript or at least half the manuscript?

Dr. Huth:

The numbers I have are so small that I am not sure that they would be accepted as valid evidence. Within the last 12 months, of perhaps 200 papers published, I know of two instances of some variety of repetitive publication that involved my journal and another journal. Dr. Coffey mentioned one.

Dr. Rennie:

The case that Dr. Coffey cited of the identical submissions was in a sense plagiarism, which leads me to ask Dr. Marsh whether he has any comments about the fact that the American system of teaching children to write and then calling what they do research is a perfect way of teaching plagiarism; this is very striking to researchers who come here from other countries. I was disappointed to hear that Harvard hasn't adopted the guidelines about the number of publications to be considered in promotions. At Rush Medical College in Chicago, where I was on the promotion committee, such guidelines were adopted a long time ago; and at the University of California, San Francisco, one is allowed to submit even fewer papers for consideration.

Dr. Marsh:

Is teaching someone to write the same as teaching plagiarism? No. I think plagiarism is an issue of character, and the issue of nurturing character is really a bit aside. On the face of it, encouraging good writing is entirely beneficial. But I think the cue that is picked up—that the quantity, and not the quality, of the work is important—is a problem.

Dr. Coffey:

There is an old saying: If you steal one thing, it is plagiarism; if you steal 100 things, it is research. But I think everyone in science has seen examples of plagiarism. I asked five investigators whether they had been plagiarized, and they all said yes; and I am not talking about just the idea, but about sentences, paragraphs, and even pictures that had already been published. Dr. Huth, how often do people write to you to say that something has been plagiarized?

Dr. Huth:

Only once or twice in 5 years has it been called to my attention.

Mr. Whitney:

I have several journals, and it is not difficult for me to prevent multiple publication in these journals. But we get into a problem when we have articles that are written by a physician, a pharmacist, and a nutritionist, and each one wants the article published in a journal of his or her own discipline. Another question is what to do when a journal reaches a milestone like an anniversary and its editors want to republish some classic papers. Is such repetitive publication desirable or undesirable?

Dr. Huth:

I think that editors have failed to define precisely the varieties of repetitive publication that are unacceptable. I am glad that Dr. Coffey brought up the episode that he did, because I was involved. Looking back, I very much regret having possibly injured the careers of the authors. It is now clear to me that we do not state explicitly in our journal what the varieties of possibly unacceptable repetitive publication are. I intend to correct that.

Dr. Bracker:

"Salami science" is a form of repetitive publication; short papers written on related topics often include overlapping information. I have heard many comments here about encouraging more comprehensive papers. However, as editors we are talking out of both sides of our mouths. I can think of instructions for authors in a couple of journals that say something to the effect that authors should not be seduced into writing papers as results come to hand, but instead should wait until a more comprehensive analysis can be reported. Farther down in their instructions, the same journals remind authors that papers must not exceed eight pages or so. I know of young authors who try to stick to those limits and simply break their papers into pieces to conform. As editors, we must be prepared to adapt to longer papers that are more comprehensive, because, after all, not all comprehensive and classic papers will fit into a short space.

Dr. Koshland:

I don't think that our editorial responsibilities can be changed acceptably by the fact that there is a lot of pressure to publish. Bank tellers have to deal with lots of cash, but we don't condone stealing. Full disclosure is all right, but I think that most people know that repetitive publication of primary data in primary journals is not allowed. The question is what we do when we confront it. We have had two cases recently, one in physics and one in medicine. The reviewers—in this case, we picked the right reviewers—had reviewed identical manuscripts for other journals. What is the appropriate response? In another case, a paper appeared in two primary journals a number of years ago, and the authors had not let either journal know that they had submitted to the other; the authors were banned from publishing in both journals for a time. Those two journals were not the only ones in the field, so one could argue that it wasn't much of a punishment. What would be an appropriate punishment? Should the authors be banned from a larger group of journals? Should we circulate the information? In one of the recent cases, we haven't decided what to do yet; when we do, should the information be circulated to other journals? Should it be published? What is our legal liability if we do that? It seems to me that the minimal response is some kind of ban by our own journal.

Dr. Coffey:

Everything is fine until you use the word "punishment"; once you use that word, it is a legal question, because the person being punished has rights and you have rights. I think we have to get legal counsel, because the issue turns to defamation of character and a lot of other things. What would I feel personally? Suppose that there were no chance of a lawsuit. Most of our journals are published by societies. I think those cases have to be brought to the society, and the society should decide the punishment—whether the offenders should be put out of the society and whether they should be prohibited from publishing in the journal. Some journals are not published by societies, and I think in that case the problem is more difficult. But I think you should be banned from publishing in that journal. If the offense is flagrant, there should be some public humiliation.

Dr. Huth:

The undesirability of out-and-out duplicate publication is generally acknowledged, but I do not think that it is a major problem. We get into gray areas; in the episode at Johns Hopkins that was described, the authors believed that they had some justification for their double publication: the piece first appeared in a non-peer-reviewed supplement. From my point of view, and I pointed this out to the authors, *Lancet* is also in large part not peer-reviewed; what is more important is that *Index Medicus* does index that supplement, so it appears in the journal literature. However, I accept the opinion that editors have some distance to go in making clear exactly what they see as the problem and in defining the limits more precisely for authors.

To summarize: We have heard of the pressures to publish and the climate in which there are urges to spread one's material around and extract more in terms of publication in behalf of one's career, reputation, and tenure. We have also heard that editors have a substantial responsiblity to develop policy and—perhaps even more important—not to develop policy in a vacuum among ourselves, but to take into account the problems for scientific investigators in the real world.

Legal and Ethical Risks: Real or Perceived?

Barbara Mishkin

Journal editors are caught in the firestorm surrounding scientific misconduct, because the publication of retractions and of articles that are critical of previously published reports can affect the reputation of scientists and erode confidence in science generally. The first duty of a scientific journal is to publish research in accordance with accepted standards. If a journal unwittingly publishes an article that is seriously flawed, it has an ethical responsibility to correct the scientific record.[7] Moreover, a brief review of the law of defamation strongly suggests that the often-expressed fears of liability[5,12] are largely without foundation. The risks of responsible reporting can be contained by adherence to established policies and by concern for due process,[8] whereas failure to correct the scientific record can jeopardize both scientific progress and public health.

THE DIFFERENCE BETWEEN BEING SUED AND BEING LIABLE

When an attorney is asked whether a journal can be sued for publishing a particular article, the answer invariably is yes. Anyone can sue, and the only way to prevent lawsuits entirely is not to publish at all. Although litigation can be costly, failure to maintain the integrity of the scientific literature could be even more costly. Accordingly, it is better to ask, "If the journal is sued, how likely is it to lose?"

In cases of formally confirmed or admitted scientific misconduct, it is highly unlikely that a journal would be held liable for publishing a retraction without the permission of all authors. Similarly, a paper that criticizes a previously published article can be written to protect against liability. If care is taken, lawsuits will not result (despite the threats), because the journal would be protected by the truth of the factual statements made, the privilege of "fair reporting," the absolute protection of genuine opinions by the First Amendment to the U.S. Constitution, and due diligence in reviewing the manuscripts.

TRUTH IS A DEFENSE

If a formal investigation finds that research reported in a published article was fabricated,[1] there should be no liability for reporting that fact. If a journal's report of fabrication is incorrect in a few minor details, but the essence of the matter in question is accurate, the person claiming libel will not prevail.[10] Not only will the plaintiff lose, but the journal's attorney could obtain a summary judgement or dismissal and thus avoid a prolonged proceeding and trial.[11]

Of course, a plaintiff can appeal the dismissal, and the journal would then be involved in further litigation. At some point, however, lawyers will advise potential plaintiffs not to initiate such proceedings, because judges can impose penalties on attorneys who bring groundless suits to the courts. An Arizona court recently ordered a physician and his lawyer, who had brought a groundless suit against members of a medical peer-review committee, to pay attorney's fees for all the defendants. When they appealed, not only was the order affirmed, but the appellate court added the costs of the appeal to the original penalty.[3]

THE FAIR-REPORTING PRIVILEGE

The privilege of "fair reporting" protects journals against liability for reporting matters of public interest and importance, including matters related to health.[4] For example, a university professor recently circulated a letter to sports magazines and athletic organizations, criticizing a questionnaire that purported to identify psychologic traits that predict athletic success. The psychologist who developed the questionnaire sued and lost, because the professor's criticisms were based on extensive research and his motive for publishing was to inform others in his profession of the unreliability of the questionnaire.[6] Moreover, the psychologist had adequate opportunity to respond.

The fair-reporting privilege clearly should apply to publication of an official statement of the findings of a formal investigation from an academic institution or a federal agency. Similarly, it should not be necessary for a journal to insist that only the author of an article can request retraction, or that all coauthors must agree, if there has been a formal finding that an article is unreliable and if the retraction is reasonably designed to reach those who might have relied on information in the discredited article. The fair-reporting privilege should work as long as the journal has no reason to believe that the critique was written with malicious intent. Fair reporting incorporates the principle of due diligence.

GENUINE OPINIONS ARE PROTECTED

As the U.S. Supreme Court has observed:

> Under the First Amendment, there is no such thing as a false idea. However pernicious an opinion may seem, we depend for its correction not on the conscience of judges and juries but on the competition of other ideas.[2]

That principle affords broad protection to opinions critical of published materials. To enjoy the protection, authors must use language that clearly expresses a genuine opinion, rather than a fact. For example, scientists might express puzzlement at their inability to replicate previously published findings, rather than saying that the previous authors clearly fabricated their data, because the latter would be an assertion that the previous authors had engaged in serious misconduct. The principle does not, however, protect assertions of fact masquerading as opinion. Thus, the statement "In my opinion, Dr. X is a fraud" would not be protected as opinion, despite its characterization as such.

DUE DILIGENCE AFFORDS PROTECTION

Even when erroneous statements are published, a publisher generally can avoid liability by demonstrating care in the review process. For example, a nutritionist recently sued a New York publisher for printing an article that falsely reported that she had been "instrumental in preparing [a] marshmallow-based diet to help . . . readers lose up to a pound a day."[9] In fact, it was a reporter for the newspaper who had created the diet. In its defense, the paper described its review process. An editor had requested and received the names, titles, and telephone numbers of the persons with whom the reporter claimed to have spoken. The editor also obtained a list of the dates of the conversations. A rewrite editor improved style and clarity. The assignment editor reviewed both the original copy and the revised version and made further changes. The editor approved the article for publication. And the entire issue of the paper was submitted to outside counsel for libel review.

Although no one had attempted to verify the nutritional validity of the diet, and the published statement was both incorrect and professionally embarrassing to the nutritionist, the court granted summary judgment to the paper, because it had not shown "gross irresponsibility" in publishing the article. In fact, the paper had met generally accepted standards of responsible publishing, including accepting work from a source whose prior publications had never been challenged, having several editors check the work carefully, and subjecting the article to review by libel counsel.[9] Moreover, the court found that, although the author was paid for the article, he was not an employee of the paper, so the publisher could not be held responsible under any theory of vicarious liability. The stylistic editing done by the editors did not confer responsibility for the content of the article.

Although the states have substantial latitude in defining standards of liability for defamation, "so long as they do not impose liability without fault,"[2] it is improbable that a scientific journal that follows generally accepted review practices would be held liable for unwittingly publishing false statements in an article submitted by a scientist whose reliability the editors have had no reason to doubt.

DUTY TO CORRECT THE RECORD

Once there is reason to believe that an article is unreliable, journals should place the burden on the authors to prove the reliability not only of the article in question, but of others published previously. A journal need not require proof of reliability or conduct its own review of the primary data, a process being proposed by the Food and Drug Administration. A journal should require proof of published claims, once they have been called into question, as does the Federal Trade Commission. Like damaged goods, fraudulent scientific reports can waste consumers' time, and they can be dangerous.

Similarly, adding the names of scientists to research for which they have no responsibility is false labeling: It misleads the consumer by promising a level of quality associated with a respected source. Accordingly, it is in the interest of good science for journals to develop and insist on proper standards for authorship. Journals also must report misconduct once reliable and fair procedures reveal wrongdoing.

Adoption of a uniform policy, such as that proposed in 1987 by the International Committee of Medical Journal Editors,[7] would provide protection to individual journals in the event of libel suits. In addition, journals might consider establishing a risk pool, or self-insurance fund, to defend against legal actions or to participate in a test case to establish precedent from which all scientific journals would benefit.

If editors were to develop sound policies and procedures with the assistance of legal counsel, they could remain steadfast in the face of scientific misconduct and thus preserve the integrity of their journals and of science itself.

REFERENCES

1. Freedman DX. Request for retraction [letter]. Arch Gen Psychiatry 1988;45:685-6.
2. *Gertz v. Robert Welch, Inc.* 418 U.S. 323, 339-340, 347 (1974).
3. *Gilbert v. Board of Medical Examiners* 745 P.2d 617 (Ariz. Ct. App. 1987).
4. *Hoffman v. Washington Post Co.* 433 F. Supp. 600 (D.D.C. 1977), *aff'd.* 578 F.2d 442 (D.C. Cir. 1977).
5. Hostetler AJ. Fear of suits blocks retractions. The Scientist 1987;1(23):1-2.
6. *Institute of Athletic Motivation v. University of Illinois,* 170 Cal. Rptr. 411, 413, 418 (Cal. Ct. App. 1980).
7. International Committee of Medical Journal Editors. Retraction of research findings. Ann Intern Med 1988;108:304.
8. Mishkin B. Responding to scientific misconduct: due process and prevention. JAMA 1988; 260(13):1932-6.
9. *Nelson v. Globe International, Inc.* 626 F. Supp. 969, 971, 976-979 (S.D.N.Y. 1986).
10. *Tavoulareas v. Piro,* 817 F.2d 762 (D.C. Cir. 1987) (en banc).
11. *Vachet v. Central Newspapers, Inc.* 816 F.2d 313 (7th Cir. 1987).
12. Woolf PK. Ensuring integrity in biomedical publication. JAMA 1987;258:3424-7.

Should Science Go to Law?

JOHN MADDOX

Editors of scientific journals can no longer behave as though the law does not exist; however, the intrusion of the law into their editorial business is not yet as extensive as it might become. Science proper is similarly threatened. Why "threatened"? Because it would be comforting for a field of inquiry whose success depends on open communication and free speech, as does science, to be untrammeled.

The two obvious points at which science and the law interact are property rights and personal reputations. Both differently constrain people's freedom to say and do what they wish. Much of the trouble arises because rights and constraints are not clearly defined. Differences between legal systems in different countries are a source of confusion.

Much of the difficulty regarding property rights arises because of the understandable conflict in scientists' minds between the virtues of the two most obvious rewards of innovation—approbation in the scientific community and riches. The conflict is sharper in Britain than it is in the United States, because of the British rule that any disclosure before application prevents the grant of a patent.

One way of resolving the difficulty is the standard consent agreement by which innovators supply research materials to others in return for the understanding that their use will be for research only, not for commercial purposes. That might satisfy the lawyers, but the mere need for an agreement is a constraint. A curious inversion of the process, also a constraint, is that in which a genetic probe is distributed on the condition that it be used not for research, but only for diagnosis.

Where will all this lead? By what means can researchers be made more free, yet less fearful of losing their intellectual property?

The issue of a person's reputation is more confusing. Publication, for example, is a means by which ideas are communicated and a means by which reputations are enhanced. What is the consequence of a journal's publishing an article by Author A, whose reputation is enhanced by the publication, but whose reputation is later diminished—perhaps to a point below its previous level—by the publication of a criticism of Author A's work by Author B in the same journal? There is no case law on the issue; most journals and their contributors would avoid the problem by couching their criticisms in language that had meaning only to those already in the know and by giving Author A the opportunity to reply to the criticism. We are all familiar with how an admission of error can be hidden in a sufficiently combative piece of prose. Would it not be better if we followed the convention that even the best people sometimes make mistakes?

Other circumstances can be even more corrosive of the intellectual climate. Recent accusations of fraud in science have usually been followed by bouts of recrimination about its antecedents—the responsibilities of senior scientists, referees, journals, and coauthors. These are also circumstances in which individual reputations can be damaged. Curiously, people are as much offended by the suggestion that they might not have been fully effective coauthors as by any other. But is that not unavoidable and also not a case for running off to the law?

It would be pleasing and consonant with the simple view of science—as a means by which reseachers altruistically collaborate to advance the frontiers of understanding—if it were possible to assert that science never goes to law. But that would be not only untrue but unrealistic. The research profession is a profession like others—medicine or accountancy, for example—in which people seek to secure rights to which they believe they are entitled or in which they seek to defend their professional reputations and thus their potential enjoyment of the benefits of professional success, fame and fortune, or both.

It is therefore not surprising that most journal editors from time to time find letters from lawyers in their mail. *Nature* might publish three or four issues each year that entail legal questions. Most often, we have letters from authors or their lawyers, threatening legal action of some kind; we can deal with many of the complaints informally without asking our own lawyers to reply and usually without consulting them. But there also are occasions when we think it prudent to consult our lawyers before deciding whether to publish an item; usually, this involves news items that seem potentially defamatory.

What follows is not a lawyer's account of the problem—I am not a lawyer—but an anecdotal impression of my experience. First, I should register the following general qualification and reservations.

At a time when most scientific journals have become international, in the sense that their readers and their contributors are no longer concentrated in a single country, it is a nuisance that the law on intellectual property and on defamation varies enormously from one country to another. For example, under European patent law, prior publication of a report about an innovation in a scientific journal invalidates a patent application. United States patent law, however, appears to allow inventors a year's grace after first publication before patent applications are automatically invalidated.

The defamation laws are even more variable. As I understand it, in the United States, the truthfulness of a published statement is always a sufficient defense against a libel action. It is even possible that untruthful published statements can escape legal sanction, provided that they are not willfully untruthful. A reporter who seeks to publish a charge against a named person can do so with relative impunity, if the person charged declines to speak to the reporter on the telephone. But if the person charged does speak and insists that the charge is false, an unvarnished report of the allegation would be risky; the parallel publication of the charge and its rebuttal would be defensible. That is exactly what you would expect in the land of the First Amendment. In Britain, where there is no written constitution to amend, the shoe is on the other foot. British libel law places the burden of proof with the defendant in a libel suit, not with the plaintiff, as in other civil suits. Moreover, truthfulness is not a sufficient defense. A client might hold a true statement to be libelous because it is not germane to the purpose of the article in which it appears, it might have been published maliciously, or its appearance is not demonstrably in the public interest.

British libel laws are not hard to live with, but editors must be aware of differences between the laws in different countries in which the same journal circulates. In a recent case, the *International Herald Tribune* had to pay damages of £25,000 in a libel suit that could have been brought to trial only in Britain. In one particularly difficult negotiation with lawyers representing a potential litigant, I was clearly reminded that the litigant would be free to bring an action in whichever jurisdiction seemed more appropriate.

I don't want to give the impression that *Nature* is in and out of the libel courts. To my knowledge, we have lost only two libel suits in 15 years. In one, the reviewer of a book written by a well-known eccentric used the words, "If only Professor Bloggs were honest with himself, he would admit. . . ." Our lawyers told us that the sentence implied dishonesty so we paid £50 to Professor Bloggs and printed an apology. It also cost us £50 when I published a tortuous sentence to argue that one should not judge an institution by the source of its funds; I repeated an allegation about the Church of England that had been the subject of a libel suit in the 1930s.

The scientific profession differs from the rest of scholarship in the degree to which it relies on the published literature to establish and maintain professional standards, good science, and good scientists. Most other professions have formal mechanisms for setting standards, such as professional associations or structures that validate the curricula of professional degree courses.

It is remarkable that the scientific profession delegates this crucial task to its journals, many of which are commercial. The arrangement has the important advantage of openness. Important innovations and discoveries emerge in the most unlikely places, and the general accessibility of the scientific literature is good for the field. This process illustrates the importance of bibliographies in research-grant applications and explains why peer reviewers should carry out their thankless tasks unpaid—they are influencing the standards of quality in their own fields of research.

But the dominant role played by the literature in determining scientific quality also has disadvantages. The scientific literature is ill suited to what many insist is its primary function—pure communication. If communication were the primary goal, the literature would be more artful, more frank, and more literate. I would welcome an erosion of the dominance of the literature in the determination of quality in research. There are some signs of change in that direction, but they are not especially significant.

Given the role of the literature in determining the quality of research, it is remarkable that there appear to be few legal suits involving journals and the contributions with which they are entrusted by authors. These may be more litigious times than in the past, but the surprise is that they are not much more litigious.

INTELLECTUAL PROPERTY

At *Nature,* we are currently involved in a legal dispute that involves two authors, A and B, who live in different countries and had collaborated on a project. At some point, they parted ways, and A sent B a letter summarizing what he had learned from the collaboration. It emerged later that this summary was the outline of a paper that A planned to submit for publication. B was intrigued by the letter's central hypothesis, which he had not heard before, and used already published data to demonstrate that the hypothesis was valid. B submitted his paper to *Nature* and sent a copy to A, who then claimed that B had stolen his idea. We believed that was true. A asked that B's paper not be published until his own version had appeared. A's lawyers asserted that A's letter constituted a copyright of the hypothesis and consequently that B would be violating the copyright if B's article were published first.

We have decided to publish B's article, but we have insisted on two changes in the text. First, B must reference A's letter and credit A with providing the inspiration for B's idea. Second, B must provide a notice regarding A's forthcoming paper. You might not choose either A or B as a drinking companion, but it is my belief that an interesting, even important, idea should not be kept out of print for 6 months because collaboration between two authors has broken down.

Despite the growing importance attached to the commercial exploitation of intellectual property, disputes of this kind are still much more common, to my knowledge, than are those which arise from patent law. Researchers' concern with establishing their priority as the originators of interesting ideas is related directly to the function of the literature as the chief determinant of standards.

The commercial side of research will probably become more obtrusive. I have seen a steady growth in the requests from patent lawyers asking us to provide affidavits confirming that copies of *Nature* have reached subscribers by a specific date. The British government has been impatient with British science during the last 10 years, because no arrangements have been made to secure patent protection for monoclonal antibodies, introduced through publication in *Nature* by César Milstein in 1976. The explanation is, in part, that the authors believed that by publishing their discovery they had put monoclonal antibodies in the public domain. They did not have a year's grace, which is allowed in the United States, for patent protection.

A ticklish administrative point arises here. Authors often ask that their articles be considered for publication, but that publication be delayed until patent formalities have been completed. The objective seems to be to establish priority and secure a patent. I do not agree and am concerned with avoiding the conflicts of interest that could arise from delaying publication.

In general, probably little can be done to avoid the difficulty arising from those discordant legal procedures. Perhaps a uniform rule on prior disclosure might be negotiated among the major industrial nations.

Should it be a condition of publication that authors make research materials available to others working in the field or deposit data generated with the appropriate data banks, or both? The first suggestion most legitimately is based on the belief that many crucial research materials—cell lines, for example—cannot be specified precisely in the published literature; only a physical sample of the material will suffice. The suggestion challenges researchers' rights to their intellectual property in obvious ways.

The lawyers, always ingenious, have devised sensible ways to allow researchers to share materials without losing property rights; consent forms by which people undertake not to use others' cell lines or oligonucleotide probes for purposes other than research have become common. What are the implications of the demand that all research materials be made available to some general class of inquirers, or that all nucleotide sequences be submitted to a data bank, before a manuscript is accepted for publication?

Are all cell lines free of hazard? Who is liable for damages? Which competitors and colleagues constitute the class of legitimate inquirers? Who meets the cost of distributing materials and of maintaining a stock of them so that delayed requests can be honored? Are inquirers required to say why they need the materials or data? How will materials be transferred? How will the data be acknowledged in later publications? Should commercially based researchers be treated differently from other inquirers? In what ways?

Data supporting published conclusions should be generally accessible. Requiring transfer of data to data banks eliminates the possibility that researchers will neglect to store data and make them generally available.

I accept that the publication process is imperfect, in that crucial evidence, such as a cell line or a nucleotide sequence, might not accompany the ink-on-paper version of a paper. But if the evidence is indeed crucial, does the responsibility not rest with the journals to find ways of ensuring that the data are accessible? That question needs discussion before we decide that our contributors should be coerced into practices with disadvantages that might not yet be evident.

To the extent that the common interest of editors is that literature be freely accessible, all restraints appear as abridgments of a contributor's freedom.

These questions deserve more thought than they have been given. *Nature*'s policy is to encourage compliance with the rules, but not to insist on it. Among other things, we doubt whether we would be effective.

DEFAMATION

If I am correct in saying that the published literature is the principal determinant of quality in science, it is not surprising that authors are sensitive to published criticism of their work. But I would like to argue that the very same convention—that science can in some cases be equated with the published record—provides journals with an opportunity and even a freedom to be critical, not merely of what they publish, but also of what appears elsewhere.

An author publishing a paper is not merely contributing to the accumulation of knowledge, but is staking a claim on an appropriate share of the credit. For the sake of understanding, it is important that the literature be a valid record, as free as possible of spurious and misleading assertions. Although researchers will often come to conclusions about the merits or faults of particular articles, they rarely challenge them in print. One consequence is that the scientific literature is not an entirely satisfactory record of the process of discovery. The peaks are the frequently cited papers; the false leads fade away.

That is unsatisfactory. It would be better for science if the literature were more explicit. It seems essential that journals provide opportunities for readers to criticize what has been published. Potential critics often bite their tongues; the responsibility then falls on the shoulders of editors.

As I understand it, the law is not constraining in this regard. Authors who claim credit for a discovery invite criticism and cannot complain later if their work is shown to be less important than they originally believed. It is exactly the same when a publisher sends an editor a book to review and then complains if the review is hostile. As a matter of equity, the authors of both the article and the book can complain if the criticism is unjust; this requires vigilance from editors in telling the difference between legitimate and illegitimate criticism. As a matter of law, hostile criticism should fall short of libel. For example, it would be allowable to argue that Dr. Bloggs's proof that water runs uphill is experimentally unsound, but not to suggest that Dr. Bloggs has published his conclusion because he is hoping to raise venture capital to form an antigravity-propulsion company.

Nature has been involved in the last few years with two publications of a critical nature. One was the paper by Stewart and Feder[2] on the publications of Dr. John Darsee, who was found to have been responsible for fraudulent data at Harvard Medical School and, earlier, at Emory University. The high interest in that paper was due to its demonstration that coauthorship can be "honorary" to the point of being symbolic. I believe that to be an important comment on the practice of research. Some complain that publication is unwarranted because the allegations are untrue; others claim that publication is unwarranted because the allegations are so true that science will look foolish. Our legal difficulties with that paper had to do simply with the avoidance of libel—not merely to avoid damages, but to avoid being unjust.

In the case of our more recent account[1] of the work of Dr. Jacques Benveniste and his colleagues in Paris, the issue is whether we should have published an article that reported sensational data and a remarkable interpretation of the data and then have criticized the paper on the grounds that the data were gathered so unsystematically that the conclusions could not be sustained. Some have complained that it was a publicity stunt, but it might be described as a public service. Science needs to know more clearly what is being done in the name of science.

My hope is for a scientific literature that is more self-critical than at present and that will become more human in allowing researchers to acknowledge that they can make mistakes. My worry about the spate of allegations of fraud over the last few years is that it is now more difficult than ever to allow for honest mistakes.

REFERENCES

1. Maddox J, Randi J, Stewart WW. High-dilution experiments a delusion. Nature 1988; 334: 287-90.
2. Stewart WW, Feder N. The integrity of the scientific literature. Nature 1987; 325: 207-14.

Communicating Public-Health Information Through the Mass Media

BRUCE B. DAN

Public-health information is of little value unless it can be communicated effectively and clearly to those who will benefit most from it—the public. Until very recently, most people learned what little they knew about health and medicine from talking to their personal physicians. Those conversations, carried out in cramped examining rooms, were brief exchanges at best. Indeed, most of those infrequent encounters were held in a setting in which modern communication theory predicts that little or no information can be transmitted. But now it seems that most Americans get most of their medical information from sources other than their doctors—newspapers, magazines, health newsletters, diet books, fitness tapes, radio talk shows, and television.

Interpersonal communication is marked by a single source and single receiver. A homogeneous relationship exists between the source of the information and the receiver, and there is immediate feedback. In contrast, mass communication has many participants as sources and many receivers. The audience is diverse and heterogeneous, and feedback is delayed, if it exists at all. Physicians are trained in interpersonal communication, but they have virtually no formal experience in mass communication. Yet survey after survey suggests that most people get their information from the mass media.

Recent A. C. Nielsen studies on the viewing habits of the public show that an average American watches 7.4 hours of television a day. More than any other form of mass communication, television is tightly limited by the constraints of time and audience. The average news segment is 60-90 seconds long, and this compression leads to oversimplification and distortion of information. More disquieting is that television audiences are highly skewed as to socioeconomic levels. In a national survey conducted by one advertising company, 88% of people whose median income was less than $10,000 said that they had watched television the day before, but only 50% had read a newspaper. More than 75% of those with an income of more than $35,000 had read a newspaper, and television viewing was correspondingly lower.

Even more dramatic are studies showing that during a crisis (defined here as a crucial event involving danger) virtually everyone with access to television uses it as the primary source of information; almost 99% of Americans own television sets. In the last half of the twentieth century, at least in the United States, society not only has become directly linked to the mass media, but is often defined by them.

News of medical importance, whether it originates in articles published in the leading medical journals, in papers presented at scientific meetings, or in government publications, such as *Morbidity and Mortality Weekly Report,* is first filtered through and then disseminated by the mass media. That process undeniably modifies the form and the content of the message.

Television is used by a variety of information providers, many of whom have a vested interest in the message and in how it is presented. Since 1986, the Federal Trade Commission has encouraged food producers to make health claims in their marketing campaigns to communicate health-related information to the public. More recently, to hype its bran cereals, the manufacturer of Kellogg's cereals has promoted information disseminated by the National Cancer Institute to the effect that high-fiber foods can reduce the risk of colon cancer in some people. That campaign not only increased sales, but increased the overall consumption of other manufacturers' fiber cereals.

Campbell's soup advertisements suggested that eating soup can help to reduce the risk of cancer and that soup is a good source of calcium (perhaps to sway women who had already been bombarded by television messages about the dangers of osteoporosis). The facts that the source of calcium was the milk that consumers add in preparing the soup and that canned soup also is high in sodium were not addressed.

Quaker Oats has waged a campaign to convince the public that eating oatmeal will lower serum cholesterol concentration. That approach obviously meshed nicely with messages from the National Institutes of Health, suggesting that Americans need to lower their serum cholesterol to reduce the nation's high death toll from heart disease. The Center for Science in the Public Interest stated that the Quaker Oats campaign was a "gross exaggeration" and "proved the food industry can't even make responsible claims for decent foods" (according to Bruce Silverglade, Director of Legal Affairs, in conjunction with a complaint filed with the Federal Trade Commission in 1988).

In another attempt to capitalize on America's latest fitness craze, Kellogg's Special K was advocated to help dieters to "keep the muscle and lose the fat." The National Advertising Division of the Better Business Bureau countered that people would be better off eating protein in a more concentrated and higher-quality form in fish, meat, or poultry.[1]

But using advertisements to get health messages to the public is not limited to food manufacturers. The pharmaceutical industry has recently embarked on direct to-the-consumer advertising. Bypassing the usual controls of the Food and Drug Administration, drug companies are transmitting subtle messages to the American people. Squibb began a "Quality of Life" campaign after the *New England Journal of Medicine* published an article in 1986 about an antihypertensive medication that was purported to cause fewer side effects than similar drugs do.[2] The thrust of the campaign was an only slightly veiled innuendo that men taking Squibb's drug would suffer lower rates of impotence.

Patients were urged to "contact their physicians if they were not feeling like their old selves."

In the midst of these sudden changes in the way the public receives medical information, news directors of local and network television stations were receiving results of a poll by the Radio and Television News Directors Association (RTNDA) and Roper suggesting that not only was the public getting most of its health information from television, but two-thirds of the public wanted more information than was currently available (according to a preliminary report presented at the RTNDA 1986 annual meeting, in Salt Lake City).

The clear indication was that putting doctors on television would be good business. Physicians could translate the day's medical news, and they could offer perspectives on the complex medical world. Doctors began popping up on television screens in virtually every local market, and several have been assigned as network medical experts. Doctors appear on popular morning shows, evening newscasts, and late-night special broadcasts. Although many of the physicians who appear on the air serve merely as specialty reporters with an interest in the medical beat, others have begun to offer medical advice. Some actually host live call-in shows, during which viewers can give brief medical histories, have their illnesses diagnosed, and have treatments suggested on the air. Several legal experts have stated that we will soon see the first malpractice suits against doctors who practice in the broadcast media.

Regardless of these unusual and perhaps transient trends, there is no doubt that the public will continue to receive most of its health information through the mass media. Understanding the new "mass medicine" is imperative, if we are to understand and protect the public health.

REFERENCES

1. Better Business Bureau, National Advertising Division. Case report #2576, March 21, 1988. New York, N.Y.: Better Business Bureau.
2. Croog SH, Levine S, Testa MA. The effects of antihypertensive therapy on the quality of life. New Engl J Med 1986;314:1657–64.

Open Discussion

Dr. Dan:

I appreciated Ms. Mishkin's comments about editors' having a stiffer backbone. The *Journal of the American Medical Association* has guidelines that would help. The journal has been, of all things, dissuaded from publishing book reviews that recommend against readers' buying a book. The journal's legal counsel has said that such a recommendation could be construed as restraint of trade, and perhaps a review as forceful as that should not be published.

Ms. Mishkin:

If book reviewers simply say that they dislike a book, the reviewers and the journal are safe. What is harmful is advice to readers not to buy a book.

Dr. Dan:

Is that not covered by free speech and opinion? Is that really restraint of trade?

Ms. Mishkin:

I think it is an overstatement, but if you wanted to be careful about it you would simply tell reviewers to express opinions forcefully, but to let readers make up their own minds about book purchases.

Mr. Maddox:

It is very hard to restrain book reviewers from making that kind of recommendation if, indeed, they feel strongly about a book. It seems to me that, even in repressive old Britain, it would be fair to let the recommendation stand. The rule that we have come to appreciate the hard way is that, if a book reviewer says that the price of a volume is outrageously high and for that reason the book should be disliked, the chances are that the reviewer doesn't understand enough about the economics of publishing to state that opinion. We seem to worry more about that sort of recommendation than about the advice, "Do not buy the book; it will be bad for your students."

Dr. Bracker:

If I say that an author is dishonest and I can't back it up, that is actionable. If I say that it is my opinion that an author is dishonest and I can't back it up, that is not actionable?

Ms. Mishkin:

That is the strict distinction. If you say, "In my opinion, she is guilty of murder," then, even though that is your opinion, it is actionable, because you are accusing someone of illegal conduct.

These examples must be looked at in context. I hate to keep saying, "It depends," but lawyers like to use those terms. It really would depend on the context of what was being said and on what a normal reader of that publication would understand from the statement.

Dr. Angell:

It is refreshing for a lawyer to tell us not to worry too much about lawyers. But Ms. Mishkin also said that, in this country, the only way to be certain of not being sued is not to do anything. Then she suggested that journals might want to pool resources to share risks.

At the *New England Journal of Medicine* we have been lucky so far. Do you know of cases in which journals have been sued for going about their business in more or less appropriate ways and what the outcome has been?

Ms. Mishkin:

I don't know of a lot of cases, but I think it would be worthy of study. I think that fear of lawsuits is greatly exaggerated and exists without a great deal of foundation. It would be nice to have some data on that from journal editors, who are in a better position than I am to know how frequently they get these letters and how much time is used in negotiations and settlements. We see only cases that actually make their way through the courts.

I am greatly encouraged to hear that the *New England Journal of Medicine* has not had a lot of problems with this, because it is a journal that is willing to take stands. If that does not lead to legal problems, then the case is pretty well stated. Perhaps those who think it does lead to problems ought to have the burden of proving it.

Dr. Koshland:

Some speakers have discussed the problems of dual publication. If journal editors devised a mechanism to circulate the names of offenders, would that be libelous? Could we be sued for such an action?

Ms. Mishkin:

My view of due process begins way up front with prophylaxis, and that is to make your procedures clear to anyone who wants to submit articles to your publication. For example, your policy might be that, if someone submits an article to two journals without disclosing this information, the editor will make it known to other journals and, in egregious cases, to the readers. If you give warning, have an established policy, follow your procedures, and apply your rules fairly and consistently, you are on much firmer ground in taking whatever action you choose. If you simply cite the fact that both you and another journal received identical papers and give the dates, that is a factual statement. Readers can draw their own conclusions from it.

Dr. Koshland:

So, your answer is that, if a policy is clearly stated in a journal's instructions for authors, authors violate the policy, and an editor makes that violation public, the editor should be successful in a lawsuit?

Ms. Mishkin:

You certainly increase your likelihood of being successful.

Mr. Maddox:

I think that there is a fine distinction between whether an editor's redress is to publish a notice of a violation in the journal or to inform the editors of other journals, even privately, that they should not accept papers from specific authors. I would have thought the first course of action to be more defensible than the second.

Ms. Mishkin:

I agree, because informing other journal editors privately that they should not accept papers from authors goes beyond merely stating that an author has submitted the same paper to two journals. If editors want to ensure that other editors understand such a recommendation, they can publish the facts of the situation as stated and then send reprints to editors of other journals. I don't see anything wrong, for example, with journals in a particular association or consortium agreeing to share information, as long as that policy is clear to those who submit papers to those journals.

Dr. Friedman:

In our letter to journal editors regarding the Slutsky affair, we stated that we understood the act of retraction to be a tacit admission of fraud on the part of Dr. Slutsky. We then stated the university's opinion of the matter. Half the journals that printed our statement deleted the statement about tacit admission of fraud. From what you say, I gather that that was a perfectly acceptable thing to do, because it was clearly an expression of our opinion.

Ms. Mishkin:

That is why I had difficulty in responding to the question of whether it is acceptable to say, "In my opinion, she is guilty of murder." I don't think that a journal can really protect itself adequately against what is clearly an allegation of misconduct by saying, "In our opinion, he is a fraud."

Dr. Friedman:

Is the journal protected? That was the point, not whether the university is protected by saying that it has written a letter that contained the statement as part of a longer one.

Ms. Mishkin:

I would probably advise the journal to ask Dr. Friedman to rephrase the statement.

Dr. Friedman:

If a journal editor learns something, either by allegation or by convincing proof, about the bad publication practices of an author, whether it is plagiarism, fraud, or whatever, what governs the editor's ability to communicate that to the institution before having absolute, clear proof?

Ms. Mishkin:

I think the journal editor would be wise to raise the question with the institution, unless the editor has the resources and the inclination to do a full-scale due-process review under journal auspices. I doubt that that is often an option. It seems to me that the wisest course is for the journal to request some clarification from the institution and to ask the institution to investigate.

Dr. Dan:

As you can imagine, most associations have lawyers whose primary duty is to defend the association against all assaults, and they interpret that a letter from a lawyer implying a threat of lawsuit is an assault, which takes up their time and resources. The American Medical Association is considered a conservative organization—a large one, certainly—and has a large body of rather conservative attorneys.

Such a philosophy or attitude restricts the creative artistry and imagination that allows journals to do what they really should be doing: exploring new ground and taking issues to the edge. The legal community tends to bring us back to the things that are precedent, things that are well known and traditional.

Mr. Greenberg:

Nature chose to publish the Feder and Stewart paper, and *Science* chose not to. I would like to ask Dr. Koshland whether there were legal considerations in the decision.

Dr. Koshland:

The answer is no; the manuscript that we received was not the same as the one that John Maddox of *Nature* received. It went through many versions.

Dr. Dan:

Was that an attempt to evade the question, Dr. Koshland?

Dr. Koshland:

Absolutely not, but we don't discuss why we reject papers.

Ms. Ohman:

If someone writes a letter to the journal, saying that an article in our journal was terrible, and we send the letter to the author for reply, does that automatically protect us from any problems arising from the letter?

Ms. Mishkin:

Suppose the letter said not only that the article is awful, but that Dr. X is guilty of serious fraud and misconduct, inasmuch as everything in the article is fabricated. There might be a problem, because the letter-writer is accusing Dr. X of serious misconduct. You could ask the letter-writer to rephrase it and say, "We have tried without success for 2 years in this laboratory and various others to replicate your findings. We are curious about what the problem is. Perhaps Dr. X could enlighten us."

Ms. Chalk:

Dr. Lock described an informal survey that he had conducted among his colleagues at various medical schools and journals in England and Australia. He identified 72 cases of scientific misconduct in the biomedical sciences. I would like to hear Mr. Maddox's opinion about the prevalence or incidence of unreported cases of serious misconduct. I am interested in cases of deliberate deceit or deliberate distortion of data that constitutes substantial deviation from research standards.

Mr. Maddox:

Obviously, one can't be dogmatic about anything. What we know exists in the way of serious misconduct is, generally speaking, what has been brought to light by other people. We, like most other journals, are conscious during the reviewing process of how often reviewers ask for further information that authors, for one reason or another, are reluctant to provide. Quite often authors have it, but believe that it would be better kept out of the paper. I think there is a fair amount of deliberate obfuscation of the literature going on when, for example, researchers report the amino acid sequence of a peptide, but are reluctant to provide the structure of their oligonucleotide probe, and so on. In those circumstances, it is the editor's responsibility to make sure that the data are available, although not necessarily published. It is becoming increasingly hard to do. That is not necessarily serious misconduct.

I would not want *Nature* to be thought of as a kind of journal vigilante in this respect. Perhaps publication has too much importance in determining the quality of scientific work; I would like to see that diminish a little bit for the good of science. I would like it to be easier for scientists who have made mistakes to acknowledge their errors without being made to suffer.

There are good reasons why biomedical research is particularly vulnerable to unreported cases of serious misconduct. Some years ago, I traveled from India to the United States through Japan. The last person I saw in India was a distinguished scientist, who proudly presented me with his bibliography, which ran to more than 1,400 references. I asked how he could have such a large bibliography; he said that he had very willing graduate students. The first person I saw in the United States was the dean of a distinguished medical school. When I told him about the man with the 1,400 references, he looked at his shoes and said, "Look, let's face it. It is important for somebody in my position, who has to belong to study sections and who has to persuade his colleagues in the study section that he is active in research, to do a bit of that himself." So, long before the Feder and Stewart paper, I was vividly informed of the extent to which people acknowledge that honorary coauthorship is, in fact, common for one reason or another.

I would like to get away from honorary coauthorship: It would help to make the scientific literature more like literature and the scientific profession more like other professions.

Dr. Huth:

I have been in this business for 27 years, and I am aware of only two legal actions involving journals. A recent one in Philadelphia had to do with an effort to force identification of a peer reviewer. I was asked to give a deposition about peer review and simply to state that it is a normal process and that in most journals it is carried out anonymously. I don't know the outcome of that case. The other case is, in my view, an important suit brought against the *British Medical Journal*, which involved a matter that I thought was normal scientific criticism. Yet, the journal was tied up for some time defending itself.

Twice within the last 2 years, I have been asked by a congressional committee to produce information having to do with peer review. I could not respond, because we have a standing rule in the office that we discard records after 3 years, simply as a practical matter.

Ms. Mishkin:

A request from a congressional committee presents an interesting question in and of itself. I know of instances in which federal agencies have turned over to congressional committees individual patient records or individually identifiable records of research, without taking care to black out the names of the people involved. Once the documents get into the hands of a congressional committee, despite their perhaps good intentions to keep them confidential, they sometimes do not remain confidental.

I suggest that a journal editor resist as long as possible until faced with a subpoena; it might be interesting to try resisting even then. You would have to get the courts or the committees to prove that they truly need your information before you would turn it over, because if the information of confidential reviewers is going to be available for frivolous reasons, then your reviewers will be aware of this and will not be able to do a good job of reviewing.

Dr. Lock:

Some 20 years ago, an article from an academic department of anesthesiology reported a new technique of conservative dentistry: A practitioner gave an intravenous injection of anesthetic and then rushed to fill the patients' teeth with no other person present. There had been considerable alarm about this in our newspapers, and, indeed, something like 10 deaths had been associated with this procedure. The academic department carried out some research with the particular technique and showed that blood oxygen fell to dangerously low levels; the researchers suggested that this probably accounted for the deaths. The dentist who introduced this technique said that he was in private practice and his entire income and reputation had been libeled. We didn't have a legal opinion on this article, because it seemed to us straight science; consequently, we didn't have it validated. We did accompany it with an article that was peer-reviewed.

The court was no place to determine scientific truth. In any event, an eminent professor of anesthetics, who supported the dentist, thought that many of the deaths were caused by the patients' fainting. The patients in question had fainted; their tongues had obstructed their breathing, and they died. The case never came to judgment.

Ms. Mishkin:

What was the outcome? Did you settle it?

Dr. Lock:

We had to settle it. We paid our own costs. Our insurance company was going to settle in its own way, and we had decided to fight the case ourselves, because we thought it was so important. I object to the idea of a consortium, because if you have a consortium, sooner or later your insurance company is going to dictate policy. If the insurance companies are going to settle, it doesn't matter whether scientific truth is at stake.

Ms. Mishkin:

But a consortium could work the other way. Because you would be in effect self-insured, you wouldn't be obliged to do as your insurance company's counsel advises.

Dr. Lock:

An audit of how often we use legal procedures would be valuable. We use a libel reader, a barrister, about four or five times a week. Probably three times a week, we actually pick up potential problems.

The Myth of "Passing Peer Review"

Lawrence K. Altman

Peer review in scientific journalism is repeatedly described as a linchpin of science and one of its venerable traditions. It is something that most scientists have come to accept uncritically, almost like a religion. Yet we have only a hazy understanding of how scientists have applied peer review in past decades and of its impact on science and society today. My spot checks and interviews make it clear that many doctors and scientists have an inadequate understanding of what peer review is and that they have not fully assessed its strengths and flaws. Nevertheless, the lack of a clear understanding of the process does not stop many from passionately defending peer review.

Whatever peer review is, it is becoming a contentious, controversial public-policy issue for several reasons. Much of the controversy springs from the secrecy with which peer review is conducted. There are concerns about built-in potentials for abuse and conflicts of interest. One concern is that the system relies on rivals—anonymous referees who vie for the same research funds with the authors of the papers they judge at a time of heightened competition, when a steadily increasing percentage of proposals that get high ratings go unfunded.

Another concern is a perceived lack of accountability of journal editors to authors and the public. Journals generally limit acknowledgment of submission and rejection of manuscripts to the authors of the paper involved and will not disclose this information to others; readers can judge only from what is published. Accountability is crucial here, because of the huge taxpayer support given to science and medicine in recent decades. This financial support has drastically changed the way scientific research, education, and medical practice are carried out. Science and medicine are no longer private enterprises, but public institutions. Taxpayer funds partially underwrite the costs of most peer-reviewed journals. In our culture, any secret system that involves public funding is a target of inquiry. It is likely that peer review will come under increasing public scrutiny.

We need a clearer understanding of peer review and its ramifications, because the secrecy with which peer review is conducted has far-reaching ramifications. It governs access to publication and money, and it contributes to the making of scientific reputations. Favorable peer review can help to build careers; unfavorable peer review can help to destroy careers. Because a scientist's curriculum vitae is crucial in gaining academic promotions, peer review helps to mold the composition of universities, medical schools, and research institutions.

Peer review is also being reassessed because of the many claims that scientists make for it as a means of scrutinizing data in trying to separate solid from weak or false scientific research.

Scientists have impressed on the public the benefits achieved by peer review, but they have talked much less openly about its limitations. A principal one is that peer review cannot weed out false claims when it has no access to original data. Although this may be obvious to most journal editors and to many scientists, it is not to the public. Thus, the public is surprised when it learns of serious mistakes, findings of dubious validity, and fraud in the very medical journals that have claimed so much for the quality of their peer review. Such surprise increases public skepticism and leads many people to question the process.

A theme that will run through my remarks here is that, for all its benefits, peer review has been oversold. From my viewpoint, the phrase "peer review" contains a large element of jargon, because it reflects a simpler word—editing. Do not misunderstand; peer review involves hard work, requires long hours, demands technical knowledge, and can improve manuscripts if it is carried out correctly. Reviewers, however, do not do the experiments; they critique them. As I see it, that is a form of editing. Such jargon can confuse the public and scientists and can lead many people to believe that peer review is capable of doing what it cannot do. Good peer review does what good technical editing does. Bad peer review does what bad editing does.

We are talking about print journalism, which dictionaries define as the reporting and editing of material of current interest in newspapers or magazines. Scientists generally tend to think of journalism in popular terms—confining the term to newspapers, magazines, radio, and television. However, that is too restrictive a view, because it overlooks the numerous scientific publications that include the word "journal" in their titles. Editors of scientific publications are journalists; certainly for the hours of the day when they edit, journal editors practice one of the many forms of the journalistic craft. If you doubt that scientific publication is journalism, recall that the *Journal of the American Medical Association* relied on the Illinois journalism-shield law to protect itself against a subpoena to reveal the name of the author who wrote the famous peer-reviewed "Debbie" article about euthanasia.[12]

In discussing what the public should expect from peer review, I will draw on my own observations as a reader of medical journals and from the small literature on the subject.[2,10,11,13,14] I will concentrate on a few random aspects of peer review to which only limited attention has been directed and that would benefit from further study. I will close with some specific suggestions for improving peer review.

DEFINITION

A logical beginning is to define "peer review." Despite the expectation that leading medical and lay dictionaries would define such an important and common phrase, I could not find a definition in any source that I consulted. Instead, many people seem to play on Supreme Court Justice Potter Stewart's statement about pornography—"I know it when I see it"—when they define peer review. That is because journals vary in their peer-review processes. We should reflect on why the foremost dictionaries do not define something that scientists and physicians consider a cornerstone of their profession. For those who doubt the importance of a definition, I refer to the traditional claims of the precision and reproducibility of science—the type of standardization that a definition affords.

PEER-REVIEWED JOURNALS

Lack of a standard definition of peer review makes it all the more difficult to define "peer-reviewed journal," because the extent of peer review varies among journals. Only occasionally do journals publish clear statements about their peer-review policies in their instructions for authors.[15,18] *Index Medicus* is the standard reference of citations in the medical literature, but officials of the National Library of Medicine have told me that they do not have a standard definition of "peer-reviewed journal" to determine whether to cite a particular journal's articles in *Index Medicus.*

The bulk of what is published in some journals that claim rigid peer review is not peer-reviewed. Consider an entire issue of a scientific journal. Epidemiologically speaking, the denominator would include all advertising pages for journals that carry advertising. The advertising-to-text ratio varies widely among journals.

Many journals do not carry advertising, although the practice of page charges raises questions about the definition. A three-line note that appears in most articles of the *Proceedings of the National Academy of Sciences* (PNAS), a journal that carries no advertising, says: "The publication costs of this article were defrayed in part by page charge payment. This article must therefore be hereby marked 'advertisement' in accordance with 18 U.S.C. 1734 solely to indicate this fact." Many scientists will dispute that such peer-reviewed articles are advertisements. But when the government pays the scientists' bills, it can and does make the rules.

Unlike PNAS, other journals are thick with advertising. A few have an advertising-to-text ratio that is weighted in favor of advertisements. Although journals have criteria for accepting advertisements, it would be the rare journal that peer-reviews its pharmaceutical advertisements. I am not saying that advertisements should be subjected to the peer-review process; I am saying that generally they are not in peer-reviewed journals. You cannot dismiss the advertisements lightly. In considering the impact of each issue of many journals, it is the advertisements that influence what doctors prescribe. If you doubt that statement, then why do drug companies spend large sums of money to advertise in peer-reviewed journals, if practitioners, including academicians, do not respond?

As to the text of peer-reviewed journals, many sections are not always peer-reviewed. Among the examples are letters, editorials, and proceedings of conferences and seminars.

Thus, peer review seems to be confined to a small portion of many journals—the original articles and some of the other papers. Portions that are peer-reviewed are not marked by an asterisk (for example) to alert the reader. Nevertheless, all sorts of astonishing claims are made for publication of non-peer-reviewed material (as well as peer-reviewed material) in peer-reviewed journals. Those claims are also used to justify journal policies. In this provocative spirit, let me ask: Is it false advertising and promotion for journals to describe themselves as peer-reviewed journals if not everything within their pages is peer-reviewed? Similarly, should everything published in peer-reviewed journals, even parts that are not peer-reviewed, be cited in *Index Medicus?* Or should only the peer-reviewed material be cited?

REVIEWERS

We know little about who the peer reviewers are and how they are selected. Among the long-debated questions about peer review is this one: Should editors seek peers for their objectivity or for their biased views? There are valid reasons for either or both.

The public has every reason to expect that all reviewers selected are competent and well trained for the task. But, inasmuch as we know little about the criteria for choosing referees, can we assure the public that it is getting the quality it expects? There are disturbing hints that quality is lacking. Several journal editors and referees have told me that they believe there are not enough good reviewers to serve all journals. Moreover, it is widely believed that referees are often chosen for their political connections and friendships, rather than for their skills as reviewers. This view, whether valid or not, might reflect the paranoia of authors and conflicts inherent in the academic town-gown relationship. But the impression exists, particularly because there seem to be no standard, published criteria for selecting reviewers.

Must peers pass some test for imagination? I raise that question because of Dr. Rosalyn Yalow's statement that, of the "many problems with the peer-review system," "perhaps the most significant is that the truly imaginative are not being judged by their peers. They have none!"[20] Dr. Yalow's biting humor reflects her experience with *Science,* which she said rejected the key paper that led to her Nobel prize, and the *Journal of Clinical Investigation,* which published the paper only after extensive negotiations.[21] That has become a famous anecdote and involves Nobel-prize-winning research; we would benefit in our analysis of peer review if an independent person studied the episode in close detail.

Journals are concerned with new ideas and discoveries, but one of the most common criticisms of the peer-review system is that it has a built-in bias against highly innovative work. Indeed, journals have rejected novel and life-saving advances. We have spoken of Dr. Yalow's experience. Another example is William Jenner's smallpox-vaccination technique, which led to the eradication of the viral disease—the only naturally occurring disease to have been wiped out. We do not know how many papers were never published because they did not pass peer review, but would have led to important contributions. The reason is the old story of being unable to know what is not known.

Dr. Yalow's comment raises several key questions that have not been debated as widely as they should be:

- Are peer reviewers consultants to the editor or to the author? One journal editor, Dr. Alfred Soffer, said he was disturbed by the philosophy espoused by an unidentified editor of another medical journal, who said: "The comments of our editorial board members and out of office reviewers are for our use primarily and only secondarily for the author's consideration. Sometimes we return detailed comments, often we choose to send only a letter of rejection."[17]
- Do peer reviewers have too much power—or not enough—over a final decision about publication of a paper?
- Are peer reviewers too often simply convenient cloaks behind which editors hide when they reject manuscripts?

What criteria do journal editors use in answering the question: Who is a peer?

Is the answer determined by the extent of a referee's training in a specialty? Training in a particular line of research? By virtue of publication in the field? Must a peer be an outsider? Or may a peer be on the staff of a journal?

I raise the last two questions about outside review because all too often the terms "peer" and "peer review" are confused with the relationship of the referee to the publication. Members of the staff of a journal might be technically qualified as peers. The issue is independence.

My point is that the phrase "peer review" is misused when it is applied to the issue of outside versus inhouse review.

FOLLOWUP

It is often said that peer review should not and does not end with publication of an article—that readers provide the ultimate peer review. If so, claims of the accuracy and benefits of peer review imply that authors and editors will responsibly follow up their original reports. However, neither authors nor peer-reviewed journals have an exemplary record in that regard. For example, some journal editors have been known to refuse to publish letters of retraction from authors of peer-reviewed papers that they themselves had published.[1]

Some medical-journal editors say that journalists should not report any medical advances until they are published in a peer-reviewed journal. Consider the following anecdote. Dr. Anthony Fauci, who now heads the National Institute of Allergy and Infectious Diseases and is a leading researcher on AIDS, suggested, in an editorial in a peer-reviewed journal, the *Journal of the American Medical Association,* the possibility of catching AIDS through casual contact. That editorial accompanied a 1983 peer-reviewed article that said: "Our experience suggests that children living in high-risk households are susceptible to AIDS and that sexual contact, drug abuse, or exposure to blood products is not necessary for disease transmission."[16] In May 1983, in an editorial accompanying several papers on AIDS in homosexuals and in children, Dr. Fauci said: "First, it is possible that AIDS can be vertically transmitted. Perhaps even more important is the possibility that routine close contact, as within a family household, can spread the disease. If, indeed, the latter is true, then AIDS takes on an entirely new dimension."[8]

The American Medical Association issued a news release that highlighted those statements. The media were criticized for reporting them, even though they included statements by a key government public-health AIDS worker released by the largest private medical organization in the United States. In one sense, not to report the story could be perceived as censorship, because it involved statements by key health officials in major journals.

Neither Dr. Fauci nor the *Journal of the American Medical Association* has corrected Dr. Fauci's statement. However, in January 1984, Dr. Fauci said in another peer-reviewed journal, *Annals of Internal Medicine:* "There is no evidence that the acquired immunodeficiency syndrome can be transmitted by routine household or social contact."[7] What should journalists believe when the same public-health official makes decidedly different statements in two peer-reviewed journals? When does the second statement overtake the first, if the first is not corrected? Or is the first correct, and the second in error?

STANDARDIZATION IN PEER REVIEW

Any contention that peer review is a purely, or even largely, scientific process is nonsense. Of course, it involves scientific knowledge, but peer review is a form of editing, and as such it is vulnerable to all the whims, fancies, and biases of the subjective process that characterizes editing. To some, peer review means editing by or with independent consultants or review. To others, it means editing by the staff. To still others, it combines the two.

One way in which editors can influence the outcome of the peer-review process is to assign a manuscript to a reviewer known to favor a particular point of view. Another is to pick a reviewer who is likely to be lenient in judging work submitted by a friend or close colleague. Leading journals strive to avoid injecting such biases in choosing referees. Nevertheless, the secrecy of the system encourages speculation that bias is more widespread than editors say it is. We know little about how most editors choose reviewers, except for the general statement that a knack is needed in choosing skilled reviewers. Surely there must be a knack. But we know less than we should about how these "skilled reviewers" actually carry out their critiques and how editors apply the results to the pages of their journals.

There seems to be no standard agreement on how many peers peer-reviewed journals customarily use or should use to judge a manuscript. The numbers vary. Two and three seem to be the most commonly cited figures. But at least one scientific journal, *Current Anthropology,* has routinely selected 15 reviewers.[3] Several reasons were cited: to counter bias, to discern differences of opinion, and to avoid the perceived dangers inherent in selecting a smaller number.

If peer review were a scientific or truly objective process, it would be conducted blindly in a manner similar to that of an experiment or a clinical trial. Editors would remove the names of the authors and their affiliations and randomly select reviewers from a pool of qualified persons.

QUALITY

Another consideration is the thoroughness of peer review. For example, most reviewers and editors do not check references to be sure that they have been cited correctly. Two recent studies have identified substantial numbers of errors in reference citations—not only in misstatement of page numbers and misspelling of the names of authors, but also in the assertions made about cited papers that sometimes cause untruths to become "accepted facts."[5,6]

We might learn a lesson from our lawyer friends. Law-review editors see to it that each reference and citation is checked before an article is published, and they generally rely on students to do the checking. Perhaps there is a way to involve graduate students in the scientific publishing process. With or without such students, the budgets of scientific journals would rise substantially if they were to adopt a system of independent verification of references and citations. Lack of funds, however, is an inadequate defense against installing some mechanism for improving the precision of reference citations, if scientists are to continue to make the claims they do for the accuracy of articles published in peer-reviewed journals.

Many editors take the position that peer review protects the public against unwarranted claims. We have only their testimony that peer review corrects many errors that would otherwise make their way into scientific journals and that peer review has led authors to reverse their conclusions. Undoubtedly, that has happened. But where are the data to prove the contention? How many and how serious were the errors? Were they of such magnitude that the scientific community and the public would have been seriously misled if they had not been detected by peer review? Or do the overwhelming majority of the errors fall in the categories of failing to dot i's and cross t's, poor organization, and poor writing?

We know that, at times, peer reviewers have failed to detect statistical and scientific flaws before publication. We do not know how often.

Dr. Yalow says that her practice is to read the paper being reviewed and previous papers by the same authors and then to try to determine whether their papers are cited by others in the field.[20] Is she exceptional? Is hers the customary practice? Should it be?

DISAGREEMENT

Readers know little about peer disagreement concerning papers published in peer-reviewed journals, and that situation raises several questions.[4] When referees claim to have found serious flaws in a manuscript, how often do journals assume that the referees are correct and the authors wrong? Editors justify the need for peer review on the basis of their lack of sufficient specialized knowledge to evaluate a paper. Presumably, the lack of expertise can also handicap an editor in evaluating a referee's critique. It would be useful to know how often authors get the opportunity to rebut referees' criticisms. How many journals allow for appeal? And how often are authors successful in reversing a decision?

The basic issue is how to settle serious controversy among authors, journals, and referees. Should the disputes be argued broadly by the scientific community at large or confined to an editor and a few referees? Disagreement is highly informative, not a liability. When readers are deprived of the lively debates that could help them to evaluate the merits of a paper, they might miss some key points and carry away an unrealistic view that there was more agreement than dispute about the findings.

Although journals ostensibly use different methods for determining publication when referees seriously disagree with each other and with the editor, it comes down to the editor's decision, as is proper for editing and journalism. Several editors have told me that they have rejected papers that got high praise from reviewers, because those papers were not suitable for the journal or because too many papers on the same subject had appeared in recent issues. But does it take the peer-review process to determine that a journal has already published too many papers on a specific topic? Several editors have told me that they have published papers that the referees unanimously panned. How often? We do not know. Such a situation is valid, even commendable, because in journalism it is the editor's task to decide—even if it means overruling referees. But the system should be explained more clearly.

What is not commendable is the practice to which at least one editor has admitted privately: sending a manuscript of a paper that the editor wants to publish to enough referees to ensure that two recommend its publication.

OVERALL IMPACT

We have no measure of the fate of rejected articles and thus no way to assess the overall impact of peer review on all scientific journals.

The occasional studies done on that point have suggested that most papers rejected by leading journals get published—often in other leading journals.[19] If the anecdotes I have heard are true, a paper is sometimes published in Journal B in virtually the same form in which it was rejected by Journal A. How often is unknown. We also do not know how often authors revise their manuscripts to take into account criticisms raised by reviewers from journals that reject the original submission and ultimately publish the revised papers elsewhere. It is not known to how many journals authors will send papers before finally giving up. Nor do we know the costs of that effort—to journals, to authors, to taxpayers.

If the overwhelming majority of papers are published, even after rejection by many journals, we must ask what purpose the peer-review system serves. If bad research is being published because there are too many journals that need to fill their pages, what does that say about peer review? And about the quality and value of the scientific research for which the public is paying? If the research is not bad and needs to be published, we should expect to see data that weigh the risks and benefits of the practice. What did peer review contribute? How much did peer review delay publication?

THE MYTH OF "PASSING PEER REVIEW"

Because so many in the field do not fully understand the limitations of the peer-review system, a misleading impression exists that the appearance of a paper in a peer-reviewed journal is something equivalent to its being stamped with the *Good Housekeeping* seal of approval. This has created the myth of "passing peer review"—a myth that misleads many into believing that peer review by supposedly unbiased reviewers alone determines the fate of a manuscript. It tends to reinforce the misimpression that peer review is a scientific process, when, as noted, it is largely a tool used in editing.

Many physicians and others have told me in interviews that they believe that published papers reflect unanimous or majority decisions from referees and editors and, more important, that referees' decisions are binding on editors. In citing findings to bolster a position in a controversy, many of those people say that the findings came from a paper that "passed peer review," implying that the results are necessarily valid. Scientists should read all new findings critically and with a healthy skepticism. The widespread acceptance of the myth, however, often has the opposite effect. The assurance that findings have been scrutinized by peers and then published leads many readers to be less critical than they should be. Perpetuating the myth will not serve scientists and the public well.

PROPOSALS

Having reflected on the role of peer review in scientific publication, I offer several tentative thoughts about how to improve the accountability of editors, authors, and reviewers.

First, in describing peer review, editors should acknowledge that it is a form of editing, albeit a special and valuable one. That must be done to avoid further misleading scientists and the public that peer review is a scientific process and that publication in a peer-reviewed journal is synonymous with receiving the *Good Housekeeping* seal of approval.

Second, do the research that is needed to answer valid questions raised by responsible critics. There is widespread agreement that there has been little research on the role of peer review. Substantial research is imperative, if the scientific community is to continue to use peer review to justify some of its publishing policies. The meeting on peer review in scientific journalism sponsored by the American Medical Association is the first of its kind, long overdue, and a step in the right direction.[9]

Professional societies and private companies that own peer-reviewed publications are profiting from this policy, and what they publish bears on public policy. Shouldn't they help to fund independent studies of the system? We could profit by learning how the peer review now practiced compares with that conducted in decades or centuries past, and we should encourage historians of science to help us in that task.

Systematic use of secret peer review was not a common practice of many scientific journals until after World War II. Even then, some leading journals were edited by one person who did not seek outside review for the papers the journal published. In the nineteenth century, much of the peer review took place in public. The impression that I and others have from reading papers of that era is that it was common for scientific journals to publish debates over major scientific issues. We should learn more about the alleged benefits of anonymous versus open reviewing, not simply accept the former.

In a publicly supported system, shouldn't editors offer more supporting evidence of the need for anonymity in the peer-review system? Would we benefit more from an open reviewing process in which referees had to defend their views before their peers? Many defenders of the peer-review system insist on scrutiny of data before publication, but the very system that scientists rely on to make such assessments has itself not been subjected to similar scrutiny. We need independent polls and other ways of learning more about the scientific community's preference for open versus secret peer review. But the scientific community must gain a better understanding of the peer-review system before polls are taken. Otherwise, polls will be meaningless.

Third, journals should be more open about peer review and should publish much more information about their peer-review policies. Surveys of journals would be helpful in determining what their policies are.

Fourth, publication of more corrections, revisions, and other details would help to provide more followup and keep many topics fresh to readers.

Fifth, as an experiment, arrange for spot checks of published papers to help verify the accuracy of the raw data and to help ensure that the experiments were done as described. This idea has been around for several years, and it is getting renewed attention from Drummond Rennie and others.

In summary, you need not abandon peer review. Just define it. Recognize it for what it is—a good tool for scientific editing, and not a scientific process. Clearly state each journal's policies in applying it. Emphasize the limitations of what peer review can do. Tell us more about the reviewers and the disagreements among them concerning the merits of published papers. And try not to oversell peer review.

REFERENCES

1. Altman LK. Columbia's medical chief resigns: ex-associate's data, fraud at issue, N.Y. Times Aug. 9, 1980:1.
2. Bailar JC, Patterson K. Journal peer review: the need for a research agenda. N Engl J Med 1985;312:654-7.
3. Belshaw C. Peer review and the "Current Anthropology" experience. Behav Brain Sci 1982;5:200-1.
4. Colman AM. Editorial role in author-referee disagreements. Bull Brit Psychol Soc 1979;32:390-1.
5. DeLacey G, Record C, Wade J. How accurate are quotations and references in medical journals? Br Med J 1985;291:884-6.
6. Eichorn P, Yankauer A. Do authors check their references? A survey of accuracy of references in three public health journals. Am J Pub Health 1987;77:1011-2.
7. Fauci AS, Macher AM, Longo DL, Lane C, Rook AH, Masur H, Gelmann EP. Acquired immunodeficiency syndrome: epidemiologic, clinical, immunologic, and therapeutic considerations. Ann Intern Med 1984;100:92-106.
8. Fauci AS. The acquired immune deficiency syndrome: the ever-broadening clinical spectrum. JAMA 1983;249:2375-6.
9. Guarding the guardians: research on editorial peer review. Selected proceedings from the First International Congress On Peer Review in Biomedical Publication. May 10-12, 1989, Chicago, Ill. JAMA 1990;263:1317-441.

10. Harnad S. Peer commentary on peer review. Behav Brain Sci 1982;5:185-6.
11. Ingelfinger FJ. Peer review in biomedical publication. Am J Med 1974;56:686-92.
12. "It's over, Debbie." JAMA 1988;259:272.
13. Lloyd JE. On watersheds and peers, publication, pimps and panache. Florida Entomol 1985;68:134-8.
14. Lock S. A Difficult Balance: Editorial Peer Review in Medicine. London: Nuffield Provincial Hospitals Trust; 1985.
15. Lundberg GD, Carney MJ. Peer review at *JAMA*—1985. JAMA 1985;255:3286.
16. Oleske J, Minnefor A, Cooper R, Jr, Thomas K, dela Cruz A, Ahdieh H, Guerrero I, Joshi VV, Desposito F. Immune deficiency syndrome in children. JAMA 1983;249:2345-9.
17. Soffer A. Peer review in medical journals; proponent view. Chest 1987;91:255-7.
18. Williams E. The process of peer review of scientific manuscripts. JAMA 1988;260:1761.
19. Wilson JD. Peer review and publication: Presidential address before the 70th annual meeting of the American Society for Clinical Investigation. San Francisco, California, April 30, 1976. J Clin Invest 1978;61:1697-1701.
20. Yalow RS. Competency testing for reviewers and editors. Behav Brain Sci 1982;5:244-5.
21. Yalow RS. Radioimmunoassay: a probe for fine-structure of biologic systems. Science 1978;200:1236-45.

Beyond Rejection: A User's View of Peer Review

Thomas P. Stossel

"Peer review" is the official name of a process for making value judgments that decide the distribution of resources, such as research funds and journal space. It is a complex mixture of technical analysis and priority assessment, the latter supposedly based on the integration of some higher wisdom with technical scrutiny. Priority decisions ultimately allocate resources and are what really matter to the supplicant.

Peer review in practice is so diverse as to be nearly indefinable. Widely divergent approaches fulfill the analytic and priority-determining functions. Sometimes, authorities, such as editors and bureaucrats, determine priorities after others, deemed experts by the former, do the technical examination. The experts are often called "referees," an inept analogy to sport; in the latter, referees are never the players for the competing team, as they often are in the scientific peer-review process. In other settings in science, authorities do both analysis and allocation. In yet other settings, when the applicants can acquire resources on demand, they themselves provide the expertise and priority-setting.

The criteria for evaluation have been extensively codified:

> Thus long standing critics justly reigned
> licence repressed and useful laws ordained,[2]

and detailed criteria are enumerated in checklists on forms sent by journals or granting agencies to referees. Reviewers are supposed to enforce standards of evidence, assess interest and relevance, and ensure appropriate attribution. But what is "licence"? What is a "useful law"? What are the standards of evidence? Who deserves credit? Who decides? "Peer review" is served up as though it were a machine driven by objective calculation. It is, instead, especially in the theory-deficient world of biomedicine, ineffable and subjective— a process shaped by the reviewer's personality, upbringing, professional education, and environment. It is, moreover, definable only in the context in which it operates.

The context here is the journal system, encompassing thousands of competing periodicals of extraordinary diversity. The system is hierarchic. At the top sit the usually interdisciplinary high-prestige journals, which automatically attract—for various reasons, including tradition, marketing, and vagaries of fashion—increasingly spectacular science. They compete for it with promise of speedy publication, association with the stars of science, wide circulation, and embellishments of news, commentary, and review. In the middle are the more archival interdisciplinary journals and many so-called specialty journals, which can also be prestigious, but in general are less so than journals in the first category. They put out what does not make it to the top. At the bottom reside the other periodicals, which exist so that everything can be published somewhere.

Peer review differs among the three classes of journals. The low-prestige journals publish nearly everything submitted to them. Arguably, experts of all but the lowest status will not referee papers for them or enforce high standards. The middle echelon attempts to maintain a dialogue between authors and peers[4] and thereby makes the largest proportional investment in a peer-review process. That approach, however, results in difficulty in finding enough "good" referees[3,5] to sustain the effort. On the average, this estate of journals ends up publishing about half the papers received, although the variance around this average is large and the time from receipt to publication varies enormously. The high-prestige journals have very high rejection rates and publish papers on the average more rapidly than do the other classes of journals, on the grounds that papers are of unusual interest and importance.

In its competitive disorder, the journal system resembles the prestige hierarchy and fierce competition of American colleges and universities. Is what has made American higher education great applicable to scientific discourse?

I think not. When educational institutions are successful in competition, the success is parlayed into better performance of their educational, research, and athletic missions. The success of the most prestigious journals often translates into profits for shareholders, for private persons, or for parochial interests that bear little relationship to the consumers and producers of knowledge. The American economy, for all its problems, can sustain the diverse university system. The declining resources currently available to science might be squandered on its journals. A prestige university might produce a better educated student; a prestige journal will not improve a bad paper—if anything, it might mask how bad it is.

Journals exist to serve scientists; it is not the other way around. Scientists themselves should determine the behavior of their journals. What do scientists want? I accept on the authority of Robert Merton[1] that, beyond the satisfaction of problem-solving for its own sake, scientists want respect and recognition by peers. That kind of peer review has only a peripheral relationship to journal or grant peer review, which, as I said, is a technical process for allocating resources.

Who should serve as a peer or gatekeeper for resource allocation? A British lord? Someone of equivalent legal status? Someone with no conflict of interest, who must therefore know little about the details of a field? A highly critical pessimist? A fatuous optimist who loves everything? An expert, who cannot possibly be free of conflict? Editors say that they can navigate these treacherous waters by knowing the complex human characteristics of their authors, their readers, and their reviewers. I agree with that. But I also say that editors do not discharge their responsibility adequately.

I argue that, in comparison with the middle-echelon journals, the high-prestige periodicals are editorially thin. They retain, in comparison with the middle journals, few editors who are working scientists, although they have responsibility for triage decisions. They can afford, because of market demand, to be arbitrary. That creates a temptation to emphasize "pest control," a barrier of vague excuses that minimizes rebuttal, instead of dialogue with potential authors. Contributors have the impression that these journals indulge the temptation; yet we support the system and react with bovine acceptance or masochistic frenzy. Consignment to the lower ranks of journals, we think, will mean obscurity or, worse, not being funded. The situation regarding journals has its counterpart in the setting of grant funding. In affluent times, incisive technical analysis can provide constructive criticism for better use of allocated resources. In constrained times, like today, any criticism at all can mean abandonment.

What, if anything, should be done? My first, admittedly quixotic, suggestion is to purge original articles from interdisciplinary prestige journals, and restrict these journals to news, policy statements, and gossip (at which they increasingly excel), in addition to simple authoritative reviews, easily comprehended by the nonspecialist majority of readers. Those who must read the original articles that currently appear in these periodicals will easily find them in more specialized high-quality journals. Editors will, of course, contend that their journals already contain the kind of reviews that I am advocating. But those reviews are written for specialists, narrowly defined. Only objective evidence that the editors themselves can read and understand the esoteric reviews will convert me to a defense of the status quo.

Failing this first goal, I advocate the opening of the high-prestige journals to more articles of high quality, diminishing the emphasis on immediacy and priority, and increasing attention to editorial dialogue, which would permit authors to refine papers for eventual acceptance. We ought to be more concerned about getting papers into the literature than about keeping them out. Diligent editorial work can improve more papers to the community standards of acceptability.

Objections to my proposals are predictable. "If we reject fewer papers outright, we invite confusion by congesting the literature with uninteresting papers." The response to that assertion is that the researcher already is overloaded by having to scan multiple journals for articles of possible interest. Few scientists read any journal cover to cover. With today's indexing and filing systems, picking and choosing is easier than ever. Good investigators know what they like. They pick bits and pieces from the bazaar of raw material, and what they pick reflects their taste. Journal prestige has not prevented confusion. Confusion can be reduced better by having professional groups, department chairs, deans, and study sections devalue numbers in favor of the quality of papers.[6] Then there would be less incentive to emit fragmentary signals to overcome noise.

Another objection is this: "We'll lose the special flavor of our general journals." I reply that the original mission of those journals is not always consistent with current practice. Ad hoc rationalization of historical accident and social conformity should be recognized as such. Why should a regional medical journal, for example, be viewed as the ultimate repository of medical truth? The editors of such a journal will deny the foundation of any such view of a journal, but I have not seen them encourage news reporters to look elsewhere for comparisons.

A third objection is that "it will cost too much to publish more papers." My response is that journals can afford it. It is virtually impossible to lose money publishing a journal. Journal economics include advance revenues and a predictable market. The top-echelon journals are hugely lucrative. The middle journals might or might not be highly profitable, depending on circulation and interest to advertisers. Wired to specialty societies and subsidized by page charges, reprint revenues, and advertising, they cannot lose. Even the pedestrian periodicals break even and are profitable to publishers.

A fourth objection is that, "if we omit original articles from interdisciplinary prestige medical journals, we will fail to educate the medical practitioner about the latest advances." The answer is that we know what practitioners tell us they read. But we do not know what they really read or retain or what impact it has on practice, if any. The commercial advertisements, those editorial blind spots, give some indication of the level of comprehension.

The final objection is often stated as a suggestion: "Why not simply abolish peer review altogether?" The police do not prevent all crime. The fire department does not stop all fires. They both help, however, and the better the public safety officers, probably the more effective they are in practice. Criticism in science, as in art, has a legitimate place. For all its flaws, peer review is helpful in refining scientific work. If taken more seriously and supported better, it can do it more effectively.

In conclusion: Refine more, accept more, entertain less.

REFERENCES

1. Merton RK. Priorities in scientific discoveries. Am Soc Rev 1957;22:635-59.
2. Pope A. Essay on criticism (1709). In: Selected Poetry and Prose. New York: Holt, Rinehart and Winston; 1961:63-84.
3. Shevach EM. Annual report of the Editor-in-Chief, Journal of Immunology. American Association of Immunologists Newsletter, 1985; Summer: 6-7.
4. Stossel TP. Refinement in biomedical communication: a case study. Science, Technology & Human Values 1985;10:39-43.
5. Stossel TP. Reviewer status and review quality. N Engl J Med 1985;312:658-9.
6. Stossel TP. Volume: papers and academic promotion. Ann Intern Med 1987;106:146-9.

The Value of Peer Review

ARNOLD S. RELMAN

Editorial peer review, the process by which manuscripts submitted to scientific journals are assessed by outside experts, has recently come in for more than its share of criticism—much of it, in my opinion, undeserved. It is easy to find flaws in the system, but it is difficult to think of something better to take its place.

I do not mean to say that improvements cannot be made. As practiced today by even the most reputable of biomedical journals, peer review has defects that can and should be corrected, or at least mitigated. But it seems to me that those who now call for elimination or radical reform of the system, or who question its usefulness, either misunderstand its purposes and processes or have not seriously considered what journals would be like without it.

In this brief essay, I discuss the value of peer review, as well as its flaws. I shall tell how I think it ought to work and why it sometimes fails. I shall also give my views of what a successful peer-review system can be expected to achieve and what it cannot. In so doing, I hope to explain why, after a professional lifetime as an editor, author, and reviewer, I still believe that editorial peer review, despite its limitations, is an essential part of biomedical science.

The effectiveness of peer review depends on the way the participants behave; therefore, as in all human endeavors, there are bound to be flaws. The three key participants are the author, the reviewer, and the editor.

For the system to work properly, authors must first of all be honest. That is the basic assumption on which everything else rests. There is no need to assume that authors are correct in their choice of experimental design and methods, in the way they conduct their study, or in their analysis and interpretation of the data and their conclusions. The system, in fact, assumes that authors might well be wrong in any or all of those respects, and one of the prime functions of peer review is to put such matters under scrutiny. But when authors say what they did and what they observed, there must be a presumption of honesty, because reviewers and editors cannot know what occurred in the laboratory. Occasionally, internal inconsistencies or implausible results might raise suspicions of malfeasance, but it is usually difficult, if not impossible, to recognize fraud solely from perusal of a manuscript. Detection of fraud or other malfeasance is the responsibility of the author's co-workers or supervisors at the institution where the work was done, not of reviewers or editors. Those considerations are overlooked by critics who cite failure to detect fraud as evidence that the system is futile. As I hope to make clear, the system is far from futile; it is simply not designed to investigate an author's honesty.

Authors are also expected to address in good faith the legitimate concerns of reviewers and editors. They need not agree with all the substantive criticisms and suggestions, but they should consider them carefully, attempt to rebut those with which they disagree, and respond constructively to the others. The system works best when authors try to work with editors and reviewers to reach an agreement. When authors and reviewers cannot agree on a technical matter, the dispute must ultimately be resolved by the editor—often with the help of additional consultants—but editors should ensure that authors are given a reasonable opportunity to defend their views. When the issue concerns style or exposition, editors should be more firmly in command, and authors—although they should be heard—have less say.

Reviewers are, of course, at the heart of the peer-review system. They should be asked in advance whether they will accept their assignment and complete it within the required time. They should receive clear instructions from the editor as to their responsibilities and the form in which their evaluation is to be rendered. Reviewers should serve as consultants to the editor, not to the author, and therefore should never communicate directly with the author. They should hold a manuscript in strict confidence and should not make a copy for their files, discuss the manuscript in public or (except with the editor's permission) in private with others, or use information in the manuscript for their own purposes.

Reviewers should be expected to give manuscripts a careful and unbiased review, making their criticisms as rigorous and yet as constructive and unrancorous as possible. The review should be detailed and specific enough to be helpful to the author and the editor. Most editors ask that reviewers prepare two separate sets of comments: 1) detailed technical criticisms, for transmission to the author; and 2) more general opinions about the quality and suitability of the manuscript, for the editors only. If the second kind of comment is sent to the author, it might constrain the editor's freedom to make the final decision and cause much difficulty with the author in the event that the editor's decision is not consonant with the reviewer's opinion.

Reviewer anonymity and reviewer blinding have been much debated. I believe that reviewers are more candid and rigorous when they are not required to sign their reviews. Therefore, the policy of the *New England Journal of Medicine* has been to leave the choice of signing to reviewers. About 85% of our reviewers have preferred to remain anonymous. As for blinding the reviewers (i.e., concealing the author's identity from them), that option—whatever its merits might be—is simply not practical in most instances. Even with the removal of authors' names, most manuscripts have identifiers of one sort or another in the text, illustrations, or references. Removing all the clues (including watermarks on the paper) would be nearly impossible.

Editors—the third element of the system—have the crucial responsibility of overseeing the peer-review process and making it work properly. Most defects in the system can be attributed to the editor's inattentiveness to the task or to failure of the editor's judgment. First, the editor and the editor's staff must assign each manuscript to appropriate reviewers. The reviewers selected not only must be expert in the field, but should be able and willing to produce, in a timely fashion, a careful and unbiased review. Beyond their scientific involvement in the field, reviewers should have no vested interest in the manuscript, no close personal association with the author or the research project, either positive or negative, and no economic interest. To select competent experts and ensure that the responsibility of reviewing is widely shared among those qualified for the job, editors need to have extensive files that are continually updated to reflect the availability and recent performance of reviewers. Some journals, ours included, allow authors to suggest possible reviewers and also those to whom the manuscript should not be sent. In my view, the latter type of request should be honored, but the list of reviewers should be regarded only as suggestions to the editor.

It is also the task of the editor or the editor's staff to keep the review process moving at a reasonable speed. One of the most commonly voiced criticisms of peer review is that it takes too long; unfortunately, that is often true. Delays are usually due to dilatory reviewers, but sometimes manuscripts languish in the editorial office. Some delays are unavoidable, because of special problems with the review, but in most instances editors should be able to give the author an initial decision within 6-8 weeks of submission. In a few cases, when the research is of urgent public concern, editors might want to take special steps to expedite the review process, but the expedient must be used sparingly, if order and fairness are to be preserved.

The most important role of the editor is to act as the impartial moderator of the review process, with particular attention to the protection of the legitimate interests of the author. To the editor falls the task of ensuring that the reviewers' criticisms are thorough, yet fair and temperate. Reviewers often disagree, and the editor must be prepared to resolve the impasse. When the issue is purely technical, the editor might have to seek additional expert advice; but when it is primarily of an editorial nature, the editor will have to deal with it alone. In the last analysis, reviewers are consultants to the editor, and it is the editor and the editor's staff who must make the ultimate decision whether to publish and how much revision to require.

After a review, if the decision is negative, the editor owes the author an explanation. If the reasons are purely editorial, they should be explained in a covering letter; if the reasons are technical and scientific, the editor should ensure that the comments transmitted to the author are sufficiently explanatory. When a decision is deferred pending revision, the editor must see that the comments and criticisms are clear, consistent, and detailed enough to give the author a fair chance to produce an acceptable manuscript. The tone of the comments should be constructive and courteous. Nothing is more wounding to an author than to have a paper rejected with denigrating comments. Review, whether positive or negative, should be a civil discourse among colleagues, intended to improve the quality of research and its communication. There is no place for acerbity in this exchange.

If peer review is to be a discourse among colleagues, authors must have a reasonable opportunity to respond to the reviewers' criticisms. Sometimes, the latter are so decisive that the editor feels confident in making a firm and final negative decision after the initial reviews. Often, however, the editor will want to see how the author responds before making a decision. Occasionally, a manuscript will be rejected, but the author will be invited to submit a new version if additional data or a new analysis can be produced. Such negotiations between editor and author are, of course, justified only when the editor has determined that the manuscript is potentially acceptable. If it seems clear that the manuscript is not suitable for the journal, the editor should not waste the author's time and should inform him or her promptly of the decision. Some manuscripts submitted to a peer-reviewed journal should not even be reviewed, if the editor determines that they are not appropriate for the journal. A brief statement to that effect is generally all the author receives, although some authors seem to feel that they are always entitled to a detailed review of their manuscript, regardless of its suitability for the journal. Although that policy would undoubtedly be useful to authors, few journals have the resources to provide such a service—particularly if they must reject the great majority of the manuscripts they receive.

Whatever the reasons for rejecting a manuscript, the editor should always be open to appeal from the author, because the peer-review process is not infallible. Reviewers and editors sometimes make mistakes, and authors who feel that they have been unjustly criticized on scientific grounds should be given a second hearing. Even manuscripts rejected without review for purely editorial reasons deserve at least another look, if the author can mount a cogent appeal. Editors usually have absolute authority over the decision to publish, but precisely for that reason they should give appeals to their decisions every possible consideration. The danger is not so much that editorial decisions might be mistaken as that they might be capricious or arbitrary.

Contrary to common belief, even the most careful and competent peer review cannot certify the validity of a manuscript. Many people, particularly those outside science, think that a manuscript that passes rigorous peer review can be presumed to be true. When later work proves that not to be the case, they conclude either that the review was lax or that the process itself is not worthwhile. But, even at its best, the system can guarantee the truth of a manuscript no more than it can the honesty of an author. Rather, its function is to hold a scientific report to the best current standards, to ensure that the design and method are acceptable by those standards, and to ensure that the data are properly analyzed and reasonably interpreted. As knowledge in a field advances, new developments will improve methods and modify older concepts. Even the best current research will probably be superseded by more sophisticated and insightful work, which might reveal unsuspected limitations or flaws in previous reports. Conscientious peer review is an indispensable aid to that process of scientific advance and renewal. By setting high standards for the publication of research reports, it encourages good work while discouraging excessive and inappropriate publication. Given the pressures to publish and the size and diversity of the biomedical research community, there can be no doubt that in the absence of peer review the research literature would be far more unwieldy than it already is and more burdened with flawed, redundant, trivial, and unreliable papers. The good work would still be there, but for the average reader the task of identifying it in the mass of inferior reports would be overwhelming.

A final point: Not all papers rejected after peer review are of inferior quality. Given the limitations of space and the large number of submissions, most prominent journals must make decisions based on editorial priorities, as well as scientific merit. For example, most of the scientific manuscripts rejected by the *New England Journal of Medicine* are thought to be basically sound, but unsuitable for the *Journal,* because they would not be of sufficient interest to a general readership, because they do not add enough to the existing literature, or for other reasons not related to the technical quality of the work. Most of those articles are ultimately published in other journals, thus demonstrating that peer review not only screens out unsound papers and improves the quality of those which are published, but also distributes manuscripts among different types of journals. The value of the latter should not be underestimated, for it results in predictable differences in content among biomedical journals and helps readers to select the few journals they want to read from among the hundreds they might otherwise have to peruse.

Even if it is conceded that peer review serves useful purposes, might there not be a more effective method of monitoring the communication of scientific reports? Perhaps there is, but no one so far has suggested a practical better alternative. Peer review, it seems to me, is an essential part of the self-criticism on which science depends. We probably can do it better, but I doubt that we can do without it.

Open Discussion

Mr. Hancock:

If peer review is really editing, what is "editing"?

Dr. Altman:

Peer review is a particular kind of editing. It requires a high degree of technical knowledge. One works over data, charts, graphics, and a variety of statistical methods. Those are scientific processes, but my definition of "editing" implies that they are being applied by someone reviewing or critiquing the work, not by someone doing the experiments themselves. The reviewer is not reproducing the experiment, not trying to confirm the experiment. That is the distinction.

Editing is a matter of judgment. You apply some criteria of fairness, of accuracy, of backing up statements, of flow of thought, and of clarity of presentation and cohesion. That is what an editor does, whether it is on a newspaper, where a reporter is handing in something and an editor is challenging it, or in a journal, where the author is sending something over the transom and the editor is evaluating it.

Dr. Bracker:

Followup of what is published might not be systematic and might not be cataloged for easy retrieval, but it is done all the time in review articles and in papers from laboratories that evaluate what other laboratories have done and build on and criticize it.

Dr. Altman:

Yes, but it is not easy for someone from the outside, who is not expert in a field, to find the followup publications.

Dr. Anderson:

I would like to note one other task or one other virtue of the peer-review system. Many of the sciences increasingly rely on illustrations in data presentation; indeed, some morphologic sciences rely extremely heavily on illustrations. The fraudulent investigator can use many techniques in presenting illustrations, and I find that the reviewer is often our best ally in assisting in the detection of such misuse of material—and, on the positive side, in identifying good science that is presented in subtle ways.

Dr. Berkow:

Dr. Relman, with regard to the question of further study and evaluation of the peer-review process, I am left with the impression that you feel that that can't be done or that you already have the data.

Dr. Relman:

We can learn some things. We are not going to learn as much as we think, because an important part of peer review has to do with subjective quality judgments. It has to do with the kinds of judgments that we make in every field of science and the humanities about what we think is quality. That is often a matter of opinion and current style, and it is flawed; it is fallible. My challenge to those of you who say we should throw peer review out unless we can demonstrate that it is valid (and you will never be able to do that) is: Tell me what you think it would be like without any peer review, and also give me a better practical system that could take its place. I have not heard a satisfactory response to that challenge.

Dr. Dan:

I have looked superficially at the possibility of blinding reviewers to authors' identities. I looked at 57 papers, and it took me a total of 131 hours. It is almost impossible to blind a paper, so that no one would know where it came from, without destroying some of the data that are important for understanding the paper. It can be done, but it is not worth the effort.

Dr. Relman:

You would have to rewrite part of the paper. You would have to eliminate references in the text to previous work, many references in the bibliography, and even the watermark on the paper. You would have to worry about institutional identification through the illustrations. You would have to have a kind of a CIA mentality to go through and delete parts and rewrite parts—and even then you couldn't be sure.

Dr. Altman:

Has anyone put it to the test?

Dr. Yankauer:

This problem is different in different fields. We have been blinding reviewers for years. We cannot always do it. We have polled reviewers; not only did they want to be blinded, but they claimed that they usually could not identify the authors.

Mr. Whitney:

We do it with all papers. In fact, we did a survey that showed that 18% of journals are blinding their reviewers. I don't think that *JAMA* and the *New England Journal of Medicine* are representative of the large number of journals throughout the world or the country. Those are "megajournals." The average journal is different, and we don't find blinding to be that difficult.

Dr. Gallagher:

Dr. Relman, most of your rejections are not on technical, scientific grounds, but on editorial grounds?

Dr. Relman:

Most rejected scientific papers have had a review, and there are usually technical, scientific problems, but the decision to reject is an editorial judgment.

Dr. Gallagher:

Could you not have rejected many of those manuscripts earlier without sending them out for review? What does the review process add?

Dr. Relman:

Some we could, and some we do. But some we can make a confident judgment about only after we have gotten expert opinion. The issue might have to do with the novelty or the importance of the paper or its significance for the field, and we need the reviewers to tell us about that.

Dr. Zuckerman:

I don't think we can take the personality or professional conflicts out of peer review, but I do want to comment on Dr. Relman's point about financial conflicts. I work for the House of Representatives Subcommittee on Human Resources and Intergovernmental Relations, chaired by Representative Ted Weiss. We have had a couple of hearings on scientific misconduct, and a few weeks ago we focused on financial conflicts of interest.

My question deals with reviewers who know about financial conflicts that the authors might have. It is my understanding, from my experience as a reviewer and from reading articles, that most journals require authors to say who funded their research. For example, some journals ask that authors who are writing about the effectiveness of a drug disclose any stock holdings they have in the manufacturer. I don't know how many journals do that. I don't know how many journals give that information to the reviewers. I think that it is very rare (possibly never) that reviewers know whether an author gets honoraria or consulting fees from a company that makes a product that is being evaluated in the paper.

I think that most people would agree that $500 in honoraria doesn't amount to much. But what if it is a half-million dollars? Where do you draw the line?

Obviously, reviewers should also be free of conflicts of interest.

Dr. Relman:

It is desirable that reviewers not have financial conflicts of interest. But we are not trying to do what *JAMA* apparently is trying to do: Ask for conflict-of-interest statements from reviewers and not send manuscripts to reviewers who have such conflicts of interest. We routinely do what, as far as I know, every other journal does: We expect authors to give the source of their support. In addition, we do what only a few other journals do, as far as I know: We tell authors that we are going to review their paper without requiring any advance information about financial conflict of interest, unless they choose to tell us, and without saying anything to the reviewers. We do not think it relevant to the scientific technical review. We think that the first step is for a paper to be reviewed on its scientific merits, with the fundamental assumption that the authors are honest.

If we are going to accept the paper, we ask the authors to tell us about any kind of conflict of interest; we talk it over by telephone or mail and decide whether and how such information ought to be revealed.

Dr. Stossel:

My first reaction is that we are creating an enormous manual of behavior that presupposes that reviewers are on clouds with little halos over their heads. There are enormously complicated conflicts. This is a very complicated personal process. And in the economic sphere, there will be short-term ramifications if a paper gets published and stock goes up. It does create some additional problems.

Dr. Relman:

You seem to imply that the peer-review system requires supernatural, unrealistic, idealistic standards of behavior for reviewers.

Dr. Angell:

What I heard was three people not disapproving of the peer-review system. Dr. Altman is saying that it is not being honestly advertised. Dr. Stossel is disapproving of its use in the upper echelon of journals—in a particular few journals—although he sounded as though he approved of it in the middle groups.

Dr. Altman:

I have not called for throwing the peer-review system out; I have called for improving it. And I have made several observations and offered suggestions. I also have to ask why there is so much misunderstanding. What are journals doing to educate people about the system?

Dr. Relman:

There is much misunderstanding in part because the journals have not done as much as they should in informing authors and the world at large about peer review. I accept that criticism; we could do better. But also there is much misunderstanding because of the mass media. The public and government are misled, it seems to me, by the lay press. The lay press constantly attacks peer-reviewed journals as being valueless because of fraud or because a paper published in a prestigious journal is later found to be in error. Science deserves a much more sympathetic and much more knowledgeable commentary than it sometimes gets in the public press on the subject of peer review.

Dr. Rennie:

I have already said that I believe a survey or audit of articles would be scientifically appropriate, useful in a practical way, and extremely useful politically. Would Dr. Altman comment?

Dr. Altman:

If the scientific community uses objective methods in doing experiments and conducting clinical studies and uses the medical literature system and makes so much of the peer-review system, why is the peer-review system itself not analyzed objectively? If a random audit showed that everything is as claimed in the papers, that would reassure the public and the profession about the peer-review system. Without it, the system is open to the question of what is going on. It is a secret system. Competitive factors are involved in the financing of studies and in a gamut of other matters.

Dr. Berkow:

I think that the problem begins where Dr. Altman started his talk—with an undefined term that could be misleading. Maybe we really ought to call this "editorial consultations," because we are using the so-called peer reviewers as consultants for editors. That might make it clearer what the process is.

Ms. Randal:

Dr. Relman, you were unhappy that the lay press reports instances in which journals have been hoodwinked or whatever. I wonder what you would suggest instead. Isn't that part of the function of the press?

Dr. Relman:

I think that there is abroad in the press a general misunderstanding of what peer review is and what it can do. Dr. Altman says that we haven't explained what we do, and that is a fair criticism. We haven't done as much as we should, but I must add that he also hasn't explained it very well either. With all due respect, I don't think Dr. Altman fully appreciates what goes on in the editorial offices of a peer-reviewed journal.

If you sat at my elbow or sat around the table when we discuss reviewers' comments, if you read the reviewers' comments and saw the kinds of issues that were discussed, the kinds of changes that were made, and if you were to follow the history of a manuscript, I don't think you would say that peer review is just like editing a lay newspaper or magazine.

In your definition of peer review, the peer reviewer has to get into the laboratory and audit the work. If you choose to call that peer review, give me another name for what we do, which is certainly not the same thing that your newspaper editor does when he edits one of your articles.

Dr. Altman:

I have sat at the elbows of editors at the *New England Journal of Medicine* and other journals, and I do not think that they are materially different.

The *New York Times* or the *Washington Post* or any other newspaper or magazine or whatever is not peer-reviewed, is not edited in the same way as a scientific paper. I am not saying that. But the process is editing, and I submit that the critiques and the extensive reviews are editing. (It is called "vetting" when it is done outside in lay journalism.) Many magazine articles go through the same type of critique. It is done much more extensively in scientific publications, as it should be, but it is an editing process.

Dr. Relman:

Peer review is simply an attempt to hold articles to scientific standards that will improve the articles, that will make it more likely that bad material will not be published, and that will separate out the better from the worse. It is no guarantee of absolute truth, and it certainly is not protection against fraud.

Dr. Balaban:

I am against audit, because I think audit is sort of peer review on peer review. But there is honest error, not only fraud, and we have to be careful to differentiate between them. All progress has some error.

Dr. Hollander:

The National Science Foundation has oversight-committee reviews of its programs every 3 years. This depends on honesty on the part of everyone who is involved, but programs are asked to nominate people to come in and take a look at how they have been handling proposals. They nominate some who have been awarded and some who have been turned down. Every oversight committee is to ask standard questions about the process and its outcomes and can ask specialized questions if something seems to be particularly important to look at for the future.

If you are concerned about how the journal peer-review process is working and how institutions are doing in their laboratories or in their research, if you are concerned about integrity and the perception of integrity in the processes that you are involved with, NSF might provide a model.

Dr. Lock:

I think that the government expects too much. We all tend to think that we are living in an ideal world. I have no idea of the processes of a newspaper. How often does one of these newspaper barons actually interfere with a leading article or with policy? How often do they direct things?

We live in an imperfect world. Many of our readers—most medical readers—have a fair degree of skepticism. In my country, 90% of articles will be wrapping up the fish and chips within 3 years. If we could predict which ones they were going to be, we wouldn't need all this. What we are trying to do is to put some aside. We know that 85% of articles are going to be published somewhere.

Certainly, if you have a humdinger of an article, even if it is relegated to a journal that is minor with respect to citation analysis or something like that, it will get into the public domain pretty quickly. It will get picked up by the journalists. They look at all the minor journals. It will get evaluated. It will get into ordinary medical practice.

The peer-review process is imperfect, but we have to live in the real world. We have to remember that we don't give the reviewers anything except brickbats. There is no reason why any of us should take part in this process all the time. Why should these people spend their Sunday afternoons evaluating papers for us all the time?

I am sure that we should do much more research on peer review. I wish that someone could tell me how I could do a proper powerful study of blind reviewing and what my "gold standard" should be, and so forth.

EDITORIAL POLICY COMMITTEE, COUNCIL OF BIOLOGY EDITORS

John C. Bailar III, MD, PhD, Chair
Office of Disease Prevention and Health Promotion
Department of Health and Human Services
Washington, D.C.
and
Department of Epidemiology and Biostatistics
McGill University Faculty of Medicine
Montreal, Quebec, Canada

Marcia Angell, MD
Executive Editor, New England Journal of Medicine
Boston, Mass.

Sharon Boots, PhD
Managing Editor, Analytical Chemistry
American Chemical Society
Washington, D.C.

Evelyn S. Myers, MA
Consultant, American Psychiatric Association
Washington, D.C.

Nancy Palmer
Publications Manager, Association of Official Analytical Chemists
Arlington, Va.

Melanie Shipley
Managing Editor, American Journal of Psychiatry
American Psychiatric Association
Washington, D.C.

Patricia Woolf, PhD
Department of Sociology
Princeton University
Princeton, N.J.

AUTHORS OF CONFERENCE PAPERS AND INVITED PARTICIPANTS

Lawrence K. Altman, MD
New York Times
New York, N.Y.

Donald S. Coffey, PhD
Director, Research Laboratory, Department of Urology
Johns Hopkins Hospital
Baltimore, Md.

Constance C. Conrad, MD
Department of Community Health
Emory University
Atlanta, Ga.

Bruce B. Dan, MD
Senior Editor, Journal of the American Medical Association
Chicago, Ill.

Stephen E. Fienberg, PhD
Dean, College of Humanities and Social Sciences
Carnegie Mellon University
Pittsburgh, Pa.

Paul J. Friedman, MD
Dean, Academic Affairs
School of Medicine
University of California, San Diego
San Diego, Calif.

Barry D. Gold
Office of International Science
American Association for the Advancement of Science
Washington, D.C.

Vernon N. Houk, MD
Director, Center for Environmental Health and Injury Control
Centers for Disease Control
Atlanta, Ga.

Edward J. Huth, MD
Editor, Annals of Internal Medicine
American College of Physicians
Philadelphia, Pa.

Donald Kennedy, PhD
President, Stanford University
Stanford, Calif.

Daniel E. Koshland, Jr., PhD
Editor, Science
Washington, D.C.

Stephen P. Lock, MD
Editor, British Medical Journal
London, U.K.

John Maddox
Editor, Nature
London, U.K.

James D. Marsh, MD
Department of Medicine
Brigham and Women's Hospital
Boston, Mass.

Barbara Mishkin, Esq
Hogan and Hartson
Washington, D.C.

Robert G. Petersdorf, MD
President, Association of American Medical Colleges
Washington, D.C.

Arnold S. Relman, MD
Editor-in Chief, New England Journal of Medicine
Boston, Mass.

Drummond Rennie, MD
Deputy Editor (West), Journal of the American Medical Association
Chicago, Ill.

Richard J. Riseberg, Esq
Chief Counsel, Public Health Service
Rockville, Md.

Maxine Singer, PhD
President, Carnegie Institution of Washington
Washington, D.C.

Thomas P. Stossel, MD
Massachusetts General Hospital
Department of Medicine
Harvard Medical School
Boston, Mass.

Michael A. Stoto, PhD
Institute of Medicine
Washington, D.C.

Miron L. Straf, PhD
National Research Council
Washington, D.C.

Stephen B. Thacker, MD
Center for Environmental Health and Injury Control
Centers for Disease Control
Atlanta, Ga.

Samuel O. Thier, MD
President, Institute of Medicine
Washington, D.C.

OTHER CONFERENCE PARTICIPANTS

Peter Adams
Editor, Physical Review B
Deputy Editor-in-Chief, American Physical Society
Ridge, N.Y.

Paul J. Anderson, MD
Editor-in-Chief, Journal of Histochemistry and Cytochemistry
Mt. Sinai School of Medicine
New York, N.Y.

Miriam Balaban, PhD
National Council for Research and Development
Rehovot, Israel

Robert Berkow, MD
Editor-in-Chief, Merck Manual
Merck & Co., Inc.
Rahway, N.J.

Charles E. Bracker, PhD
Associate Editor, Experimental Mycology
Department of Plant Pathology
Purdue University
West Lafayette, Ind.

Rosemary Chalk
Institute of Medicine
Washington, D.C.

Eugene B. Gallagher, PhD
Editor, Journal of Health and Social Behavior
Department of Behavioral Science
University of Kentucky
Lexington, Ky.

Daniel Greenberg
Editor, Science and Government Report
Washington, D.C.

Charles C. Hancock, Jr.
Manager, Journal of Biological Chemistry
Bethesda, Md.

Rachelle Hollander, PhD
Program Director, Ethics and Values Studies
National Science Foundation
Washington, D.C.

John M. Last, MD
Editor, Canadian Journal of Public Health
Canadian Public Health Association
School of Medicine
University of Ottawa
Ottawa, Ontario, Canada

John C. Nemiah, MD
Editor, American Journal of Psychiatry
Hanover, N.H.

Ruth R. Ohman
Executive Editor, Journal of the American College of Cardiology
New York, N.Y.

Frances E. Porcher
Chief, Publications and Graphics
Center for Infectious Diseases
Centers for Disease Control
Atlanta, Ga.

Judith Randal
Washington, D.C.

John F. Sherman, PhD
Executive Vice President, Association of American Medical Colleges
Washington, D.C.

Harvey A. K. Whitney, Jr.
Publisher and Editor, Drug Intelligence and Clinical Pharmacy
Harvey Whitney Books
Cincinnati, Ohio

290

Alfred Yankauer, MD
Editor, American Journal of Public Health
Department of Family and Community Medicine
University of Massachusetts Medical Center
Worcester, Mass.

Diana Zuckerman, PhD
Human Resources and Intergovernmental Relations Subcommittee
House of Representatives
Washington, D.C.